SEQUEL TO HISTORY

Indexed in

EGLI 1992

SEQUEL TO HISTORY

POSTMODERNISM AND THE CRISIS OF REPRESENTATIONAL TIME

Elizabeth Deeds Ermarth

PRINCETON UNIVERSITY PRESS   PRINCETON, NEW JERSEY

Copyright © 1992 by Elizabeth Deeds Ermarth
Published by Princeton University Press, 41 William Street,
Princeton, New Jersey 08540
In the United Kingdom: Princeton University Press, Oxford
All Rights Reserved

Library of Congress Cataloging-in-Publication Data

Ermarth, Elizabeth Deeds.
Sequel to history : postmodernism and the crisis of
representational time / Elizabeth Deeds Ermarth.
p.   cm.
Includes bibliographical references and index.
ISBN 0-691-06930-1—ISBN 0-691-01517-1 (pbk.)
1. Postmodernism (Literature) 2. Time in literature. I. Title.
PN771.E7   1991
809'.93384—dc20   91-21077

This book has been composed in Linotron Galliard

Princeton University Press books are printed
on acid-free paper, and meet the guidelines
for permanence and durability of the Committee
on Production Guidelines for Book Longevity
of the Council on Library Resources

Printed in the United States of America

10 9 8 7 6 5 4 3 2 1

10 9 8 7 6 5 4 3 2 1
(Pbk.)

To Cronopios Everywhere

The unfortunate image of a "road" to which the human mind has become accustomed (life as a kind of journey) is a stupid illusion; we are not going anywhere, we are sitting at home. The other world surrounds us always and is not at all at the end of some pilgrimage.

    —Vladimir Nabokov, *The Gift*

Until at last it came to me that time was suspect.

    —Albert Einstein, writing in old age
      about his discovery of the
      Special Theory

Contents

Preface

THE AIM of this book is to show that postmodernism involves a reformation of temporality. While unsettling questions about time have long been raised in contemporary science as well as in postmodern narrative writing, most theoretical treatments of postmodernism still either ignore temporality altogether or take old habits for granted in discussing it. Postmodernism transforms the historical construction of temporality that took shape in the Renaissance and that informs the humanistic tradition, and it is in this way that postmodernism most radically undermines both realist and humanist practice.

Although this book touches on many different theoretical and disciplinary fields—postmodernism, surrealism, and feminism; the arts, anthropology, economics, literature, discourse analysis, philosophy, and physical science—all fields remain primarily resources for considering my main subject: the construction and experience of time. Discussions to which those issues are not central do not get extensive treatment here. Even quite specific scientific parallels get fairly short shrift owing to space limitations, but wherever possible I do indicate directions for further conversation in the interest of homogenizing the conversation about postmodernism and its implications. The reader who sees neglected opportunities for developing similar arguments in other fields or directions will be having precisely the kind of response that I hope this book will generate.

My own writing here has been influenced by a wish to make discussion of postmodernism more accessible than some of its theoretical incarnations have done; at the same time I have written so as to call attention to the power of style. If I have accomplished this without being quirky or without detracting from the points being made, I am content that I have kept my own writing consistent with my argument. Postmodern textualization, that is, writing in a postmodern style about postmodernism, is something I do not attempt in any extensive way, although I do employ paratactic repetitions that best become apparent over the course of the whole manuscript. The problem of what writing style to use in coping with this subject certainly is one I have had in constant view. Negotiating between theoretical writing and other kinds has been part of the fun of writing this book.

For the thoughtful reader who does read for more than hollow calories but who may not be thoroughly familiar with now classic texts by Hélène Cixous, Julia Kristeva, Luce Irigaray, Jean-François Lyotard, Jacques Derrida, and Michel Foucault, I have occasionally summarized what is essential for understanding my point. The use of fairly "canonical" texts of post-modern writing will not limit the scope of my argument for informed readers, and for those coming to some of these issues for the first time such texts are necessary. My own relation to these sources is hard to characterize. For example, in writing I have found Foucault perhaps the most powerful single influence even though I probably do not agree exactly with any particular sentence he wrote. These kinds of influence, as George Eliot once noted of Thomas Carlyle, generate not information but powers, not solutions but the means by which solutions may be wrought. That seems to me the greatest tribute. I cite Kristeva, Cixous, and Irigaray, three of the most original writers I know who are not novelists, but I do so without at all subscribing to psychoanalytical interpretations of anything. I discuss for general reasons some differences between Lyotard and Jürgen Habermas, but I'm not particularly interested in negotiating between them. I cite Martin Heidegger without being a Heideggerian.

Within the limits of my subject and human endurance I have consulted the relevant scholarship and theoretical writing in order to find out, among other things, what has already been done on my subject. I myself detest reading bright books by people who repeat points I have long since made in my own writing, and I recoil from inflicting that experience on others. Given the variety of disciplinary fields in which I pursue my subject, it is practically impossible to read everything or even to cite everything I have read. In selecting my bibliography I have emphasized primarily work that I have found to be either useful or relevant or both.

My bibliography records mostly recent reading but says little about the books that have grown along with this project over many years, including those that helped in the formulation of my study of the construction of historical consciousness from Leone Battista Alberti to Henry James (*Realism and Consensus in the English Novel*, Princeton, 1983): a book that was inspired in part by my wish to base my work about antirealism on a better analysis of realism than I found available. It seems inappropriate to cite works I used in that volume (by, for example, St. Augustine, Alberti, Miriam Bunim, Ernst Cassirer, William Ivins, Jr., Gabrielle Spiegel, Alfred North Whitehead, and many others) and yet misleading to omit them, so I mention such sources here in a generic way.

My most general debts, cited or not, will be evident throughout: to the painters and writers who have undone the neutrality of space and time and who, consequently, have undone the secure spectator positions and subject positions that made such space and time possible; and to those in all fields engaged in the exploration of language in practice.

Many years, many rhythmic returns, and many conversations have gone into this book. The hybrid influences in the actual writing, which could only be classified perhaps by Ceferino's system (as elaborated in Julio Cortázar's *Hopscotch*, chap. 133), include Japanese novels, George Eliot, Josquin de Près, Marguerite Duras, Rome, King James, Michel Foucault, feminist practice in the United States, Filippo Brunelleschi, jazz, French theoretical feminists, Sils-Maria, Vladimir Nabokov, Virginia Woolf, and many, many more. I am grateful to them all for being there.

The women of the 1988 Dubrovnik conference on "Women and Writing," by their interest in new kinds of writing, have helped to confirm my belief that in pursuing my objectives here, I am not sailing off the edge of the world. Finally, considerable inspiration has mysteriously flowed from the memorable advice to critics that I once extracted from the German novelist Martin Walser, who advised me always and above all to "write in a personal voice."

It makes a world of difference to my writing to be able to share my thoughts with colleagues at conferences. I am grateful to the editors of *Novel*, both for their invitation to speak at a conference on the novel held at Brown University, where I explored some relations of postmodernism and feminism, and for their permission to reprint in Part Three, Section I, certain passages of that talk, later published in *Novel*. Thanks, too, to George Levine for his invitation to speak about postmodern time at a conference held at Rutgers University on the current situation of "Realism and Representation."

The University of Maryland has provided financial and research support for this project over several years, thereby significantly hastening the work. Sally Hearn, Simona Simmons, and the generous staff of the Albin O. Kuhn Library have made my day on many, many occasions when research and writing would otherwise have been frustrated. Thanks to Anna Oldfield, who turned research assistance into an art form, and to Denise Murphy, who multiplied hard copy with incredible dispatch.

"Thanks" hardly seems enough to say to the heroic people who read manuscripts for other people and give them specific advice about nagging problems monumental only to the writer. Thanks to Katherine Hayles, who poses in humane ways in her own work the questions raised by postmodernism and who gives excellent methodological advice. Thanks to Stephen Tyler for his useful work and for his intelligent and encouraging reading of the entire manuscript. Thanks to Samuel Hynes for reading a troublesome section of this while he was finishing a book of his own, and to John McGowan for valuable comments on the whole. Thanks to Kathryn Deering for help with Part Three and to Anthony Deering for his care in reading and restraint in giving advice, and to both of them for their friendly interest. I am grateful to my students over many years who have listened to me and talked back, especially in a 1976 seminar where I first formulated many of the ideas developed here. Robert Brown at Princeton

University Press has made the process of publication more a pleasure than a chore, and for that I am very grateful indeed. Janet Wilson has edited the manuscript line by line with care and precision, helping the author to make sense and building for typesetters that beautiful bridge between manuscript and print.

Winter and summer, year in and year out, slings and arrows notwithstanding, Thomas Vargish has read the dratted drafts, given me good advice, and in a thousand ways made my free time freer. It is my good luck to live with someone who not only can share my professional and personal life but who also shoulders his full half of the time-consuming work that every single day requires: what Adam Smith, most unjustly, calls "unproductive labor."

SEQUEL TO HISTORY

Prologue _____

Why Text?

THIS BOOK is about postmodern temporality, and about the multivalent crises of historical thinking that appear across a very broad spectrum of cultural practice. I sketch these broad arguments in three main parts, often using literary analogies to specify a point, and then I punctuate the argument with a final "Rhythm Section" on one narrative text. This is, then, not precisely literary criticism, nor is it precisely social, philosophical, political, or cultural analysis. It is all of these and none. A conventionally disciplined reader might question this mixing of species, regarding it as an unnatural act. A more theoretically up-to-date reader would take a different line but one that also arrives at a difficulty: since I accept the expanded use of the term "text," which includes artifacts ranging from architecture to events, why not use historical events as examples instead of literary narratives? In other words, and from both sides of the interpretive situation, "Why Text?"

First, and for the empiricist who believes that rocks and stones and trees are more "real" than play and poetry, and that, like minerals, political systems belong to nature not art, my implicit argument is this now familiar one: that the distinction between what is invented and what is real is one that for many reasons we can no longer afford. As Claude Simon, the 1985 Nobel Prize winner has said, art and literature meet human needs as basic as hunger and thirst. Second, and for the collegial discourse-analyst who finds textuality in historical events, my explicit argument is this: that the term "event," like "text" or "self" or "historical," retains the essentialism that postmodernism challenges. In a postmodern process, every event may be a text, but no text is single. It is the nature of the process, the series, the sequence that most interests me in this book and that can scarcely be called an "event" in any traditional sense. The revision of sequence at the level of language is where the practical, embedded resolutions of postmodernism become available.

The complex answer to the question "Why text?" turns on the new priority postmodernism gives to language in defining any system. Postmodernism conceives language as a system of signs, that is, as something internally coherent and not merely a neutral collection of traveling pointers with which we indicate "real things." While this may be widely understood, its implications, I think, are not. The materiality of language is always in view in a postmodern text, and any putative "neutrality" that language might once have appeared to possess remains conspicuously absent. Language is not neutral and not single. In postmodernism, language means residence in a particular discourse, and alternate semantic systems or discourses are not just alternate views or versions of "a reality" that remains beyond them. This is just as true of the "languages" of socialism, capitalism, feminism, sexism, or fashion as it is of French or Spanish or English. Language, in other words, is the constant by which we compare forms of "writing" in the expanded sense that postmodernism gives to that word: writing, that is, conceived as a unique, finite, and local specification of a particular sign system. Considered as discursive "writing," activities are not instruments of production but the activation of different opportunities of residence and of engagement. A "text," furthermore, is no longer a singular "thing" because it is constituted by the process of enactment that engages this or that particular personnel or material.

The term "postmodern" has acquired considerable currency in recent decades, spreading from architectural theory and linguistic esoterica to sweater advertisements in the *New York Times*. This multivalence, this "play" in the term, certainly contributes to its vitality, but it means quite different things in different contexts, and these differences need to be acknowledged. In architecture, for example, postmodernism succeeds and copes with the results of early twentieth-century modernism, particularly the razing effects of Bauhaus and the reduction of detail in favor of Euclidean forms. In philosophy and discourse analysis, on the other hand and partly as a result of Nietzsche's influence, postmodernism succeeds a modernism formulated in a much broader sense, going even so far as to consider postmodernism the successor to a "classicism" traceable to the Greeks.[1] It is important to achieving some political focus on postmodern-

---

[1] Charles Jencks, for example, wants for reasons of his own to limit the historical frame and to distinguish Post-Modern from Late-Modern in the twentieth century, although he does say that postmodernism is post-Christian (*What Is Postmodernism?* [New York: St. Martin's Press, and London: Academy Editions, 1981], pp. 7–8, 38, 32–33). Fredric Jameson, who refers to architecture, also seems to find postmodernism a relatively local deformation appearing since the 1940s; this might follow if one takes history to be a permanent condition and not, as I do, an inflection of culture since around 1400 (Jameson, "Postmodernism and Consumer Society," in Hal Foster, ed., *The Anti-Aesthetic: Essays on Postmodern Culture* [Port Townsend, Wash.: Bay Press, 1983] p. 113). In localizing the definition of postmodernism, Jencks may be responding in part to Jean-François Lyotard's completely ahistorical definition of postmodernism as a constant cultural state and not historically specific (i.e., that modernity "in whatever age" is the shattering of belief and the "discovery of the 'lack of reality' of reality, together with the invention of other realities" (*The Postmodern Condition: A Report on Knowledge*, trans. Geoff Bennington and Brian Massumi [Minneapolis: University of Minnesota Press, 1984], pp.77, 79, 81). "This crazy idea," says Jencks, "at least has the virtue of being original and it has led to Lyotard's belief in continual experiment, the agonism of the perpetual avant-garde and continual revolution, a confusion in Jencks's terms with Late Modernist

ism to remember that two related but quite distinct things are at stake: first, the modernity that began with the Renaissance and Reformation, and second, the representational discourse traceable to classical philosophy and science.

In my usage "modern" indicates a period and a discourse that had pre-eminence between the Renaissance and the turn of the twentieth century; that is, I conceive "modern" culture to be the discourse that, however unevenly and gradually, supplanted medieval culture and enjoyed hegemony until fairly recently. The case for this I make at length in *Realism and Consensus in the English Novel*, my book on the construction of historical consciousness from its roots in Renaissance perspective through the complex historical forms of the nineteenth century. What succeeds *that* "modern" culture is "post-modern." What postmodernism supplants, then, is the discourse of representation characteristic of the long and productive era that produced historical thinking, or what Meyer Schapiro calls "the immense, historically developed capacity to keep the world in mind."[2] This usage assumes a broader definition of "modern" than the one synonymous with early twentieth-century "modernism," and a narrower definition than the one synonymous with "classical" discourse. The related crises of the subject and of history involve discursive conventions much newer than those of the Greeks who had no conception of history in the modern sense and no conception of the subject.[3] By taking up this "classical" discourse at the familiar fictional threshold of the Renaissance I can focus on the formation that has favored institutions that we still take very much for granted, including, to mention a few, representational government, Newtonian and Darwinian science, realistic art, and capitalism. This middle-range conception of the "modern," which is by no means unique to my argument,[4] in-

---

avantgardism" (*What Is Postmodernism?*, p. 42). Jürgen Habermas, while he laments the habit of universalizing "modernity" by finding its roots in the dissolution of archaic life (à la Nietzsche), seems to agree with Lyotard at least on this, that "the relation between 'modern' and 'classical' has definitely lost a fixed historical reference." But the "determinate negation" he finds recommended by the practice of Max Horkheimer and Theodore Adorno does not offer anything very "ad hoc" when it is grounded in "dialectic" (Jürgen Habermas, *The Philosophical Discourse of Modernity: Twelve Lectures* [*Der philosophische Diskurs der Moderne: Zwölf Vorlesungen*, 1985], trans. Frederick Lawrence [Cambridge, Mass: MIT Press, 1987], pp. 87, 4, 128; on dialectic see Part I, sect. 1).

[2] Meyer Schapiro, "Nature of Abstract Art," *Marxist Quarterly*, no. 1 (January–March 1937), p. 85.

[3] Michel Foucault, "Final Interview," in *Raritan Review* 5, no. 1 (1985), p. 12.

[4] Stephen A. Tyler (*The Unspeakable: Discourse, Dialogue, and Rhetoric in the Postmodern World* [Madison: University of Wisconsin Press, 1987]) and William Spanos (*Repetitions: The Postmodern Occasion in Literature and Culture* [Baton Rouge: Louisiana State University Press, 1987]) both take modernism to be a post-Renaissance phenomenon and, although they differ in their estimates of the value of modernism, are intent on the political dimension of the problem postmodernism poses. For Tyler, "postmodernism is the culmination of mod-

forms my estimate of the difference postmodernism makes. In terms of temporality, postmodern writing moves beyond the identity-and-similitude negotiations that characterize the construction of historical time and its rationalized consciousness. The tellable time of realism and its consensus become the untellable time of postmodern writing.

That the terminological situation with regard to these new currents is unstable and sometimes parochial seems quite understandable considering the vast implications of postmodernism. Even the term "postmodern" has emerged relatively late in the historical situation I describe, and some of the people I quote use the terms "modern" or "contemporary" to indicate the same thing I describe as "postmodern." I prefer "postmodern" over "contemporary" for discussing narrative to avoid any implication that the new writing I describe might include any of that large number of authors still writing traditional plot-and-character novels; and I prefer "postmodern" over "modern" not only for the general reasons already advanced but also because the writing I discuss differs markedly from the achievements of high modernism. The term "postmodern" is after all a mere chronological indicator, a concession to the difficulty of talking sense about one's own immediate cultural definition, and a mark of general awareness that something, indeed, is happening to discourse in the post-Renaissance, post-Reformation, and post-Enlightenment West. Across a broad range of cultural manifestations a massive reexamination of Western discourse is underway: its obsession with power and knowledge, its constraint of language to primarily symbolic function, its ethic of winning, its categorical and dualistic modes of definition, its belief in the quantitative and objec-

---

ernism's assault on the idea of representation, but unlike modernism, it also undermines the idea of form"; and "postmodernism is the writing of the history of the repression of the paradigmatic axis of reading and representation, and it is the breaking of the mirror, and the 'opening of the field' of the signifier," the ultimate goal of which is, perhaps, to return us to the world of "speech" and "quotidian talk" (pp. xi, 4, xii). Tyler attends to the important political role of language, and on postmodernism's attempt to erase the "plain style" that was inspired by science and that "above all else, seeks to erode the presence of the speaker by eliminating all marks of individuality that speak of the speaker's difference from the text" (pp. 6–7). I part company with Tyler when he opts for "dialogic" as a postmodern solution.

Spanos is interested in the political consciousness of modernism as a "Western" tradition: "the structure of consciousness into which post-Renaissance man has wilfully coerced his classical inheritance" (p. 18). He, too, is interested in language ("the authorizing logocentric forms and rhetorics of the entire literary tradition," p. 195), although his argument does not allow for what I take to be crucial to postmodern writing: that its interrogations of those forms takes place, to the extent it does take place, entirely as a phenomenon of language. It is not possible, really, to conduct this interrogation in any other way, or at least not in the conventional philosophical or "historical" terms that are themselves authorizing and logocentric. If we can speak of postmodern hermeneutics at all, it "is open ended, ongoing, (im)provisational," but it is not at all "interminably historical" (p. 218).

tive, its linear time and individual subject, and above all its common media of exchange (time, space, money) which guarantee certain political and social systems (see *Realism and Consensus* on the culture of humanism).

Because postmodernism subverts very basic habits, it is not surprising that its assertions alarm those with vested interests in the modernist order of things: an order where imaginative constructs ("art") are exported (along with "the subject" and even creativity in general) to the margins of discourse where they act as the repressed foundation for rationalist order. Feminist theory has had much of a revisionist nature to say about the repressed of Western culture, and it provides essential terms for the present argument about the postmodern collapse of the dualisms that have served modernist hegemony and its forms of transcendence. An example is the dualism between invention and reality. By refiguring fiction-making as the primary mode of consciousness (it replaces mirrors, lamps, and other such metaphors), postmodern narrative emphasizes the power of invention and fabrication to the point, as Robbe-Grillet says, of making it the foundation of discourse, the subject of the book.

The postmodern reformation that most interests me in *Sequel to History* is the subversion of historical time. The humanist construction of time is historical, and postmodern writing subverts this temporality and its projects. Given the scale and profundity of Western, especially Anglo-American and Northern European investment in this construction of temporality, its subversion merits much more attention than it has had in theoretical writing, which often seems riveted to static models. Time is often the missing link in discussions of postmodernism, which cycle through endlessly reflexive spatial and static models without ever revealing the disappearance of history and the practical reformation this implies. Usage almost invariably betrays a view of "time" that is fundamentally historical and without alternative. Habermas, for example, notes the importance of "time" but does not distinguish one construction of temporality from another. When he speaks of "a changed consciousness of time" in dada and surrealism (he calls these "aesthetic modernity"), what changes seems to be consciousness, but "time" remains the same. Habermas even seems to agree with Lyotard that "the relation between 'modern' and 'classical' has definitely lost a fixed historical reference," meaning that the sense of Big Change reappears variously "in" time which itself remains the same.[5]

The challenge in postmodern writing to this hegemony of History understandably appears threatening. At the same time, the effect of such writing is often the opposite of threatening, and it opens a sense of alternative possibility foreclosed by History. It takes only a slight disciplinary shift to

---

[5] Jürgen Habermas, "Modernity—An Incomplete Project," in Hal Foster, ed., *The Anti-Aesthetic*, pp. 4–5.

bring into view some profound preparation for this reformation of time. Twentieth-century phenomenology has massively revised the modern formulations of time and consciousness inherited largely from the seventeenth century, which formulated time as a categorical imperative "natural" to human thought and inseparable from the conception of the individual subject, the founding *cogito*, that has developed its powers since then. By focusing on a phenomenal "event" in which subjectivity and objectivity cannot be distinguished, phenomenology anticipates the always-embedded and in-process postmodern subjectivity. Like surrealism, phenomenology seeks to "bracket" preconceptions in order to make palpable a world of experience that precedes rational knowledge, including the very act of perception itself. For example, this bracketing of preconceptions is an implicit motive in the art of collage: a characteristic form of the early twentieth century that promotes the imaginary and neutralizes the principle of non-contradiction by disconnecting material objects from their "normal" (read, habitual) connections and conditions.[6] Postmodern narrative can be instructively thought of as a temporal instance of collage, or rather collage in motion.

The best-known twentieth-century revision of the modern view of time is Einstein's General Theory of Relativity, where time is no longer a constant but instead a function of relative motion, a dimension of events. Just as the classical object has been redefined in physics, so the phenomenological subject is no longer discrete, apart from the event, but, like time and space themselves, functions of specific events and bound by their limitations. And beside physics and philosophy appear other efforts that subvert historical thinking and its supporting discourse of realism and empiricism. The period of Einstein's papers on relativity and Edmund Husserl's logic, for example, also saw the publication of Franz Kafka's stories, the poetry of Guillaume Apollinaire, Sigmund Freud's papers on the unconscious, the cubism of Georges Braque and Pablo Picasso.[7]

For strategic as well as substantive reasons it is important to remember that the work of postmodernism is *not new* (it is fully evident in surrealism and, as André Breton saw, already present in romanticism), and it is *not over*. Many so-called modern and postmodern achievements are already in evidence in the nineteenth and even the eighteenth centuries, although the

[6] On collage see Robert Delevoy, *Dimensions of the Twentieth Century, 1900–1945*, trans. from French by Stuart Gilbert (Geneva: SKIRA, 1965), especially Part III: The Principle of Indeterminacy; and Marjorie Perloff, "The Invention of Collage," in *The Futurist Moment: Avant-Garde, Avant Guerre, and the Language of Rupture* (Chicago: University of Chicago Press, 1986), pp. 42–79.

[7] For an illuminating discussion of relativity theory see Delo E. Mook and Thomas Vargish, *Inside Relativity* (Princeton: Princeton University Press, 1987). I am grateful to the same authors for sharing their work in progress on relativity theory and its cultural contexts.

cultural critique they implied did not yet have critical mass. Non-Euclidean mathematics belongs to the nineteenth century, as does phenomenology, which even extends back to the eighteenth. The relativization of religious systems that began in the Renaissance got a major redirection in the nineteenth century in the German religious revolution known as the Higher Criticism, which historicized Christianity and in some forms came very near to using linguistic models. The denunciation of "this ridiculous illusion of happiness and *understanding*" belongs, as Breton says, to romanticism as well as to surrealists a century later and their postmodern heirs.[8] In other words, the work of postmodernism is quite broadly prepared for, not rootless or unmotivated.

It is also important to keep in view the politically quite stunning fact that, while there is considerable Anglo-American interest in postmodernism and its predecessors, the cutting edge of theory and practice has remained primarily based in Romance-language countries in Europe and Latin America. England and the United States may have too much invested in the empiricist models responsible for their material and political hegemony to absorb the critique of empiricism so persuasively underway elsewhere in Western culture.

The changes evident in postmodern writing cannot be ignored, but should they be resisted? While I think not, the question is important because the stakes are very high: it is not often noted how high. The critique of historical time involves a critique of everything "in" it: not just anthropomorphism, not just the metaphysics of presence, transcendence, and depth, not just the structure of the human sciences, not just the definition of subjectivity as "individuality." The postmodern subversion of historical time threatens other things still broadly taken for granted in universities and constitutional governments: the idea of "natural" or "human" or "inalienable" rights, the definition of disciplines and fields of research and perhaps the very notion of research itself, the possibility of "representation" in political as well as aesthetic terms, the nonceremonial (i.e., informational) functions of language. There are some who fear that postmodernism, by depreciating traditional causalities, portends an end to morality itself, and the fear is not unfounded so far as traditional morality is concerned. After all, how *do* we deal with each other domestically or globally when we can't be certain who or where each other is? And who, for that matter, is "we"? So how broad and practical might be the changes that postmodernism implies? Is it cause for unease, for instance, that business seems still to be conducted in empiricist not to say Aristotelian terms (profit-loss, cause-effect, ends-means, provider-recipient, product-mar-

[8] *Manifestoes of Surrealism*, trans. Richard Seaver and Helen Lane (Ann Arbor: University of Michigan Press, 1972), p. 153.

ket)? The systemic consequences of this inertial rest are becoming hard to ignore. On a more intimate and potentially more powerful level, the affairs of questionable subjects-in-process, is it just the least bit unnerving to consider that, in Irigaray's words, "if we continue to speak the same language to each other, we will reproduce the same story"?[9]

It is, as an academic must be only too well aware, quite possible to live an unregenerately representational existence in this era of postmodernism. At the same time it seems likely that the postmodern reformation belongs to an inalienable shift of cultural disposition. The description of the physical world has changed, and with it the relative importance of habits formulated prior to that mutation. We are surrounded by a world that operates on the principles of quantum theory; we are living in mental worlds that operate on the principles of Newton. The object is not simply to modernize—or postmodernize—for its own sake; Newton's mechanics still operates at the everyday level of practical affairs, like dropping the apple and lifting the bag of groceries. But in the subvisible and stellar worlds that surround us, things have changed, and those changes limit the scope and importance both of Newtonian mechanics and of historical thinking. This change may seem evident as a constraint on discourse, but methodologically few observe it, and that is because it is very difficult to do so. My intention here is not to lobby for postmodernism at the expense of history, any more than it was my intention in writing about the historical conventions of realism to lobby for history at the expense of alternative conventions; my intention is to locate a major discursive shift in our understanding of temporality and to explore some of its implications. Many irreversible events have rendered historical thinking problematic; at the same time, postmodernism is not as new as recent terminology for it might suggest. For those interested in exploring postmodern alternatives, this book shows the importance of temporality to the postmodern reformation and explores some links between postmodernism and other, older achievements; for those interested in defending historical thinking from postmodern assault, this book renders problematic the historical convention on the assumption that what remains self-evident cannot be defended or maintained.

Postmodern narrative, then, by a complex and broadly prepared act of redefinition, explores in terms of consciousness and time some reformations being explored elsewhere in the physics, philosophy, and visual art of our time. Postmodern narrative is not a translation or a marginal instance of that physics or philosophy or art; it is an enactment that redefines time

[9] Luce Irigaray, "When Our Lips Speak Together" ("Quand nos lèvres se parlent," *Cahiers du Grif* no. 12), in *This Sex Which Is Not One* (*Ce sexe qui n'est pas un*, 1977), trans. Carolyn Burke (Ithaca: Cornell University Press, 1985), pp. 205–6. Also in *Signs* 6, no. 1 (Autumn 1980), pp. 69–70.

as a function of position, as a dimension of particular events. Furthermore, both position and event are described in terms of language. While all narrative is temporal by definition because its medium is temporal, postmodern sequences make accessible new temporal capacities that subvert the privilege of historical time and bind temporality in language.

The emphasis on the reflexivity of language, on its function as a system, has proven a valuable model for the treatment of various other systems (e.g., political, social, institutional) which thus can be broadly considered as "languages" in terms of their systemic or "differential" function: that is, a system in which difference, far from being expendable, is precisely what constitutes the system. There has been considerable theoretical exploration of this and related problems since Saussure, from his own analyses of the reflexivity of signs to the deconstruction and new historicism based on Derrida and Foucault and the new theoretics of language and writing developed by Kristeva, Irigaray, and Cixous. Common to all these theoretical efforts, though voiced in different ways, is a critique of the language of rationalism on the grounds that it reinforces one discursive function at unnecessary expense to another.

For example, this postmodern critique applies broadly to the discourse of the so-called "human sciences" and their opportunistic imports of methods and categories from the restricted and disciplined realm of modern physical science into a broad range of social, political, military, and other nonscientific areas of life. Such "sciences" produce a kind of interpretation that "always 'fits' because," as Heidegger says, "at bottom it says nothing" about phenomenal and mortal being-in-the-world.[10] This broad postmodern discursive critique subverts the metaphysic that posits essences like stable, self-identical, nondiscursive identities and the transcendental "laws" that operate "in" them. Such a metaphysic simply becomes inadequate in the discourse where essence or identity is multiplied because it is always *situated*, and where the situation is always discursive, which is to say always constructed by systems of signs whose function is differential.

With "text" and "writing" conceived in this way as modes of discursive engagement, the importance of so-called literary texts and writing becomes obvious: they are among the most highly achieved, most economical exercises of discursive engagement; they take up and improve the forms of discourse we inhabit every day in sloppier, less visible versions; they make

[10] *Being and Time* (*Sein und Zeit*, 1926), trans. John Macquarrie and Edward Robinson (New York: Harper & Row, 1962), p. 108; I.3.17. Heidegger asserts the "*equiprimordiality* of whatever constitutes Being against the methodologically unrestrained tendency to derive everything and anything from some simple 'primal ground'" (p. 170; I.5.28; p. 71; I.1.10). The principle of noncontradiction (along with primal ground, origin, and end) is a conception widely violated in postmodern narrative where essence can't really be said to exist at all because "it" is always multiple.

the premises of discourse evident. And there is another, less obvious reason to use so-called literary texts. Postmodern narrative language engages pulse and intellect simultaneously and consequently permits no easy escape from practical problems. It focuses on *practices* and refuses in so many ways to accept the distinction between practice and thought, between material and transcendental "reality." Such narrative literally recalls readers to their senses by focusing acts of attention on the actual practices of consciousness and sensibility as they operate in process, and not as they might operate if the world were the rational, natural, logocentric place that so many of our models still describe. In short, postmodern narrative does much to show what the contemporary critique of Western metaphysics amounts to in practice and for a subjectivity in process. It is arguable that, at least in terms of temporality and language, novels articulate the postmodern critique more fully and certainly more accessibly than do most theoretical texts.

The most direct answer to the question "Why text?" however, is "Why not?" The separation between a world of texts and a world of affairs, between history and text, is a separation that served modern discourse; it is the same distinction as the one between politics and aesthetics. Such distinctions disappear in postmodernism along with the agendas they serve, even though the *language* that maintains these distinctions is very hard to change, even for those interested in doing so. Andreas Huyssen, for example, in one breath argues eloquently for the end to this very dualism and in another says that the postmodern emphasis on textuality is aestheticism and thus "too high a price to pay" in terms of self-limitation, thereby retaining the modernist sense of "aesthetic."[11] The language is radioactive; we will get beyond its enforcements when we stop depreciating the "aesthetic" by distinguishing it from "politics" and start writing an Aesthetics of Capitalism, an Aesthetics of Feminism, an Aesthetics of Racism, an Aesthetics of the Corporation, an Aesthetics (with national differentia) of the Cartel, an Aesthetics of the Café/Bar: in other words, when we apply to material practices the precise and sophisticated knowledge of systems that since the Enlightenment we have called "aesthetic."

A word about my use of the term "representation": it is based in part on an argument I have made at length elsewhere,[12] but even so it needs some

[11] Andreas Huyssen, "Mapping the Postmodern," in Linda Nicholson, ed., *Feminism and Postmodernism* (New York: Routledge, 1990), pp. 271, 257, and 261. Laura Kipnis links the antipopular inclination of what she calls "modernism" with a slide to what she calls "aesthetic," thus also using "aesthetic" in its post-Enlightenment and empiricist sense ("Feminism: The Political Conscience of Postmodernism?" in Andrew Ross, *Universal Abandon?: The Politics of Postmodernism* (Minneapolis: University of Minnesota Press, 1988), p. 154.

[12] *Realism and Consensus in the English Novel* (Princeton: Princeton University Press, 1983), a discussion of the construction of history and of historical consciousness from Alberti to Henry James.

explanation. While I distinguish between "realism" and "representation," it seems to me important to keep them on the same leash if we ever are going to grasp the extent to which we have confused a specific, powerful, and possibly unique discursive convention—that of representation or realism as it has been defined in the culture of empiricism typical of Western culture since the Renaissance—with a universal norm for art, for narrative, for language, not to mention for other forms of organization.[13] I have argued that history itself is the most powerful construct of realistic conventions as we have known them since about 1400. This argument implies a large discursive frame of discussion, yet the term "realism" has been confined to disciplinary usages inconsistent with discourse analysis. One could argue, for example, that an image by Matisse, which is only incidentally realistic in the sense that it uses still recognizable shapes like a woman or a goldfish, also is only incidentally representational because its governing conventions have nothing to do with the agreements that produce "objects" and that Matisse's figures therefore have little to do with empirical objects and everything to do with design, *figura*, the condition of music—in short, with a nonreferential frame. To what extent a vestigial reference can act as a commanding convention is a question to be asked about much postmodern parody.

Postmodern writing has a kind of gravitational pull that is bound to influence any writing "about" it. The reflexive qualities of my writing (e.g., the rhythm sections punctuating the macro-sequence, the paralogical pulse of particular sentences, the repetition of key quotations, phrases, and points) may cause problems for diehard representationalists, dualists, and dialecticians who will want to factor them out as "noise." This, I assume, goes with the territory. A similar problem, for those who believe in the myth of comprehensive evidence, may be the fact that although I do mention a variety of writers, I concentrate on three texts, none of them especially recent (*Jealousy*, 1957; *Hopscotch*, 1963; *Ada*, 1969). These features of the book are clues to its purpose. What interests me here is the nature of the series, which can only be considered in detailed, material, embedded practices: practices that are textual in the large sense I have described. I mean to bring into view a new set of assumptions and practices that redefine time, a considerable task given the degree to which most of us take historical time for granted. I am counting on my readers to supply other examples. So, for instance, when I discuss the postmodern emphasis on plural semantic contexts, I hope that other examples from literature or science or economics will come to mind. I want to open the door, not ransack the room. The same spirit governs my use of sources, which I confine

[13] Jacques Attali also uses "representation" for a certain phase of (primarily Western) culture in *Noise: The Political Economy of Music* (*Bruits: essai sur l'économie politique de la musique*, 1977), trans. Brian Massumi (Minneapolis: University of Minnesota Press, 1985).

mainly to footnotes in order to concentrate in my own writing on the quality of the linguistic series.

On the other hand, this text "about" postmodernism is written in the language of representation; it produces meaning, assumes a consensus community, engages in historical generalization and footnotes. In short, in my own writing I do not entirely live up to the postmodern call, a methodological problem I recognize and settle in my own conscience with several assumptions. First, I assume that one need not give up history to challenge its hegemony, although I admit the perilousness of the undertaking and the ironies of the situation in which history must recognize its own historicity. Second, I assume that the play, the alliterating thematic echoes of a text, as of a life, may be heterogeneous to "meaning" and yet remain always in sight of it. Third, the essay form, as Cortázar says (*Hopscotch*, chap. 79), permits among specialists a kind of "literature" or bridge of language that is endlessly allusive and intertextual *because* there exists a community of discourse, however problematic, in which certain questions and terms are in play; I count on that allusiveness when I write this or that phrase. Fourth, I assume a discourse community, but I write at risk. Who is my audience? Will the specialists whose work I read, read mine? Will the specialists whose work I do not read, read mine? Is judicial resolution between one discussion and another important when the fact of cultural reformation calls for sustained writerly experiment and not the same old arguments? At a time when the discourse community for such work as this is sustaining the very reformation under consideration here, to what audience can I say, "This, our text"? And yet this text makes room for an audience, takes place at the hands of and in sight of an audience: one that experience has taught me to find broadly dispersed across disciplinary, ideological, and national interests.

My thesis in brief is this: postmodern narrative language undermines historical time and substitutes for it a new construction of temporality that I call rhythmic time. This rhythmic time either radically modifies or abandons altogether the dialectics, the teleology, the transcendence, and the putative neutrality of historical time; and it replaces the Cartesian *cogito* with a different subjectivity whose manifesto might be Cortázar's "I swing, therefore I am."[14] Whether or not it is meaningful to speak of a "new" history remains an open question, although the term "history" has become so saturated with dialectical value that it may no longer be very buoyant. My emphasis on the disappearance of historical thinking does not mean that I advocate either overthrowing "history" or rallying to its defense; the

[14] Julio Cortázar, *Hopscotch* (*Rayuela*, 1963), trans. Gregory Rabassa (New York: Random House, 1966), chap. 16.

state of affairs is far more complex and interesting than such formulations imply, and more important. We face interesting questions in the history of consciousness now that the discourse which has supported historical thinking turns out itself to be discourse-bound like every other habit and belief. I attend mainly to how postmodern narrative time works, what it offers, and what its implicit requirements, gains, and losses may be. The work that undermines history also opens new questions and provides new opportunities in practice. In the postmodern frame, choice is not a question of either/or but a question of emphasis.

Each of the three parts of this book has three main sections: the first two treat some aspect or outcome of the crisis that bears on our common historical conception of time, while the third, a "Rhythm Section," grounds the theoretical arguments in a particular feat of postmodern language. There are so many writers whose narratives this book describes[15] that from sheer necessity I have chosen to focus on three novelists: Alain Robbe-Grillet, Julio Cortázar, and Vladimir Nabokov—one French, one Latin American, and one (to use his word) Amerussian—and on one novel by each, *Jealousy*, *Hopscotch*, and *Ada*. I assume that although these books are widely known, it is unlikely that many readers will be familiar with all of them. My emphasis is on the nature of the series and thus requires a detailed look at a few instances, not "coverage"; and I write so as to suggest alternative semantic systems without pursuing each possiblity. The fact that surrealism figures as an important precursor for all three of the writers on whom I mainly focus, or that Robbe-Grillet and Nabokov have expressed strong admiration for each other's work, helps confirm the choices but did not necessarily inspire them.[16] I make no claims about influence.

---

[15] Extensive lists of writers that might qualify as postmodern can be found in José Donoso, *The Latin American "Boom": A Personal History* (*Historia personal del "boom,"* 1972), trans. Gregory Kovolakos (New York: Columbia University Press in association with the Center for Inter-American Relations, 1977); Linda Hutcheon, A *Poetics of Postmodernism* (New York: Routledge, 1988); Morton Levitt, *Modernist Survivors: The Contemporary Novel in England, the United States, France, and Latin America* (Columbus: Ohio State University Press, 1987); Brian McHale, *Postmodern Fiction* (New York: Methuen, 1987); Vivian Mercier, *A Reader's Guide to the New Novel: From Queneau to Pinget* (New York: Farrar, Straus, and Giroux, 1971); William Spanos, *Repetitions* and Sharon Spencer, *Time, Space and Structure in the Modern Novel* (New York: New York University Press, 1971).

[16] Robbe-Grillet has said he feels especially close to Nabokov and William Burroughs (as well as completely different from the pseudorealism of Saul Bellow and Norman Mailer); the heroine of *The Voyeur*, who appears with a bigger role in *Project for a Revolution in New York*, "belongs to a race we call Lolitas" (David Hayman, "An Interview with Alain Robbe-Grillet," in *Contemporary Literature* 16, no. 3 [Summer 1975], pp. 273–85; quote p. 200). Nabokov, explaining his special preference for Robbe-Grillet and Borges among contemporary writers, says of Robbe-Grillet that "his fiction is magnificently poetical and original, and the shifts of levels, the interpenetration of successive impressions and so forth belong of course to psychology—psychology at its best. Borges is also a man of infinite talent, but his miniature

Many other writers and texts put in appearances or figure in the margins; My sources, for example, include twentieth-century painting, especially surrealism, contemporary antirealist narrative (Jorge Luis Borges, Cortázar, Marguerite Duras, Gabriel García Márquez, John Hawkes, Nabokov, Robbe-Grillet, Nathalie Sarraute) and antirealistic theory, especially those informed by phenomenology, linguistics, and feminism (for example, Cixous, Derrida, Foucault, Heidegger, Kristeva); Luis Buñuel and Alain Resnais make guest appearances. It will be clear throughout that I leave the business of identifying and classifying writers to others and that my objective is to explore a problematic.

Part One ("Time off the Track") describes first the difference between the modern, historical construction of time so preeminent between roughly 1500 and 1900 (Section I: "Historical Time as a Thing of the Past") and the radically different postmodern conception of "Time as Rhythm" (Section II). For at least several centuries historical time, with its linked past and future, has made possible the articulation of certain "laws" of development and has been a cultural absolute from physics to politics to narrative. Its powers are familiar, but its liabilities need an articulation that I attempt to give them here. With the developments for which 1905 stands as an arbitrary watershed, this temporal medium which had quietly assumed priority in nearly all discourse by the nineteenth century suddenly appeared not as a "natural" and constant condition of all existence but, on the contrary, as only one dimension, one variable, one function of discourse. Time ceased to be neutral. As Einstein says in the second epigraph to this book, he did not arrive at the Special Theory "until at last it came to me that time was suspect."[17] In postmodern narrative historical time appears not as a categorical "human" imperative or a fact of nature but as a formation that validates by enactment certain principles (notably the values of consensus and of transcendent subjectivity) and excludes others. Rhythmic postmodern time reinstates those excluded values. Whereas historical time is like "a road" and its life "a kind of journey," in the words of the other epigraph to this book, postmodern time belongs to a figure, an arrangement in which "the other world surrounds us always and is not at all at the end of some pilgrimage."[18]

Part Two ("Multilevel Thinking") deals with the implications and to some extent the tradition of this postmodern construction of temporality;

---

labyrinths and the roomy ones of Robbe-Grillet are quite differently built, and the lighting is not the same" (*Strong Opinions* [New York: McGraw-Hill, 1973], p. 80).

[17] Ronald Clark, *Einstein: The Life and Times* (New York: World Publishing Co., 1971), p. 84: from a letter to R. S. Shankland of the Case Institute, Cleveland, cited in *The American Journal of Physics* 31 (January 1963), pp. 47–57.

[18] Vladimir Nabokov, *The Gift*, 1937–38, trans. Michael Scammell with the collaboration of the author (New York: Capricorn Books, 1963), p. 322.

I pay particular attention to surrealism and to "the crisis of the object" it announces as a basis for exploring "the crisis of the subject" that attends and supports realistic and historicist conventions of objectivity. Postmodern temporality entails new functions for subjectivity and new acts of attention, although the critique of the subject upon which so much in postmodernism depends (for example, Kristeva and even Derrida) often stops far short of denying the existence of the subject. The postmodern critique of dialectics got special help from surrealists, whose techniques of estrangement have been adapted by postmodern novelists to linear and historical conditions. *To make the syntax appear*, such artists and writers provoke various discursive crises (of the object, the subject, the sign) that indicate the constitutive power of discourse for such apparently autonomous things as objects and subjects and even words. This problem of making the syntax appear is what novelists have inherited as a problem of temporality.

Part Three ("Language and Time") outlines the crisis of the sign that is directly linked with the crises of object and subject. A key issue in the changed definition of nonrepresentational, nonhistorical, "rhythmic" time is the invocation of language as an appropriate model. This part deals with the new emphasis on play as distinct from more productive forms of narrative activity (Section I: "Play and the Crisis of the Sign"); and in Section II, "*Della Figura* (Time and the Figure)," it introduces the concept of *figure* as the linguistic equivalent of rhythmic time. This part states most explicitly an informing theme of the book, the affinity between postmodern writing and feminism (I define that embattled term elsewhere; here my usage explains itself).[19] They are linked by their insistence that the chief political problem is one of language, and that it can only be solved by writing a new language, one uncontaminated by the old, radioactive terms (Irigaray, Cixous, Robbe-Grillet, and Derrida all explicitly mention this difficulty). Is it possible to exist *outside* history? Women know; they have existed there. Along with postmodern novelists, theorists like Kristeva, Cixous, and Irigaray have been most interested in the possible practical extensions of the now broadly accepted critique of representational discourse. Their writing engages the important questions in ways similar to postmodern narrative writing. What practice, for example, is implied by the theoretical recognition that language has a dimension of play? Where and how do the various social, psychic, literary, and other "texts" of every day accommodate disappearance of subject and object and the emergence of nonlinear models of relationship, especially temporal relationship? What is the language of a

[19] For this definition of feminism see Elizabeth Ermarth, "On Having a Personal Voice," in Gayle Greene and Coppelia Kahn, eds., *Histories/A History: The Making of Feminist Criticism* (forthcoming).

multilevel subjectivity in process? How does language behave off the linear track, and what "reality" does it offer as a possible residence?

Discarding the terms of modernist discourse, while not easy, is a necessary discipline to postmodernism. The discourse of historicism and representation remains, as Barthes said of Euclidean space, fundamentally a religious construction, and its terms will not help us appreciate postmodernism.[20] The discourse of modernism extends its media (space, time, consciousness, money, humanity) to infinity and encourages us to forget finitude and to distribute energy toward an infinite horizon. The discourse of postmodernism finds time and space warped and bounded by finite and newly defined subjective systems. Modernist discourse respects primarily the constraints of an "objective reality" that, from a postmodern context, appears to be the mediated construct of a founding subject. In postmodernist discourse the primary constraint is absolute and unmediatable finitude, a recognition that inspires reflexiveness because activity no longer can be referred to unchanging external absolutes. Such reflexiveness, furthermore, belongs to specific activity and thus is always experimental—I call it "improvisation"—and fundamentally inaccessible to generalization. The operative constraint in postmodern writing is not any transcendent "reality" beyond language but language itself: its substitutions are the events of rhythmic temporality and its figures are the unique poetry of individual life. The collapse in postmodern writing of dualisms that sustain representational distance and enable its mediations opens an unfamiliar and surprising situation where both time and consciousness belong to the linguistic figure.

[20] Although sequence creates problems significantly different from those recognized in Barthes's static, spatial metaphors: "We need to substitute for the magisterial space of the past—which was fundamentally a religious space . . . a less upright, less Euclidean space where no one, neither teacher nor students, would ever be *in his final place*." From "Writers, Intellectuals, Teachers," in *Image, Music, Text*, trans. Stephen Heath (Glasgow: Fontana/Collins, 1977), p. 205.

Part One _____

Time off the Track

> First there is a confused situation, which can
> only be defined by words; I start out from this
> half-shadow and if what I mean (if what is
> *meant*) has sufficient strength, the *swing* begins
> at once, a rhythmic swaying that draws me to
> the surface, lights everything up, conjugates this
> confused material and the one who suffers it
> into a clear third somehow fateful level:
> sentence, paragraph, page, chapter, book. This
> swaying, this *swing* in which confused material
> goes about taking shape, is for me the only
> certainty of its necessity, because no sooner
> does it stop than I understand that I no longer
> have anything to say.
> —Julio Cortázar, *Hopscotch*

NARRATIVES have various forms of cultural importance, not the least of which is the pleasure they give those who read or tell or hear them. For example, in the telling and retelling of detective stories or stories with investigative interest we not only pursue particular truths, we also reconfirm a way of approaching questions of truth; we confirm, in short, an entire discourse, one that values empirical procedure, reasoned discovery, problem solution, linear causality and temporal unfolding, individual subjectivity, and so on. Such stories exist primarily to rationalize experience: the mystery is explained, the behavior classified, and the criminal brought to justice (we note that often in this convention the victim who feels the brunt of reason gone astray has been less important). Such rationalization produces satisfaction not incidentally but as a primary effect because in that satisfaction is a confirmation, an acceptance, a re-inscription of a whole set of practices and beliefs, of which this particular act of reading is a ritual of almost religious importance.

Detective stories are merely one instance of the narrative that we can find in other and more sophisticated written forms in the novels of Stendhal and Gustave Flaubert, of Charles Dickens and George Eliot, of Ivan Turgenev and Leo Tolstoy, as well as most popular writers today. In addition, we have the vast store of unwritten narratives that support our political and social assumptions: stories that we tell ourselves or ask to be told and that, though they are less obviously literary and often, as on the nightly news, less satisfactory than those in novels, nevertheless also constitute the matrix for our most important practices. Our narratives, then, function as legends always have, as collective myths that confirm various primary "truths" about "the way things are."

A primary formulating maneuver of these now familiar narratives is the convention of historical time, a convention that belongs to a major, generally unexamined article of cultural faith (chiefly in the West and chiefly since the Renaissance and the Reformation): the belief in a temporal medium that is neutral and homogeneous and that, consequently, makes possible those mutually informative measurements between one historical moment and another that support most forms of knowledge current in the West and that we customarily call "science." History has become a commanding metanarrative, perhaps *the* metanarrative in Western discourse.

Historical time, in fact, may be the most powerful value confirmed by the narratives of Western, especially Anglo-American, culture; it informs much of what we tell ourselves about individual and collective life. This convention underwrites the many touchstones of social, scientific, and economic thought in the West since the seventeenth century, for example, what is said or implied by the United States Constitution, Darwinian biology, and Marxist philosophy. The convention of historical time also underwrites certain kinds of research and writing, including this book and notwithstanding that its subject matter concerns the disappearance of the very convention that supports it. That convention even underwrites the distinction between subject matter and treatment, content and form, that I have just made in describing my project in this book. In short, it would be hard to overestimate the scope and importance of the convention of historical time and everything it implies about individual subjectivity, collective endeavor, proper uses of language, the nature of power or thought, and, perhaps most of all, the nature and uses of knowledge.

This chapter deals with the shift in postmodern narratives from one time to another: from the linear track of historical time to the conjugating rhythm that Cortázar describes. I do not mean to suggest, however, that this shift is a simple exchange of one model for another; on the contrary, it belongs to an extensive and complex set of redefinitions necessarily simplified by discussion. Implicit in this shift are new definitions of subjectivity. Because the individual subject is largely a construct of historical conventions, the revision of historical temporality necessarily involves, among other things, the replacement of the Cartesian *cogito ergo sum* with a new formulation, "I swing, therefore I am."[1] In postmodern narratives temporality has little to do with historical conventions; instead it is multivalent and nonlinear. Whatever the advantages of this new temporality, they are gained at the expense of certain preconceptions that are commonly held to be essential, "natural," even sacred, and so the narratives that inscribe it can strike an unwilling reader particularly hard. Take the individual subject, for example, which disappears along with historical time: Richard Rorty explains that there is more to modernism than "that famous 'subjectivity.' "[2] Maybe so, but as I argue elsewhere, "that famous 'subjectivity' " does found the consensus that constructs historical time in the first place and, consequently, is instrumental in maintaining all the other agreements of modernist and empiricist culture. Representational "time" is history, and "the subject" is its constituting alibi. The loss of the medium of time (as of realistic space) in postmodernism, along with the crises of their subjects and objects and language, may seem to give an unmotivated quality to postmodern art for those who wish to continue assuming long-habitual definitions. If one conceives of narrative or political art in terms of unified temporal sequences of action—sequences that can be formulated in terms of cause and consequence—the absence of such sequences and powers seems tantamount to the absence of motivation itself or, even worse, a symptom of authorial self-display and self-indulgence. Behind such reactions often lies an explicit anxiety that postmodern art reflects a breakdown of the bases of morality and order. I have argued elsewhere that historical thinking is an attempt to "save the essences" comparable to the medieval effort to "save the appearances."[3] The efforts are similar in magnitude, and so is the revision of historicism evident in postmodern writing. The reformation signaled by changes in narrative temporality, however, belongs to a much larger cultural deformation and critique and, like it or not, one that cannot be deterred by any amount of dismissal.

Postmodern time is coextensive with the event, not a medium for recollecting it in tranquillity. Just as the neutral homogenized space of realism has largely disappeared in pictorial art since cubism, which often treats realistic space and the technologies for creating it as themselves phenomena, so similarly the neutral, homogenized temporality of realism has largely disappeared in postmodern novels like *Jealousy* or *Hopscotch* or *Ada*, which treat that (historical) time as itself a phenomenon. Where the older con-

---

[1] Julio Cortázar, *Hopscotch* (*Rayuela*, 1963), trans. by Gregory Rabassa (New York: Random House, 1966), chap. 16.

[2] Richard Rorty, "Habermas and Lyotard on Postmodernity," in Richard Bernstein, ed., *Habermas and Modernity* (Cambridge, Mass: MIT Press, 1985), p. 170.

[3] For a summary of both kinds of saving see Ermarth, *Realism and Consensus*, pp. 8–24; and for a longer discussion of the medieval effort see Owen Barfield, *Saving the Appearances* (New York: Harcourt Brace and World, n.d.).

ventions of space and time—and they are conventions essential not only to novels but to cultural narratives of all kinds, as well as to empirical science and technology—provided common ground in the media of time and space, postmodern narrative looks elsewhere for its common ground. To put it in other terms, the constant in postmodern narrative—the controlling denominator that makes possible all other definitions relative to one another—is no longer the time of history, the time of project, the time of Newton and Kant, the time of clocks and capital. Narrative no longer inscribes the time that makes possible the perception of invariant identities like "subject" and "object"; instead it concentrates phenomenologically on the reader-events that collapse the distances between object and subject, inside and outside. In postmodern narrative we experience temporality as an imaginary ambience containing tensions, fields, tectonics, values. Time, too, can stumble, we learn in *One Hundred Years of Solitude*, "and splinter and leave an eternalized fragment in a room."[4] Time, in other words, is not neutral and absolute but a function of position, literally of reader position. In short, postmodern temporality makes temporality itself part of a system of value and emphasis. The sentence read *is* time and time is a sentence: a defined part of a defined sequence that comes to an end before another sequence, another *conjugation*, begins. The "distance" or perspective necessary for maintaining historical time simply is unavailable where time is defined by such specific formulations.

This focus on the reading event collapses the distinction between invention and reality, a distinction that is another form of the habitual inclination toward transcending the moment and the detail that is fostered by historical thinking. Nineteenth-century narrative, even at its most reflexive, for example, in the novels of George Eliot or George Meredith, still did not ask readers to make this new move of considering one's own responses as text; rather this earlier narrative asked readers to consider readable parallels that were "like" life, and most popular novels in the 1980s still permit readers this detachment; that is their particular charm. The purpose of such reading is still the same: ultimately it is a way of reaffirming the existence and operability of historical time together with the beliefs it makes possible.

Postmodern narrative denies the dissociation of art from life, making the act of reading and interpretation the subject of the book. (In Part Three I discuss at greater length the collapse of this familiar dualism.) In these redefinitions, acts of reading and interpretation take on new meaning. Readers must continuously recognize that when they read, as when they do other things, their consciousness is active, not passive; that reading time is

---

[4] Gabriel García Márquez, *One Hundred Years of Solitude* (*Cien Años de Soledad*, 1967), trans. Gregory Rabassa (New York: Harper & Row, 1970), p. 322.

not a separate arrangement where one brackets or neutralizes life but instead a full exercise of that life. To read any text, whether or not it is a printed book, is to participate; it is to continue to undergo the warps and deformations that never-neutral life always entails. As we read and decipher, we coinvent; and this active attention to reader awareness belongs to a broad redefinition of what constitutes a "text." We are always deciphering a text: the Republican convention, the intentions of a friend, Hiroshima, the emergence of mass media, *glasnost*, the behavior of a relative, the invasion of a country, the painting of Paul Klee—all are texts; all are constructs; all are readable inventions. To read is to interpret and to interpret is to reinvent, or coinvent, the text. To say such things are inventions, moreover, is not at all to deny their reality or their profoundly consequential and material existence; it is not mere aestheticism to say that life literally is art because postmodern writing collapses the dualism between what is real and what is made that supports aestheticism as well as historicism.

If art is not dissociated from life, it follows that life is not dissociated from art: every maneuver that we make as we pass through our days and our lives is an act of interpretation, and thus an act of projective invention. Furthermore, we participate almost miraculously in various acts of *collective* interpretation and invention—what Cortázar calls "the colorless fire" and "the whatsis of the race" (chap. 73). Once we begin to see our mental maneuvers as inventions, they become not "neutral" and "natural" ways of behaving but instead modes of exercising responsibility and freedom. No longer *fixed* by an inflexible conception like point of view, the postmodern reader can practice deliberately the inevitable invention, perhaps even collaborate differently in collective solutions that are, by this logic, also inventions. Unlike the older narrative conventions that naturalized themselves and thus effectively neutralized the active moment of participation entailed by deciphering a text, postmodern narrative constantly reminds us that each day, in countless and intensely realized details, we reinvent Paris, Detroit, and Gaza. To read postmodern narrative is to participate self-consciously in the invention and deformation of value. Neutrality, that commanding value of historical consciousness, is precluded by the bounded character of each embedded moment.

There's no place like a Borges story to discover the priority of invention and the link between that invention and time. In "Tlön, Uqbar, Orbis Tertius," for example, the reader must endure the gradual revelation that a fictional world is taking over the so-called real one. In this fictional world everything is subjective; heresy is "materialism" or faith in a verifiable objectivity. The foundation of its geometry is "the surface, not the point. This system rejects the principle of parallelism, and states that, as man moves about, he alters the forms which surround him. The arithmetical system is based on the idea of indefinite numbers." This counterintuitive system (es-

pecially counterintuitive is its depreciation of the idea of "truth" and its
denial of time) belongs to a culture with values diametrically opposed to
the culture of representation and science:

> The metaphysicians of Tlön are not looking for
> truth, or even for an approximation of truth; they
> are after a kind of amazement. They consider
> metaphysics a branch of fantastic literature.
> They know that a system is nothing more than the
> subordination of all the aspects of the universe
> to some one of them. . . . One of the schools in
> Tlön has reached the point of denying time. It
> reasons that the present is undefined, that the
> future has no other reality than as present hope,
> that the past is no more than present memory.*
>
> . . . .
>
> * Russell (*The Analysis of Mind*, 1921, page 159) conjectures that our planet was
> created a few moments ago, and provided with a humanity which "remembers"
> an illusory past.

This story forces readers gradually into the position where the invented
country of Uqbar and *its* invented country of Tlön eclipse the "real" world
like a black hole suddenly visible. This invented—literally fantastic—world
becomes the primary reality to which the rationalist's researches become
strictly marginal. This universe is "a series of mental processes, whose unfolding is to be understood only as a time sequence" and not as a spatial-
ized universe of causality.[5] Looked at one way, novels like *Anna Karenina*
or *Middlemarch* are precisely this: a series of mental processes whose unfolding is what we call time; but neither Tolstoy nor George Eliot sought
primarily to make readers aware of that fact. The difference in postmodern
narrative is that the novelist seeks precisely to make that mental unfolding
evident to the point of making it the main business of the text.

As for history, Borges celebrates it as the mode of fantasy that founds
entire cultural formations. The true historical date, as he writes in "The
Modesty of History,"[6] is not the day of an action but the day of its perpet-
uation. This act of recording is an event unparalleled even by the battle
recorded or the retort between royalties. But Borges's historian is a writer,
not the social scientist scanning developments from past to future, and as
such he points toward an alternative view of history. The Borgesian histo-

[5] *Ficciones* (1956), English trans. (New York: Grove Press, 1962), pp. 24–28.
[6] *A Personal Anthology* (*Antología Personal*, 1961), English trans. (New York: Grove Press,
1967), pp. 179–83.

rian is the one who introduces into language and thus into the reservoir of human awareness a theme that was previously unformed or mute.

Section I: Historical Time as a Thing of the Past

Among the various interdisciplinary critiques of Western discourse and its metaphysics, one of the potentially most subversive and, perhaps for that reason, the most incompletely theorized is the critique of historical time. Various forays on the subject of time by theorists from Nietzsche to Kristeva have not yet reached critical mass in the way that other theoretical discussions have done. Unquestioning use of terms like "history," "time," and "the past" reappear regularly in the most putatively radical critiques of discourse, of theory and practice. While no other term can any longer be taken for granted and all terms are used in a deconstructive atmosphere of constructive suspicion, sometimes treated with quotation marks, cross-out marks, or other typographical antibiotics against infection from old, old habits, the word "time" still seems to remain largely transparent and functional in much the way it has been used since its culture took hold in the seventeenth century. This culture remains popularly preeminent today, especially in Anglo-American societies, despite its evident uneasiness as it teeters on the brink of who knows what transubstantiation. In this context the work of postmodern novelists becomes especially important because it is here that the problem of time, one of the most practical of problems, receives the experimental exploration lacking elsewhere. Novelists who simply abandon historical time as a convention, along with all its baggage including preeminently the stable individual subject, provide an alternative practice that illuminates as no theory has yet done the limitations of historical time.

Historical time is a thing of the past in its own terms as well. The past, however diffuse or hard to specify, is always seen in hindsight from a future vantage point which discovers a past that is by definition embedded in a controlled pattern of significance. A brief account of the primary values and assumptions entailed by historical conventions is essential preparation for my main discussion of postmodern narrative. Those conventions which presume that time is synonymous with historical time still have enormous scope and applicability, to the point that "history," as Claude Lévi-Strauss has said, "has replaced mythology and fulfills the same function."[7] As I have discussed at length elsewhere the construction of history and its conscious-

---

[7] Claude Lévi-Strauss, *Myth and Meaning* (New York: Schocken Books, 1979), p. 43. By "same function" he means insuring the faithfulness or commensurability between past, present, and future, thereby implicitly acknowledging that there is more than one (our historical) way to accomplish this.

ness from the Renaissance to the late nineteenth century, the briefest summary must suffice here.[8]

The medium of historical time is a construct and itself a representation of
the first magnitude. This "history" may be one of the most specifically
modern achievements. Without the production of history by modern culture, that is, without the production of a neutral time analogous to the
neutral space evident in realistic painting, we would be without that temporal medium that makes possible an activity unknown in classical times:
the mutually informative measurement between widely separated events
that underlies modern empirical science, modern cartography and exploration, certain forms of political and artistic organization such as representational government and tonal music, and certain habitual conceptions of
identity, simple location, structure, consciousness, the subject, and social
"laws" that govern our metaphors of psychic as well as corporate existence.[9] It is demonstrable that "history" belongs to the same descriptive
conventions that made possible the painting and architecture of the Renaissance and the empirical science of the sixteenth and seventeenth centuries.
     A familiar and immediately accessible instance is the technique of single-
point perspective, which coordinates pictorial space so as to produce a
common horizon for all potential perspectives. As opposed to the space of
medieval painting, which was either a frankly virtual space for icons or a
quasirepresentational space fractured by competing vanishing points, the
space of Masaccio, Piero della Francesca, and a large company of Renaissance architects and painters was a homogenized, neutral medium in which
mutually informative measurements could be made and in which the logic
of spectator awareness was absolute. From any viewpoint available in the
common horizon—either the one arbitrarily assigned by the artist to viewers or any others potentially available in the representational space—a spectator could grasp an invariant logic of relationships (a "world") that remained the same regardless of his or her position and that extended to
infinity, thus having the value of universal truth. This is the convention

     [8] See *Realism and Consensus*, especially the theoretical section, pp. 1–92, which specifies the
centuries-long codification of new ideas of space and time that emerge from the Renaissance
and Reformation and support the culture of empiricism. This time of "memory and project"
is what Lyotard calls the temporality appropriate to the "game of science" (*The Postmodern
Condition*, p. 26).
     [9] On musical forms of consensus see Attali: "The entire history of tonal music, like that of
classical political economy, amounts to an attempt to make people believe in a consensual
representation of the world" (*Noise*, p. 46); Ermarth, *Realism and Consensus*, pp. 24–33 esp.
p. 29n; Leo Spitzer, *Classical and Christian Ideas of World Harmony* (Baltimore: Johns Hopkins University Press, 1963), pp. 39–44; and Charles Rosen, *The Classical Style: Hayden,
Mozart, Beethoven* (New York: Viking, 1971), pp. 23–29.

that reigned, in Western European painting at least, from the fourteenth through the nineteenth centuries. It is telling that Alberti, whose *Della Pittura* articulated the new pictorial conventions, chose the word *istoria* to name the highest achievement of that art.

This technical achievement in painting belongs to the shift associated with the rediscovery of classical models in the Renaissance, a shift that changed not only the content but the entire method of understanding. One could say that the most important thing about the rediscovery of classical learning was as much the act of rediscovery as it was the creation of models. The act of historical awareness ran through the era from Piero della Francesca to Erasmus like a bolt of energy and opened the horizon, both in space and time, to exploration and conquest. From this breathtaking effort emerged the modern idea of history: the view of time as a neutral, homogeneous medium like the space of pictorial realism in painting; a time where mutually informative measurements can be made between past, present, and future, and where all relationships can be explained in terms of a common horizon. In single-point perspective sight is rationalized by a pictorial space that extends from here to eternity without encountering any disturbing fractures. The temporal analogue that links past, present, and future involves a different faculty (consciousness) and a different medium (time), but the same formation inheres. In history, that is, consciousness is rationalized by a narrative time that extends from here to eternity, perhaps encountering many disturbing warps but no disturbing fractures. In history all temporal perspectives, however widely dispersed, "agree" in the sense that they do not contradict; in this powerful sense they achieve a consensus tantamount to the creation of a common horizon in time and hence of the power to think historically.

In narrative the key feature in this convention of temporality is the much discussed, so-called omniscient narrator, or what I suggest in *Realism and Consensus* we think of as "the Narrator as Nobody." This narrator (like the professor in *Lucky Jim*) is literally "History speaking," and nothing more individualized; in fact, the term "narrator" is misleading because it refers to a range of temporal codes that far exceed the confidential opinions this narrator sometimes addresses to the reader. An individual voice is one small part of its range, just as any single vantage point in a single-point perspective painting is only one small part of the implicitly collective rationalization; more generally the "narrator" remains disembodied and indistinguishable from the narrative process itself, almost like a power of the past tense. This "Nobody" narrator, this implicitly collective historical reflex rationalizes consciousness by aligning time into a single horizon. At this level of awareness, distinctions between individual sites of consciousness, whether of author, reader, or character, seem less important than the power to slide between them, that is, the power to move between past and future. This power of transition itself is a major focus and interest of such narratives.

Such "Nobody" narrators literally *constitute* historical time by threading together into one system and one act of attention a whole series of moments and perspectives. Thus the continuums of time and of consciousness literally appear inseparable, functioning together as the medium of events even though this particular mutuality is rarely explicitly mentioned because to do so would be to compromise the whole effect and to locate a vulnerability in its presentation of objectivity, a vulnerability grasped by postmodern writers. In other words, the historical convention of temporality asserts a fundamental and powerful idea: that the neutral medium of experience, which extends to infinity and opens to an individual mind a vast power of generalization, literally is constructed by, is a product of, consensus, that is, the formal agreement among viewpoints that produces "space" and "time."

The historical convention implies a vast potentiality for human consciousness of near-universal extension; and because any particular position on the continuum of time and consciousness is arbitrary and movable, the historical convention also implies the exchangeability of consciousness between individuals, a sort of generic "human" consciousness that is the provisional sum of human capability. The collection of voices in, say, a novel like *War and Peace* all "agree"—not in the trivial sense of agreement about particular issues but in the most powerful sense of constructing and inhabiting the "same" time, which is to say, a medium in which what happens in one moment has influence upon another moment. The "narrator," that complex function without individual definition, maintains the communication between past, present, and future, and thus the possibility of causal sequences from one to another. Any realistic, that is, representational and historical narrative has as its primary cultural effect the inscription of a single, homogeneous time stretching to infinity and carrying along in its powerful current absolutely everything; it inscribes what Meyer Schapiro calls "the immense, historically developed capacity to keep the world in mind";[10] it leaves nothing aside or behind. The powers thus available to "human" consciousness are enormous. In a convention that extends to infinity the rationalized powers of human attention, no atrocity need remain unexplained, no mystery unsolved, no mistake unrectified.

When we take the historical medium for granted, what we are really

---

[10] Schapiro, "The Nature of Abstract Art," p. 83. This capacity to keep the world in mind is powerful and impressive; it is also historically specific and limited. Habermas appears to confuse it with a universal method: "Expressing the modern world in an edifice of thought means of course only reflecting the essential features of the age as in a mirror—which is not the same thing as conceiving [*begreifen*] it" (Habermas, *Philosophical Discourse of Modernity*, p. 19).

doing is accepting and reinscribing the belief—and it is nothing more or less than an arbitrary and breathtaking collective act of faith—that it is our powers of collective agreement that literally make possible historical continuity. The consciousness that goes with this historical time transcends particulars and always exceeds them. The power of this consciousness and temporality is "Nobody's" power: at once human and unspecific, powerfully present but not individualized. This historical consciousness is literally engendered by the very sequences it interprets. This flexible and composite historical medium, at once time and consciousness, literally maintains by its ceaseless relay between the past and future of events the medium of history itself as a common temporal horizon. In history this coordination is distributed over a sequence and thus depends on a collected consciousness to maintain it: a more intangible feat perhaps than the visual coordinations of homogenized and neutralized space but equally powerful in extending to infinity the human capabilities it thereby inscribes.

The "rationalization of sight"[11] that Quattrocento architects and painters produced, then, has its temporal homology in the rationalization of consciousness gradually achieved several hundred years later across a broad range of social and political discourse. The achievement of this temporal construct took place over several centuries and nations and, especially in England, transformed social and political structure by transforming the very bases of belief and knowledge. In realistic time, as in realistic space, linear coordinates establish a homogeneous, neutral medium, not warped by divine or other influence but instead a constant, universal neutrality in which human values take shape and disappear. It is a mystery worth pursuing that the specifically *temporal* manifestations of the Renaissance took so long to develop.[12]

Although by now common sense may say that these media, neutral homogeneous space and time, are "natural" bases for our mutually informa-

[11] The "rationalization of sight" is William J. Ivins, Jr.'s term for the Renaissance achievement in painting and other spatial representation. Everyone interested in discourse analysis should see both of his books on the subject: *Art and Geometry: A Study in Space Intuitions* (1946) (New York: Dover, 1964); and *On the Rationalization of Sight* (1938) (New York: DaCapo, 1973). Like postmodern theorists, although not in the same vocabulary, Ivins emphasizes the importance of architecture in the production of massive discursive deformation, and in the Italian Renaissance, specifically Brunelleschi.

[12] In England this involved the humanist reformation of church and state, the development of empirical philosophy and science, the rise of a contract society, and many other massive cultural and political reformations that could not take place overnight. Most of all, I think, the temporal manifestations of the new learning took a while to develop because they involve a deformation of the very idea of consciousness—a word that would not have had the same (if any) meaning for Homer or even Augustine that it has for us. Since the Renaissance the very ideas of time and consciousness have been so symbiotic that they are practically (I use the language of modernist representation) one and the same.

tive measurements—those all-important agreements among varied views—
the *contrary* is the case, as a historicizing of historical conventions shows.
The formal achievement that I call the realistic "consensus" has itself *created*
the media of space and time in which we proceed to make our mutually
informative measurements, arrive at our hypotheses, formulate our laws,
and produce our experiments, our capital, and our knowledge, that other
form of capital. There is nothing "natural" about it.

Historical time, and the consciousness coextensive with it, is at least potentially interchangeable among individuals because it is consciousness of
the *same* thing: an invariant world, one that changes according to certain
laws that do not change. Any individual perspective is only arbitrarily limited; it is only the "accidents" of language, nationality, gender, and so on
that obscure this potentially cosmic vision. But this condition notwithstanding, if each individual could see all the world (so the representational
convention of time goes), all would see the *same* world. The historical convention allows for practical necessity, of course; everyone is mortal and can
travel only to a few places of the mind and the planet. However—and this
is important to the postmodern critique—realism minimizes that limitation, that mortality in favor of mobility, extension, infinity. In this, perhaps, temporal realism or history betrays its religious origin.[13]

The triumph of historical time is thus an important fictional event in every
sense of the word and essentially a triumph of collective awareness, literally
collective consciousness that creates and sustains itself. This historical idea
is the modern formation par excellence. Postmodern novelists begin their
primary task of reformulating temporality by showing readers *that* such an
idea of temporality is a convention and a collective act of faith, not a condition of nature. What follows from this remains to be seen, but it is useful
to remember that even radical critique does not necessarily entail total destruction of all we hold dear. "It is not easy to say something new," as
Foucault says; "it is not enough for us to open our eyes, to pay attention,
or to be aware" because entrenched conventions influence what we see,
and such conventions have great staying power.[14]

Given the importance of these representational conventions in time as
well as space, one can understand the shock produced by work that undermines them without hope of recovery. Like the redefinition of space in

---

[13] On the Christian sources of history and of humanism see Erich Auerbach on how the
treatment of Jewish law and history as figurae for Christ and his laws gave Europeans "a basic
conception of history," in "Figura" (*Neue Dantestudien*, 1944), trans. Ralph Manheim, and
among Auerbech's essays collected as *Scenes from the Drama of European Literature* (New
York: Meridian, 1959), p. 53.

[14] Michael Foucault, *The Archaeology of Knowledge* (*L'Archaeologie du Savoir*, 1969), trans.
A. M. Sheridan Smith (London: Tavistock, 1972), p. 45.

painting since cubism, the redefinition of time that has occurred in post-modern narrative literally takes from us a medium that has been vital to Western empiricist culture and with it various important constructs, including that all-important changeling, the individual subject. Because the postmodern critique of history flies in the face of what seems to be common sense, I want to discuss briefly some of the limitations or weaknesses in the historical convention that may account in part for its eclipse. I will concentrate mainly on one of the historical convention's most powerful effects: its production of transcendence in various appealing forms.

Historical thinking entails a perpetual transcendence of, one might even say flight from, the concrete, and because of this, it offers no assistance to those who must deal with material limitation, including the ultimate material limitation of death. This fatal tendency of "history" to transcend whatever is concrete and particular has been variously noted among twentieth-century writers. This historicist weakness may be endemic to humanism, although it is worth noting that Étienne Gilson describes an ahistorical medieval humanism which, prior to the Renaissance, amounted to, in his words, "a humanism of the present."[15] In any case, the perpetual mediation of historical thinking—between aspect and depth, primary and secondary characteristics, inside and outside, public and private—requires a kind of estrangement from the present that entails dematerialization, abstraction, disembodiment. The rationalization of consciousness that supports the continuity of past and future, cause and project necessarily supports kinds of thinking that seek to *transcend* the present, concrete, arbitrarily and absolutely limited moment. Considered historically the present requires a future to complete or at least improve it, and consequently a dialectical method for getting there just as this same present has been produced dialectically by the past. By emphasizing what is linear, developmental, and mediate, historical thinking by definition involves transcendence of a kind that trivializes the specific detail and finite moment. In the mobile culture of historicism every moment *has* to be partial so that we can pursue development, so that we can seek a completion that, by definition and paradoxically, we will never actually find but that has emblems along the way: more information, more clarity, more money, more prestige, more of the constituents of heaven.

---

[15] Gilson writes in 1932: "It is often said, and it is in a sense fair to say, that the Middle Ages remained almost completely a stranger to history, at least in the way the Renaissance understood it and as we still understand it today. Its humanism is very different from the historical humanism which characterizes the Renaissance, it is a humanism of the present, or, if you prefer of the timeless." Compared with medieval humanism, says Gilson, the Renaissance and particularly Erasmian humanism displays "a passion for historical difference" (my translation). ("Le Moyen Age et le naturalisme antique," in *Archives d'histoire doctrinale et littéraire du Moyen Age* 7 [1932], pp. 35–36).

   This restless flight from material specificity and limitation that takes
place daily in a thousand practical ways depends upon a dialectical habit
imported by historicist culture from much older traditions. In the effort to
open the closed hierarchical models of medieval Europe, dialectical thinking has produced models whose horizons are in many ways the same: dualistic models that retain the same teleological and implicitly hierarchical
motives that modern thought supposedly has sought to subvert.[16] Dialectics is a common target of postmodern novelists, especially as it seeps into
the tropisms of daily living. Cortázar's *Hopscotch* is one of the most explicit,
especially on the way dialectics produces the birth of a "me," that invincible
subjectivity, which is the ultimate act of transcendence, that "personal
identity, miserable treasure."[17] Cortázar's Horacio Oliveira ruminates as
follows on this daily dialectical birth:

> The invention of the soul by man is hinted at every time the feeling appears that
> the body is a parasite, something like a worm adhering to the ego. . . .
>   I swallow my soup. Then in the midst of what I am reading, I think: "The
> soup is *in me*, I have it in this pouch which I will never see, my stomach." I feel
> with two fingers and I touch the mass, the motion of the food there inside. And
> I am this, a bag with food inside of it.
>   Then the soul is born: "No, I am not that."
>   Now that (let's be honest for once)
>   Yes, I am that. With a very pretty means of escape for the use of the finicky: "I
> am *also that*." Or just a step up "I am *in* that." (*Hopscotch*, chap. 83)

The birth of the soul is the ultimate act of departure, of transcendence; and
now this transcendental object has supported a whole cultural formation
that has reached a point of fatigue. It has made the body porous, invisible,
even nonexistent. It is difficult to describe.

> I mean something else, almost impossible to grasp that the 'soul' [my me-not-
> soup] is the soul of a body that does not exist. The soul gave man a push in his

---

[16] History, in other words, merely put dialectics on the horizontal in much the same way
Nietzsche says Enlightenment philosophy merely readjusted theological habits: "Since Kant,
transcendentalists of every kind have once more won the day—they have been emancipated
from the theologians: what joy! Kant showed them a secret path by which they may, on their
own initiative and with all scientific respectability, from now on follow their 'heart's desire'.
. . . 'There is no knowledge: *consequently*—there is a God': what a new *elegantia syllogismi!*
what a *triumph* for the ascetic ideal!——"
   As a contrast, Nietzsche cites favorably Ximénes (Xaver) Doudan, who sounds remarkably
postmodern when he speaks of "the *ravages* worked by "l'habitude d'admirer l'unintelligible
au lieu de rester tout simplement dan l'inconnu" [the habit of admiring the unintelligible
instead of staying quite simply in the unknown] (*On the Genealogy of Morals*, Third Essay,
Sect. 25, trans. Walter Kaufman and R. J. Hollingwood [New York: Random House, 1967]).
   [17] Lévi-Strauss, quoted by Julia Kristeva, *Desire in Language: A Semiotic Approach to Literature and Art* (New York: Columbia University Press, 1980), p. 127.

corporeal evolution, perhaps, but it's tired of shoving and goes on ahead by itself.
It barely takes two steps

> the soul breaks up oh because its real

> body does not exist and lets it fall down plop.

The poor thing goes back home, etc., but that's not what I After all. (chap.
80)

At least Cortázar's Horacio knows his problem. " 'I can make a dialectical
operation even out of soup,' Oliveira thought" (chap. 90). Clearly, to face
the difficulty, we must stop rising above soup if we are permanently to
change that transcendental power of dialectical thinking whose fruits—as
we can see every time we hear of the annual defense budget—are radioactive. "What can be done then with pure understanding, with haughty reasoning reason? From the time of the Eleatics until today dialectical thought
has had more than enough time to give us its fruits. We are eating them,
they are delicious, they are seething with radioactivity" (*Hopscotch*, chap.
79). This soul, born of transcendence, has become in postmodern writing
a focus of especially intense revisionist thought and experiment.

The humble birth of the soul is just one instance of the way that dialectics operates: masquerading as freedom by suppressing any current material definition in favor of a dematerialized, literally immaterial Elsewhere.
For every stomach there is a transcendental ego; for every "here" and
"now" there's a necessary "there" and "then." Ultimately there is a paradise
elsewhere that sets in perpetual motion our search and suffering, our obsession with action. By estranging awareness from the presently embodied
circumstance, especially from the embodiment of language, dialectics dis-
tracts attention from the only site where action is possible, and it produces
a negative birth of identity (I am *not* that: soup, black, woman) that is not
recognized as such. It makes all "actions" into hostage-taking. It is bent on
production, not play: on getting there, on power, on strength as force,
forging, making, doing, in short, on heroics and implicitly on a classical
system of beliefs in which truth always transcends one's grasp. Such "truth
is necessary," Irigaray writes, "for those who are so distanced from their
body that they have forgotten it."[18] There is no doubt that the dialectical
motive in historical thinking has had its own profoundly creative influence,
for example, in the Protestant modification of earlier humanist views of
temporality (see *Realism and Consensus*, pp. 24–37). The adjustment has
yet to be made between this appreciation of history and the apparently
competing appreciation of postmodern rhythmic temporality, but this
book is not the place for that negotiation.

As its opponents long have known, dialectical thinking is one of the
most insidious of habits; in the West at least it has dominated narrative and

---

[18] Irigaray, "When Our Lips Speak Together," in *This Sex*, p. 214.

language for centuries and has produced any number of rationalizations that seem to hold less and less water. It seems to thrive on repudiation. Dialectics has been partially or essentially repudiated by philosophers since Kant as "a symptom of decadence" (Nietzsche), "a genuine philosophical embarrassment" and "superfluous" (Heidegger), and a "logic of illusion" (Kant). And yet, to use Cortázar's words again, we still are "drowning" in "the falsest of freedoms, the Judaeo-Christian dialectic," which remains alive and well in a thousand events of everyday language.[19]

Practically speaking—and this is what concerns postmodern novelists—living in historical time is to live in a medium still informed by the dialectical habit, which means to live with one's immediate present effectively neutralized by the perpetual fiction of alternative possibility. To the extent we are culturally, discursively, habitually historians we always inhabit a *dematerialized present* where particular, practical, concrete, specific experience is something we can only anticipate or recollect. This convention even commits us to the paradoxical position of habitually striving to transcend our transcendence in order to arrive (ultimately) at reunion with real presence which is always posited There, never Here. Cortázar characterizes as no other novelist the monumental, paradoxical effort required for anyone to escape from these habits, and he understands fully their appeal. "Happy were those who lived and slept in history" including especially "certain communists in Buenos Aires and Paris, capable of the worst villainy but redeemable in their own minds by 'the struggle' " (*Hopscotch*, chap. 90).

This use of history as alibi is something Heidegger identified when he formulated his view of historical time as the mystification of individual finitude. Historical time, to use Heidegger's terms, is "public time" or the time of "nobody." But "nobody" never dies. Heidegger's famously difficult language is nevertheless adequate to this famously difficult subject:

> the 'they' never dies because it *cannot* die; for death is in each case mine, and only in anticipatory resoluteness does it get authentically understood in an existentiell manner. Nevertheless, the 'they', which never dies and which misunderstands Being-towards-the-end, gives a characteristic interpretation to fleeing in the face of death. To the very end 'it always has more time'. Here a way of 'having time' in the sense that one can lose it makes itself known. 'Right now, this! then that! And that is barely over, when. . . .' How is 'time' in its course to be touched even the least bit when a man who has been present-at-hand 'in time' no longer exists? Time goes on, just as indeed it already 'was' when a man 'came into life'. The

---

[19] Friedrich Nietzsche, *Ecce Homo* (1887, first published 1908), in *"On the Genealogy of Morals"* and *"Ecce Homo"* (New York: Random House, 1967), p. 223; Martin Heidegger, *Being and Time*, II, 6: p. 47; Immanuel Kant, *A Critique of Pure Reason* (*Kritik der Reinen Vernunft*, 1781) (Transcendental Analytic, Pref. to Book II), trans. F. Max Muller (1881) (New York: Doubleday, 1966), p. 118; and Cortázar, *Hopscotch*, chap. 147.

only time one knows is the public time which has been levelled off and which belongs to everyone—and that means, to nobody. (*Being and Time*, II.6.81; p. 477)

To exist in historical ("inauthentic") time is to exist as nobody and thence, Heidegger's logic goes, to act like an immortal or at least like someone able to pretend that one's finitude is not absolute and that it can be mediated by various means: achieving fame or amassing a fortune, endowing a building or a person with one's name or some other measure to guarantee survival according to the logic of historical time. But the authentic future for every *Dasein* (being-in-the-world) necessarily involves the absolute end of that being. To suppress that knowledge of death is to cripple the power to live fully, joyously, on the highest terraces of being. Death, as Miguel de Unamuno said, is the great economist.

Heidegger's most important perception, for my purposes, is this: that the idea of temporal infinity is what in practice deflects our attention from the ultimate human necessity of facing death. "Fleeing *in the face of death*" is for Heidegger the very ground of historical thinking (what he calls inauthentic temporality) because it exists in order to cover up the fact that existential time ends, and that end *is not mediated*. Dying itself is not the issue nor is it a specifically human event. But facing our necessity with recognition, living as mortals not angels, that is the specifically human challenge not only for Heideggerian *Dasein* but also for the better-humored Cortázarian cronopios.[20] It may be that in some authentic (not historical) temporality actual lived time can be experienced simply as being there, and not as being on a linear track, but this temporality has been covered up with another, grander, more teleological model of temporality constructed as a means of evading death. Heidegger's insistence on restructuring philosophical discourse so as to include the fact of death remains an important reminder of how far the conventions of historical thinking have preserved a transcendence that has enabled us to make the subject of death practically taboo. To use Duras's far more elegant and harrowing words, "People ought to be told such things. Ought to be taught that immortality is mortal, that it can die. . . . It's while it's being lived that life is immortal,

[20] Heidegger's views, despite their enormous influence in widely disparate fields, still come encumbered by his political commitments which, while they do not necessarily invalidate his words, certainly color them. But he is not alone in this critique of transcendence. Nietzsche objects to churchmen and scientists alike because in their "will to truth" they are bent on becoming "angels" (*Genealogy of Morals*, Second Essay, sect. 7). This Nietzschean conception is later deployed brilliantly in Cortázar's story "The Pursuer" ("*El Perseguidor*"), where Bruno confesses that being an "angel" is his main agenda, in *Blow-Up and Other Stories*, trans. Paul Blackburn (New York: Pantheon, 1967), p. 219. Cortázar's cronopios (a term from his splendid little book, *Cronopios and Famas*, that he sometimes applies to his most postmodern personae) embody this rejection of transcendence and dialectics.

while it's still alive. Immortality is not a matter of more or less time, it's not really a question of immortality but of something else that remains unknown. . . . Look at the dead sands of the desert, the dead bodies of children: there's no path for immortality there, it must halt and seek another way."[21]

The second weakness of the historical convention is its inclination to depreciate questions of value, and even to produce a kind of rationalist disorientation about such questions. This liability is an underside in the historical convention to its achievement of objectivity and neutrality and its emphasis on quantitative measurement. This second weakness is not unrelated to the first because if death remains perpetually outside the frame of my picture—that is, if my own inevitable finitude is not part of the discourse in which I make my choices and commitments—then questions of value can be infinitely deferred. However, if I remain aware of my own inevitable finitude, questions of value become urgent. Of course certain questions of value, for example, whether a particular use of time and attention is worth it, can never be completely avoided. But questions of value come in other less obvious and more powerful forms, and ones that the historical convention has elaborate mechanisms for disguising.

For example, historical temporality is the ultimate medium for sustaining the value of "neutrality." The historical convention creates a putatively neutral medium in which "events" take place freely, albeit according to certain laws of causality that can be "discovered" through comparisons of widely separated instances, and in which "free" human projects can be formed and pursued. Preserving this neutrality, it can even be argued, is

[21] *Dasein* (literally, Being-there-ness) is Heidegger's term for that phenomenological event of being-in-the-world. "Dasein traverses the span of time granted to it between the two boundaries (birth and death), and it does so in such a way that, in each case, it is 'actual' only in the 'now', and hopes, as it were, through the sequence of 'nows' of its own 'time'. . . . Dasein does not fill up a track or stretch 'of life'. . . . It stretches *itself* along in such a way that its own Being is constituted in advance as a stretching along" (II.5.72; Macquarrie and Robinson, pp. 425–26). The sequence of experiences is one "now" after another and not anything more cosmically structured. "The principal thesis of the ordinary way of interpreting time— namely that time is 'infinite'—makes manifest most impressively the way in which world-time and accordingly temporality in general have been levelled off and covered up by such an interpretation" (p. 476). By "world-time" he means the time that is "sighted" by the use of clocks (II.6.81, p. 474).

Marguerite Duras, *The Lover*, trans. by Barbara Bray (New York: Random House, 1985), pp. 105–6, from *L'Amant* (Paris: Les Editions Minuit, 1984), pp. 128–29: "Il faudrait prévenir les gens de ces choses-là. Leur apprendre que l'immortalité est mortelle, qu'elle peut mourir. . . . Que c'est tandis qu'elle se vit que la vie est immortelle, tandis qu'elle est en vie. Que l'immortalité ce n'est pas une question de plus ou moins de temps, que ce n'est pas une question d'immortalité, qu'c'est une question d'autre qui reste ignoré. . . . Regardez les sables morts des déserts, le corps mort des enfants: l'immortalité ne passe pas par là, elle s'arrête et contourne."

the chief purpose of thinking historically in the first place, although that purpose may not be mentioned directly. The very establishment of this medium, however, turns the present moment into a mere intersection, a neutral crossroads for various different and unrelated tracks of causality. Instead of seeing any cultural moment synchronically, as a homeostatic unit or "cultural formation," the historically minded person treats it as merely a neutral locus for the various historical threads that run "through" it. History, we might say, is the great creator of disciplines and the great segregator of culture; it diverts into separate "courses" various functions of a cultural formation that, thus orphaned, find new context in the sequence from past to future. One thinks of the disciplinary distinctions of academia, where textbooks on such fields as Western civilization are careful to segregate art from politics, one century from another, and where even a restricted field of study like literature defines everything from the curriculum to the vocabulary of scholarship in historical terms. We teach and discuss the history of genres; we teach and discuss the cultural causes of literary or textual phenomena or we see those phenomena as manifestations of cultural and historical development; we are inescapably engaged, it seems, in the language of "background" and event, the language of depth, the language of representation. And literary studies are only one instance of the massive cultural commitment to such thinking.[22] The practice of such historicism—it is a key convention in the education of young people—has the unspoken but powerful rationale of reencoding the idea that both the medium of events and the method of the investigator are imbued with a fine neutrality. My purpose here is not to deny the importance of these values but rather to render them problematic.

The neutrality habit is a complex reliance on the putative safety and "control" provided by the neutralization of questions of value. In an example that bears directly on the relation between feminist theoretics and practice discussed in Part Three, Craig Owens discusses the way women's issues get neutralized before they are put on the critical agenda (I quote at some length): "Men appear unwilling to address the issues placed on the critical agenda by women unless those issues have first been neut(e)ralized—although this, too, is a problem of assimilation: to the already known, the already written. In *The Political Unconscious*, to take but one example, Fredric Jameson calls for the 'reaudition of the oppositional voices of black and ethnic cultures, women's or gay literature, "naive" or marginalized folk art *and the like*' (thus, women's cultural production is anachronistically identified as folk art) but he immediately modifies this petition: 'The affirmation of such non-hegemonic cultural voices remains

[22] William Spanos discusses the idea, enunciated in another way by Lyotard, that academic disciplines are no longer "sites" of activity (*Repetitions*, p. 269).

ineffective,' he argues, if they are not first *rewritten* in terms of their proper place in 'the dialogical system of the social classes.' "[23] The historian is never far from making the mistake sketched in this brief critique, making value-laden distinctions that he/she regards as "proper," natural, or neutral.

Neutrality, in other words, far from being a vital resource, can be an incubus, as Cortázar is fond of showing. Here is Horacio, at the bridge once more in his epic internal war against his own dialectical habit of detachment:

> Let's see, let's take it slowly: What is that guy searching for? Is he searching for himself? Is he searching for himself as an individual? As a supposedly timeless individual, or as an historical entity? . . .
>
> It's a terrible job, splashing around in a circle whose center is everywhere and whose circumference is nowhere, to use the language of scholasticism. What is being searched for? What is being searched for? . . . It's not a question of perfecting, of decanting, of redeeming, of choosing, of free-willing, of going from the alpha to the omega. *One is already there.* Anybody is already there. . . . Nothing easier than putting the blame on what's outside, as if one were sure that outside and inside are the two main beams of the house. But the fact is that everything is in bad shape, history tells you that, and the very fact that you're thinking about it instead of living it proves to you that it's bad, that we've stuck ourselves into a total disharmony, that the sum of our resources disguises with social structure, with history, with Ionic style, with the joy of the Renaissance, with the superficial sadness of romanticism, and that's the way we go. (chap. 125)

The problem with neutrality that intimately links it with dialectics is its ineluctable flow away from the actual materialized site of life. One splashes around from alpha to omega, or even from here to there in search of what? To get where? "One is already there" or, in Nabokov's words, "We are not going anywhere, we are sitting at home. The other world surrounds us always and is not at all at the end of some pilgrimage."[24] The metaphysic of transcendence and depth, especially the seductive historical version, reinscribes without mercy a subject position that remains disembodied, outside and beyond any particular; a subject without traction, a perpetual spectator.

This subject function, one evident in the implied spectator of realistic painting and in the implied historian of realistic narrative, grew up with other forms of representation in the period following the Reformation and Renaissance. This subject function initially may have had the role of free-

---

[23] Craig Owens, "The Discourse of Others: Feminists and Postmodernism," in Hal Foster, ed., *The Anti-Aesthetic*, p. 62. He also quotes Martha Rosler to the effect that representational strategies are impoverished because they are "powerless to deal with the reality that is yet totally comprehended-in-advance by [its] ideology" (p. 70).

[24] Nabokov's novel *The Gift* provides the epigraph (p. 322) for the present book.

ing consciousness from dogma, but by now its detachment has itself become a form of dogma. Spectatorhood—the ability to look on from outside and to judge and to make projections according to objective norms—has become habitual. From sports arenas to stock-market projections we have become a society of voyeurs.

A similar point was made in a commentary on "Voyeurism in Politics" that expresses in spatial terms the problem with neutrality. It is worth attention because it focuses so well on the practical and discursive quality of the problem. Discussing the media coverage of a terrorist event abroad, James Boyle's "My Turn" column in *Newsweek* Magazine in May 1987 contrasts the "wall of coverage" with the hysteria of actual engagement on that occasion when a bomb killed American Marines in Lebanon.

> The first TV reports on the bombing were almost hysterical. Reporters did not seem to be separate from the scenes they described, but the plastic wall of "coverage" snapped back into place quickly, sliding between the viewer and the reporter. We in the public were invited to talk about the "meaning" of the event, which turned out to have nothing to do with shredded 20-year-olds hanging from broken masonry and everything to do with "America's Leadership Role in the Middle East."
>
> Two days later came the invasion of Grenada. And we were asked to predict the reaction of various entities——"How do you think the American people will respond to the decision to invade?" "What will this do to the president's standing in Congress?" "In Western Europe?" One noticeable thing about these entities is that *they are always somewhere else*.

Boyle also captures the Catch-22 of efforts that, in attempting to "deal" with the problem, merely reinforce it because it is sustained by formal agreements that have become invisible:

> I have always been sympathetic to the claim made by the philosophers of the Frankfurt school that there is no real public debate in contemporary society because political questions have been turned into technical questions and because we are all at home counting our Porsches. But there are other explanations; for example, the public sphere is empty because we are all outside of it looking in, watching others—our surrogate selves—flounder in a swamp of predictions, scandals and public-relations exercises. . . .
>
> If one had a mind to, one could plug all of these symptoms of a fear of immediacy into a general theory of social alienation, or the decomposition of politics in postindustrial capitalism. But the trouble with this kind of reaction is that it seems to repeat the very phenomenon that is being criticized. It takes a spectator's stance toward part of our political life that we should actually work to change.[25]

[25] "My Turn" column, *Newsweek*, 25 May 1987, p. 8.

In other words, and as Cortázar's Oliveira mutters, "Being an actor meant renouncing the orchestra seats, and he seemed born to be a spectator in the first row. 'The worst of it,' Oliveira said to himself, 'is that I always want to be an active onlooker and that's where the trouble starts' " (chap. 90). The displacement of subjectivity by historical conventions appears to have produced subject gridlock, and the new subject definitions of postmodern narrative belong to a completely different temporal convention.

It is true that much depends on the kind of historical thinking in question: it provides a reason to endure privation of all kinds; a motive of education and other forms of capitalism; a reason to put up with today in a certain mood for the sake of tomorrow; a reason for giving some thought to the next generation and its ozone layer, its rain forests, or its nuclear safety net. Yet paradoxically dialectics and its transcendence may interfere with the achievement of the very hopes it generates. The shadow of heaven is once again evident. The paradoxical dialectic thus renders inaccessible that same future satisfaction the achievement of which supposedly constitutes its primary raison d'être. Future solutions can never materialize when the future initially is conceived as an elsewhere and not as a present wish because locked outside this perpetual elsewhere we are never, in this the only life, ever at home.

It is precisely its insistence on practice, on value, and on the materiality of language in its most apparently trivial forms that has made feminist theory such a powerful extension of other postmodern theory based in linguistics, anthropology, and phenomenology. In a later chapter I discuss the specific implications of feminist theory and postmodern narrative language, but it is worth mentioning here the important affinity between them, however much caution is advisable in pursuing specific connections. The critique of historical thinking has been most clearly formulated in recent feminist theory that treats history as a discourse of appropriation and grasp supporting the values and the exclusions of patriarchy.

Julia Kristeva, who for example concerns herself with the "sociosymbolic contract" whereby we agree to think of "time as project, teleology, linear and prospective unfolding; time as departure, progression, and arrival—in other words, the time of history," has in view nothing less than the "religious crisis of our civilization" and the revision of "the very principle of sociality."[26] Kristeva aligns the linear convention of time with the symbolic

---

[26] "Women's Time," trans. Alice Jardine and Harry Blake, in *Signs: Journal of Women in Culture and Society* 7, no. 1 (1981), pp. 32–33. Kristeva also notes in this essay that women's experience has demonstrated that the cultural formation that supports the idea of history—and with it what Heidegger calls inauthentic temporality—has not been accessible to change from within. "The assumption by women of executive, industrial, and cultural power has not, up to the present time, radically changed the nature of this power," which has "inhaled" women and turned them into "the pillars of the existing governments, guardians of the status

disposition of language, that is, the disposition to state, qualify, and conclude rather than the disposition to play, multiply, and diversify, and she claims that this linear convention, when it is isolated from the disposition to play, fosters what a psychoanalyst would call "obsessional time": a zeal to master time in which can be discerned "the true structure of the slave." Kristeva describes this "time of history" as one that is "totalizing" in its universal sweep and, consequently, "totalitarian" towards what it excludes as "nonessential or even nonexistent" ("Women's Time," pp. 17, 21–25). Such a critique of historical time sounds very much like Heidegger's critique of inauthentic temporality; and such agendas are among the several ways in which theoretical feminism has extended and specified the postmodern experimental effort: an effort to redefine Western metaphysics and to reformulate social codes by starting with the most intimate, the most practical, the most apparently "innocent" of daily practices.

The postmodern idea that time and space are themselves defined, limited, discontinuous is so contrary to habit that it may seem almost unthinkable. Yet this is precisely what postmodern narratives establish—an alternative temporality—and precisely what they ask of their readers—to think what seems unthinkable. And in this the postmodern narrative project very much resembles the discourse analysis that has developed across and eroded disciplinary boundaries in academia and the boundary between academia and the so-called real world. As postmodern narrative breaks down the convention of historical time, it reveals the arbitrariness of its historical "neutrality," and this opening forces us to focus on precisely those questions of value and proportion that historical thinking defers. Similarly discourse analysis, especially feminist versions, permit us to shift disciplinary discussion to questions of value; and if these questions sometimes seem tautological, that is generally because they are the most important questions and because it is precisely such tautologies, unseen and unexamined, that tend to become the invisible footmen of discourse. The value of neutrality, for instance, is not so much mentioned by historical narratives as it is silently taken for granted by them. While the old historicism masks questions of value, with all their implications for commitment and choice, the new disciplinary work based on Foucault and philosophical linguistics brings such questions into focus. For example, when scholars speak in the same breath of Shakespeare and the *conquistadores*, or of Kafka and relativity physics, or of field theory and Nabokov, or of geometry and narrative,

---

quo, the most zealous protectors of the established order." Nor has the effort to outline or speak or write a "countersociety" escaped the danger of merely reiterating "in reverse ways the logic of what is supposedly being rejected." She does find, however, that a "new generation of women" is potentially moving beyond these cul-de-sacs and "is showing that its major social concern has become the sociosymbolic contract as a sacrificial contract" (pp. 19, 24–27).

they employ a method that refocuses the cultural moment as a homeostatic entity and consequently dissolves the neutrality of the present. Present moments no longer appear as neutral sites for the displacement of value but, on the contrary, as sites embedded in value-laden structures. Questions of value even leak into matters of methodology itself, wiping out any putative neutrality that may still remain there.[27]

Whatever this new effort is called, and there is considerable terminological difficulty about that at the moment, it is clearly important and difficult work: difficult largely because it involves ending one's tenure as an implied spectator or neutral historian and accepting a position in the frame of reference. To see the cultural moment as a single frame means to refocus on the difference between cultural moments and between large discursive practices, which means to see every method including my own, every value including my own, every language including my own as historically limited—even the method I use to arrive at this recognition. This is heady stuff. If I accomplished this perilous work, I would in effect de-"naturalize" my own deepest preoccupations; I would dematerialize the very ladder under my feet. I would—to use Stephen Greenblatt's phrase for one form of modernism—*improvise* my own beliefs in the act of discussing and situating them. Postmodern improvisation, that is, requires a truly "self" reflexive activity. Unlike the historian, who improvises on the beliefs of others (past generations, for example), the postmodern writer is forced to improvise on his or her *own* beliefs. Once such new practices unsettle habits, I face choices among practices and consequently I face questions of value. It is this necessity at the heart of postmodern narrative and discourse analysis that really unsettles the complacent reader-writer-citizen and that partly accounts for the reaction against it.

The costs as well as the benefits of historical thinking have by now been widely perceived, especially its entail of dissociation between discrete, textured, phenomenal experience, on the one hand, and generalized, metaphysical consciousness on the other. In fact this dissociation, of which Conrad's Kurtz is a particularly famous representative, had already proved by the end of the nineteenth century to be a definitive, determining liability. What postmodern writers inherited was the necessity to deal with the

---

[27] The interdisciplinary work alluded to includes Stephen Greenblatt's seminal essay, "Improvisation and Power," in *Literature and Society* (English Institute Essays for 1978), Edward Said, ed. (Baltimore: Johns Hopkins University Press, 1980), pp. 57–99; Thomas Vargish and Delo Mook's forthcoming book on modernism and relativity physics; N. Katherine Hayles's books on common theoretical issues in science and literature, *The Cosmic Web: Scientific Field Models and Literary Strategies in the Twentieth Century* (Ithaca: Cornell University Press, 1984) and *Chaos Bound: Orderly Disorder in Contemporary Literature and Science* (Ithaca: Cornell University Press, 1990); and my discussion of consensus as a discursive formulation in painting, mathematics, and narrative (*Realism and Consensus*, chaps. 1–3).

liabilities of a cultural discourse that had made possible world war and other world disasters, and it is only with an eye on social and political conditions of the twentieth century that we can hope to understand the phenomenon of postmodern narrative in anything like adequate ways.

The best definition of postmodern narrative might be precisely that it resolutely does *not* operate according to any form of historical time, that is, representational time, and in many cases directly parodies or disputes that time and the generalizations it allows to form. Such subversion necessarily precedes those experiments with new forms of time that postmodern narrative makes possible. In postmodern narrative, the infinite future does not exist, nor does the finite subject, or at least they are so massively attenuated that they no longer function as controlling conventions. For postmodernism, historical time is a thing of the past in more than one sense. History now is not just the convention that uses the past to hold the present in a controlled pattern of meaning: history now takes up the interesting position of confronting its own historicity.

A final figure helps to confirm the argument of this section that historical time is a thing of the past. A broadly recurring image in critiques of these historical, linear conventions of time is the image of a car on a road or a train on a track, both mechanical conveyances that carry consciousness half-involuntarily toward conventional destinations along routes already traveled. Tracking metaphors haunt the digressions of Robbe-Grillet's novels and Cortázar's stories, and it is a favorite metaphor of Nabokov's. In *The Gift*, Fyodor—riding one more time on the Berlin tram that takes him along tracks laid out by others and carrying him where he doesn't want to go to do a job he doesn't want to do—makes his major life-defining choice when he simply gets off the train and strikes out on foot across a pathless park. Cortázar's "End of the Game" links the losses that constitute childhood's end with the unforgiving motion of trains passing children at their games and carrying capitalists and soldiers to their "grown up" work. All oppose the linear juggernaut, emblem of synchronized clocks and collective rationalization, with various forms of play—childhood play, language's play, music; all raise questions about the quality of a life that maintains their separation.[28]

The same associations between time and trains appear in numerous pictorial images, notably in surrealism, where they stand as figures for what we might now call the discourse of industrial society. An especially evocative image of time and railroad trains now widely available is the poster that was made in 1929 for the French Railway system by Pierre Fix-Masseau. It shows a huge steam engine standing by a station platform and

---

[28] Although they are not discussed in this book, there are brilliant examples in John Hawkes's novels, especially *Travesty* (New York: New Directions, 1976).

dwarfing everything around it; on the wall behind it is a conspicuous clock; written on it is the word "État," and inscribed over the whole is the word "Éxactitude." The vectors of the picture insistently align the single-point perspective with the track and both with a mechanical (and political) juggernaut of linearity, regularity, and speed. The inscription "Éxactitude" alludes to the synchronizations in time and space that belong especially to representational conventions, and it reminds me of Henri Matisse's famous remark to the effect that "exactitude is not truth."[29]

Surrealism was a major force in formulating these analyses of a whole cultural disposition, and André Breton's "Manifestoes of Surrealism" continue to sound many of the themes of postmodernism. In the "Second Manifesto of Surrealism" (1930), he declares for the surrealists:

> We reject unhesitatingly the notion of the sole possibility of the things which "are," . . . ; we cannot find words enough to stigmatize the baseness of Western thought . . . ; we are not afraid to take up arms against logic; . . . we refuse to swear that something we do in dreams is less meaningful than something we do in a state of waking; . . . we are not even sure that we will not do away with time, that sinister old farce, that train constantly jumping off the track.

The time of "Western" logic, this "sinister old farce" constricts and impoverishes the human mind which the surrealists set out to liberate. Above all, Breton writes, "we want nothing whatever to do with those, either large or small, who use their minds as they would a savings bank."[30] Some are quick to note that the problem with such wide-ranging critique is that it unsettles society. Precisely so, said the surrealist; the society that has created one world war and seems bound to create another appears to *need* unsettling. At the root of that unsettling is the transformation of the individual subject into a subject function, something that is necessary because of the extent to which, as Barthes, Kristeva, and Foucault all have noted, the traditional formulation of subjectivity supports historical time. By desacralizing the author, surrealism undermined the very basis of historical temporality.[31] (I discuss this problem at length in Part Two: Section II.)

In surrealist painting one of the best-known images associating time and the steam engine is René Magritte's *Time Transfixed* (1939). The picture shows with great precision a railroad train engine coming in full steam out

[29] Quoted by Herbert Read, *A Concise History of Modern Painting*, 1958 (London: Thames and Hudson Ltd., 1974), p. 44, from Alfred H. Barr, Jr., *Matisse—His Art and his Public* (New York, 1951), p. 40.

[30] André Breton, *Manifestoes of Surrealism*, 1929, 1930, trans. by Richard Seaver and Helen Lane (Ann Arbor: University of Michigan Press, 1972), pp. 128–29.

[31] "The Author, when believed in, is always conceived of as the past of his own book: book and author stand automatically on a single line divided into a *before* and an *after*." Barthes, "The Death of the Author," in *Image, Music, Text*, pp. 146–47.

of a fireplace: its trackless motion frozen in an impossible position, its smoke heading up the chimney of a domestic hearth, the whole surrounded by the conventional classical domestic interior complete with mantelpiece, mirror, wood floors, and wainscoting. The simultaneous presence of two apparently contradictory frames of reference, the railroad and the domestic hearth, "transfixes" time (and space) by destroying its neutrality (this literally "can't happen"), thus making the rationalization of space and its ordinary representational convention and ethic of mobility at once complete and impossible. The image plays on the many analogies between clock time and locomotion, including the idea of time as a track, the historical linkage between the railroads and synchronized clock time, and the implied link between such universally synchronized time and a mechanical juggernaut. Postmodern narrative, like this image, arrests the momentum of this linear force by throwing its medium into question.

Section II: Time as Rhythm

Where a train track or a road often stands as a metaphor for temporality as it is conceived in historical conventions, the conspicuously nonvisual metaphor of rhythm stands for temporality as it is conceived in postmodern conventions. "Time is rhythm," Nabokov's Van Veen declares helpfully, an insight prompted by having got stuck on a road in Switzerland:

> Lost again. Where was I? Where am I? Mud road. Stopped car. Time is rhythm: the insect rhythm of a warm humid night, brain ripple, breathing, the drum in my temple—these are our faithful timekeepers. . . . Maybe the only thing that hints at a sense of Time is rhythm; not the recurrent beats of the rhythm but the gap between two such beats, the gray gap between black beats: the Tender Interval.[32]

In various ways each of the novelists featured in this book develops this theme of rhythmic time. In *Jealousy* Robbe-Grillet uses insect rhythms, the rhythms of song, the unintelligible ink patterns on a blotter to figure (with the reader-participant's help) what is at once regular and organized and, at the same time, utterly mysterious and irrational; and his descriptions of these are emblematic of basic patterns in the novel. Generally it is musical rhythm that best suggests the nature of postmodern temporality: Nabokov's "Tender Interval," the rhythms of Robbe-Grillet's novels as described in the next section of this chapter, and (Cortázar's favorite) jazz improvisation as the ultimate emblem of postmodern temporality. This musical metaphor has, in addition to other value, the advantage of providing an

[32] Nabokov, *Ada, or Ardor: A Family Chronicle* (New York: McGraw-Hill, 1969), p. 572.

alternative to visual models. In place of the gaze so prevalent in modern discourse, postmodernism substitutes a kinesis; whereas in the Renaissance the visual took priority over the kinetic, in postmodernism the balance is reversed.[33]

Jazz appears often as metaphor and model for the new construction of temporality in Cortázar's writing. For example, the following passage from *Hopscotch* demonstrates, as well as explains, how to "conjugate" in rhythmic form some of the most difficult philosophical problems of time. Especially salient here are two features: the important presence of death at the site of postmodern conjugation, and the substitution of a new formulation for the old Cartesian *cogito*; more plausible in the postmodern condition of embeddedness and finitude is this formulation: "I swing, therefore I am." I quote at some length from this passage because only in this way does the rhythm, the paratactic acts of attention in Cortázar's own language, become evident.

> For a moment the Ellington machine obliterated them with that fabulous sparring between trumpet and Baby Cox, the subtle and easygoing entrance of Johnny Hodges, the crescendo (but the rhythm was already getting to be a little stiff after thirty years, an old tiger who could still ripple) with riffs which were both tense and loose at the same time, a difficult minor miracle: "I swing, therefore I am." Leaning against the Eskimo pelt, looking at the green candles through his glass of vodka (we used to go to look at the fish on the Quai de la Mégisserie) it was almost easy to come to the conclusion that what was called reality deserved that disparaging phrase of the Duke's, "It don't mean a thing if you ain't got that swing," but why had the hand of Gregorovius stopped caressing La Maga's hair, there was poor Ossip, sleeker than a seal, all broken up by that distant deflowering, it was pitiful to look at him, so tense in that atmosphere where the music was breaking down resistance and was weaving everything into a kind of common breathing, the peace of an enormous heart beating for all, drawing them all into itself. And now a cracked voice, making its way out of a worn-out record, suggesting unknowingly that old Renaissance invitation, that old Anacreontic sadness, a *carpe diem* from Chicago, 1922.
>
>   Skin like darkness, baby, you gonna die some day,
>   Skin like darkness, baby, you gonna die some day,
>   I jus' want some lovin' be-fore you go your way.
>
> Every so often the words of the dead fit the thoughts of the living (if the one group is living and the other is dead). You so beautiful. *Je ne veux pas mourir sans*

---

[33] On how the visual overtakes the kinetic in the Renaissance see Ivins, *Art and Geometry*, pp. 40–42, and *Rationalization of Sight*, pp. 7–10; *Realism and Consensus*, pp. 6–23; Stephen Tyler, *The Unspeakable*, pp. 10, 22. The specular that belongs to historical discourse is not the same thing as Jean Baudrillard's "spectacle," which can be seen as "the annihilation of historical knowledge" (Jonathan Crary, "Spectacle, Attention, Counter-Memory," in *October* 50 [Fall 1989], p. 106).

avoir compris pourquoi j'avais vécu. A blues song, René Daumal, Horacio Oliveira, but you gotta die some day, you so beautiful but—And that's why Gregorovius insisted on knowing about La Maga's past, so that she would die a little less from that other backward-moving death composed entirely of things dragged along by time, so as to put her in her own time, you so beautiful but you gotta, so as not to love a ghost. (*Hopscotch*, chap. 16)

This passage provides thematic strands that will reemerge frequently in this discussion: the *carpe diem*, the problem of death, the practicalities of putting on a record and of being in a group, the multilevel thinking in which one can simultaneously take in green candles, vodka, fish on the quai, and the jazz musician's difficult, miraculous revision of Descartes, "I swing, therefore I am." Like so much postmodern narrative, this passage depends on the rhythmic, almost incantatory alternation between subjects, systems, sets of consistencies. Above all, its themes are sustained simultaneously and interwoven in a common pattern that plays, developing extraordinary syntactical extension, and then ends. The insistent rhythmic tempo of this fragment, its stretching of syntactical conventions and its risk-taking, its brooding over the relation between death and beauty belong to an effort to shift out of the time that drags backward in which La Maga is a ghost and into the time, for La Maga "her own time," in which it is possible to live.

An appropriate response to the pressures of such varied themes is not so much rationalization or clarification, not some sorting out according to a common denominator whose main business includes establishing the transcendent existence of the one who rationalizes, but instead a "conjugation," as Cortázar calls it in the passage that stands as the epigraph for Part One: "First there is a confused situation, which can only be defined by words; I start out from this half-shadow and if what I mean (if what is *meant*) has sufficient strength, the *swing* begins at once. . . . No sooner does it stop than I understand that I no longer have anything to say" *(Hopscotch*, chap. 82).[34] As long as the writer writes, as long as the reader reads, as long as the player plays, there is a time, "a time to time time" as Nabokov taps out in *Ada* (p. 585). The time ends with the play, and with the next conjugation, the next time begins. For the duration of the music Duke Ellington conjugates the group into a kind of common breathing. There is no neutrality, no infinity, nothing of historical time with its linear and rational residues or its Elsewhere. "Brain ripple, breathing, the drum in my temple—these are our faithful timekeepers."

The emphasis on rhythm is consistent with an appreciation of language as speech. Writing without the activation of a reader is, as many have pointed out, just black marks on a page; and that enactment moves easily

---

[34] The full quotation appears as the epigraph to Part One.

from silence through consciousness toward language voiced, toward language in play and in fullest life. This emphasis on speech can be found in Heidegger (the first sentence of his essay "Language" is "Man speaks"), and generally the *rhythmic* quality of speech, its kinetic energy that moves beyond form and meaning, is part of the semiotic play emphasized in postmodern theory. Stephen Tyler, for instance, faults psychoanalysts and linguists for their repression of speech: "They are both fixated on the idea of the patterning of signs, and they both repress speech as the symbol of all that is chance, contingency, narrative, and time. That is to say, they are seduced and hoodwinked by writing."[35] The tradition that precedes that of writing, the rhetorical tradition inherited from classical times, certainly emphasizes the delivery, or *elocutio*, at least as much as the thought or organization (*inventio* or *dispositio*) of a speech, although this rhetorical tradition from Quintilian, the *Ad Herrenium*, and Cicero did not emphasize consensus and did not belong to the effort at discursive rationalization that print culture produced centuries later. In any case, the value of speech is that, like other forms of improvisation, it can pluralize a verbal sequence with various rhythmic patterns and tempos. Improvisation, like good chess playing, must keep available at any moment a complex of diverse possibilities for proceeding in any sequence. The excitement of postmodern writing is not entirely remote from that of viewing a sequence from a film like *Swing Time*, where Fred Astaire's feet *are* the drum solo, and his whole body is engaged in the apparent improvisation.

Examples abound in Cortázar's writing where such improvisation is a favorite thematic voice and where jazz often suggests a kind of temporality that is an imaginable alternative to history.[36] This contrast is drawn explicitly and at some length in his short story "The Pursuer," a narrative that, like much surrealism, undercuts representational conventions not so much by abandoning them but, like Magritte's *Time Transfixed*, perfecting them

---

[35] Heidegger, "Language," in his *Poetry, Language, Thought*, trans. Albert Hofstadter (New York: Harper & Row, 1971); and Tyler, *Unspeakable*, p. 35.

Psychoanalysts and linguists share "the same desire to fix the world in an immutable pattern of necessary connections between words and images"; and Derrida repeats "the language of immortality" when he puts his faith in writing as a mode of permanence, of triumph over decay and death (Tyler, *The Unspeakable*, pp. 35, 43). While Tyler makes sense, and properly invokes the rhetorical tradition, he parts company from this argument in settling on "dialogue" as a postmodern activity because it operates with a fluid subject and "it fashions no illusory permanences" (pp. 57–58); on the problem with "dialogic" see below, pp. 57, 109. The present argument also avoids the definition of writing as something one can only do with a pen; one can inscribe things, as discourse analysis has made clear, with a voice or a gesture.

[36] See Edward Sonnenschein, *What Is Rhythm?* (Oxford: Blackwell, 1925), and J. T. Fraser, ed., *The Voices of Time* (New York: George Braziller, 1966), p. 183, where he discusses the musical value of time, its various tempos and rhythmic patterns, and the diversity and complexity of what is still a temporally and rhythmically intelligible sequence.

in the service of a figure that is not at all representational but entirely fabulous, invented, imaginary. This story brings into the "same" medium two incompatible frames of reference, thus deconstructing the one with the other, specifically two different experiences of temporality. On the one hand, there is the time roughly equivalent to historical time as I described it in the preceding section and represented here in the habits of the jazz critic named Bruno, biographer and "friend" of a jazz horn player named Johnny Carter, a thinly disguised figure for Charlie Parker. On the other hand, there is the time on the "other side" of Bruno's time, that of the jazz musician himself who plays in different planes of reality. For the musician, jazz is a way of getting out of linear time and of finding a new kind of time constituted by jazz improvisation.

"Infinite construction"—a kind of *exploratory* repetition—characterizes the musician's style and by extension what is distinctive about the temporality he keeps attempting to inhabit.

> Incapable of satisfying itself, useful as a continual spur, an infinite construction, the pleasure of which is not in its highest pinnacle but in the exploratory repetitions, in the use of faculties which leave the suddenly human behind without losing humanity. (*Blow-Up and Other Stories*, p. 185)

The time of this jazz style is a rhythm, a construction, a use of faculties. It is above all and at its fullest an *activity* and a participation the point of which, at least for the musician if not for the critic, is the doing and not any more rational or extended "point." As even Bruno puts it, "You can't just listen and promise yourself to think about it later. You hardly get down into the street, the memory of it barely exists" (p. 196). This rhythmic time of invention, of process, is for Johnny Carter far richer than the lock-step of linear time. Whether he is riding on the métro or playing his horn, Johnny knows there is more than just a minute and a half between Odéon and St-Germain-des-Prés. "We could live," he says, "a thousand times faster than we're living because of the damned clocks, that mania for minutes and for the day after tomorrow." To the professional player the Paris métro, like Fyodor's tram in *The Gift*, becomes a metaphor of the kind of time and the kind of life (the kind of life that Bruno lives) to be avoided at all costs. "To ride the metro is like being put in a big clock. The stations are minutes, dig, it's that time of yours," he says to Bruno, "now's time; but I know there's another" (pp. 194–95). The question for the musician, as for a postmodern writer like Cortázar who stretches ordinary syntax to its limit, is how far can you push it? How much stretch, how much play can the format, the syntax, the system sustain?

These questions about exploiting play in the system become insistent questions for readers of postmodern narratives, forced as they are to become co-writers. In these novels reader time is the only time that elapses, and one of the frustrations confronting those raised on historical conventions is the lack of apparent product or residue or portable meaning, the sheer fact that when it's over, it's over. Bruno complains, about the illumination he finds in Johnny's presence, that it's not something he can think about or take away with him. He gets out the door and into the street and "the memory of it barely exists." This complaint pretty well covers the experience of reading *Hopscotch* or *Jealousy* or *Ada*. These novels are notoriously hard to remember because the plot lies in the style as it is experienced by the self-conscious reader reading. It is an activity, a doing, a new form of practice. And a practice very *un*like the experience of reading a novel by Jane Austen or Thomas Hardy, where the interest lies precisely in an un-self-conscious attention to characters and events that produces the memorable rationalizations of realism. The pleasure of the postmodern text is not in pinnacles or resolutions but in the process of exploration, in the improvising and inventing in the moment, and *that* is not a virtual experience but actual living at a high degree of torque and complexity. It is not disorganized; on the contrary, it requires a high degree of technique and restraint. But the value of this kind of temporal experience differs considerably from the value of experience conceived in terms of historical time and its inexorable production of meaning.

This new experiment in writing redefines the boundaries of so-called artistic activity and extends far beyond the corral where "literature" has been kept. For example, Jacques Attali, an economist writing a political economy of music, reaches beyond the all too familiar language to a new usage and a new play in the discourse of what we're accustomed to calling economic, philosophical, and aesthetic endeavor. Attali's "composition" resembles my "improvisation." Here is Attali on composition and history:

> Composition thus leads to a staggering conception of history, a history that is open, unstable, in which labor no longer advances accumulation, in which the object is no longer a stockpiling of lack, in which music effects a reappropriation of time and space. Time no longer flows in a linear fashion; sometimes it crystallizes in stable codes in which everyone's composition is compatible, sometimes in a multifaceted time in which rhythms, styles and codes diverge, independencies become more burdensome, and rules dissolve. In composition, stability, in other words, differences, are perpetually called into question. Composition is inscribed not in a repetitive world, but in the permanent fragility of meaning after the disappearance of usage and exchange. . . . It is also the only utopia that is not a mask for pessimism, the only Carnival that is not a Lenten ruse.

Not only does this describe improvisatory rhythms, it is composed of improvisatory rhythms. This political economy of music constitutes a new kind of writing: precisely the kind of improvisation that demonstrates the renewed importance of specialized knowledge at the very moment it transgresses conventional boundaries established for the containment of that knowledge. Furthermore, this improvisation or composition "announces something that is perhaps the most difficult thing to accept: henceforth *there will be no more society without lack*." Instead of interest in commodity, production, repetition, and plenty, he announces a world transformed into an art form and life transformed into "a shifting pleasure" that is anything but trivial or narcissistic.[37] And central to this reconstruction is a new construction of time.

Jazz improvisation as a model for postmodern temporality provides several emphases, of which I mention three, the importance of which can scarcely be overstated. First, its rhythms are chiefly a basis for experiment, but experiment without any obligation to produce results; within the constraints arbitrarily established and temporarily accepted, what happens is what happens. Second, improvisation is primarily a collective activity, a collective invention, completely dependent on the collaboration of more than one and not a model given to hierarchy. Third, this collective activity, with its "common breathing," is specific, concrete, and rooted in particular configurations, not universally or infinitely extendable; its time is not a rationalized, neutral, homogeneous history extending to infinity but a time that is rhythmic and finite. Postmodern temporality, in short, does not at all do away with collective values but refigures them at their root.

In "The Pursuer," the time of rhythm, of the swing, of the Tender Interval is something intelligible to the historian, Bruno, but uninhabitable by him. Bruno is a regular man ("Good old Bruno," the musician says, "regular as bad breath"). Bruno inhabits historical time and its rationalizations and its identities as a drowning man clings to a life raft. His personal choices are always deflected onto his career and into the future; his mantra is "my house, my wife, my prestige. My prestige above all. Above all my prestige" (p. 219). He is the ultimate "professional" man. He values Johnny's music from a distance—both the music and the musician are the "sub-

---

[37] Attali, *Noise*, pp. 147–48. "Henceforth *there will be no more society without lack*, for the commodity is absolutely incapable of filling the void it created by suppressing ritual sacrifice, by deritualizing usage, by pulverizing all meaning, by obliging man to communicate first to himself.

"Living in the void means admitting the constant presence of the potential for evolution, music, and death: 'What can a poor boy do, except play for a rock 'n' roll band?' ('Street Fighting Man,' Rolling Stones). Truly revolutionary music is not music which expresses the revolution in words, but which speaks of it as a lack.

"Bringing an end to repetition, transforming the world into an art form and life into a shifting pleasure. Will a sacrifice be necessary? Hurry up with it, because—if we are still within earshot—the World, by repeating itself, is dissolving into Noise and Violence."

Nicholas Xenos discusses *Scarcity and Modernity* in somewhat different terms (New York: Routledge, 1989), esp. chap. 3 "Scarcity."

jects" of his book—and he is in perpetual flight from the contradictions
that his own experience with Johnny always entails.

> I went into a café for a shot of cognac and to wash my mouth out, maybe also
> the memory that insisted and insisted in Johnny's words, his stories, his way of
> seeing what I didn't see and, at bottom, didn't want to see. I began to think of
> the day after tomorrow and it was like tranquillity descending, like a bridge
> stretching beautifully from the zinc counter into the future. (p. 199)

The future, like a shot of cognac, relieves him of the moment and of the
insistent definitions of present actuality. Bruno's time—the time of history
and project—is a smooth hard path to the future. You can always tell the
villain in Cortázar; he is the man who keeps checking his watch. Good old
Bruno is always checking the time, the schedule, the series of appoint-
ments. All his calculations depend on keeping time and yet, as he himself
points out in a Heideggerian mood, Bruno "only lives on borrowed time"
(p. 226).

This withering attention to the historian, Bruno, is not reserved for him
alone in "The Pursuer"; doctors, representatives of "American science," are
Bruno's accomplices and counterparts in a vast game of deflection. The
musician describes the doctors who "treated" him at Camarillo Hospital
after a suicide attempt:

> and in the morning an intern came in all washed up and all rosy, he looked so
> good. He looked like the son of Tampax out of Kleenex, you believe it. A kind
> of specimen, an immense idiot that sat down on the edge of the bed and was
> going to cheer me up. . . .
>
> This cat and all the cats at Camarillo were convinced. You know what I'm
> saying? What of? I swear I don't know, but they were convinced. Of what they
> were, I imagine, of what they were worth, of their having a diploma. . . . Even
> the most humble were . . . *sure of themselves* . . . when . . . you only had to con-
> centrate a little, feel a little, be quiet for a little bit, to find the holes. In the door,
> in the bed . . . in the newspaper, in time. . . . But they were American science . . .
> didn't see anything, they accepted what had been seen by others, they imagined
> that they were living . . . completely convinced of their prescriptions, their sy-
> ringes, their goddamned psychoanalysis, their don't smoke and don't drink. . . .
> Ah the beautiful day when I was able to move my ass out of that place. (p. 214)

The doctors' confidence in their mechanical solutions is like Bruno's confidence in the future: both confidence games with deadly consequences for
the artist in this story, and for the sensibility that he represents.

"The Pursuer" is one of the more realistic postmodern stories, but it
forces readers to ask questions subversive of its own conventions. Which
is crazier, the inconsistent creativity of the jazz musician or the parasitic
confidence of those historians and scientists, with their conviction that

their psychoanalysis and their prescriptions will produce the miracles of Lourdes, and their confidence in the time stretching from a zinc counter into the future and holding out the promise of Truth that supports all their projects and experiments? The central conflict of the story is not so much between the man who keeps time and the one who does not as it is between kinds of awareness: between the man who forgets that the time he "keeps" is constructed and the man who remembers that creative premise. The usual Cortázarian reader harassment is subtle here; the verb tenses act out the focal conflict of temporalities. Initially the narrative shifts back and forth between present tense and past tense (for example, pp. 187, 229), mimicking the temporal instability that Johnny Carter thrives in. The short "sequences" of its composition (p. 225) are like small thematic developments—often controlled by some rumination of Johnny's—that start and then stop. But toward the end of the story the future tense takes over (pp. 228ff.). The effect is very sinister because it is clear by the end that Bruno has won: there's no Johnny Carter anymore, and no "now" anymore, and no rhythm but only "my house, my wife, my prestige."

For the individual subject, as this story emphasizes, the substitution of rhythmic time for historical time has significant and threatening consequences. Because rhythmic time is an exploratory repetition, because it is over when it's over and exists for its duration only and then disappears into some other rhythm, any "I" or ego or *cogito* exists only for the same duration and then disappears with that sea change or undergoes transformation into some new state of being. What used to be called the individual consciousness has attained a more multivocal and systemic identity. It is not so much what "I mean" as "what is *meant*"; instead of "I think, therefore I am," the Cartesian principle linking human consciousness with divine and universal consciousness, Cortázar enunciates the new, perhaps more modest, principle of "I swing, therefore I am." In this conjugating rhythm, *each move forward is also digressive*, also a sideways move. A postmodern narrative submits to the sequential nature of language grudgingly and at every juncture keeps alive for readers an awareness of multiple pathways and constantly crossing themes. Rhythm is parataxis on the horizontal and in motion: a repetitive element that doesn't "forward" anything, one that is always exact but never "identical." Narratives where time is rhythm give readers an opportunity to take up a new kind of residence in time, a way of staying in the narrative present—often literally or effectively in the present tense—that requires new acts of attention.

Rhythmic time—the time of experiment, improvisation, adventure—destroys the historicist unity of the world by destroying its temporal common denominator. In rhythmic time mutual reference back and forth from one temporal moment to another becomes impossible because no neutrality exists between temporal moments; on the contrary, each moment contains its specific and unique definition. Each "time" is utterly finite. The founding agreements that we take for granted in modern historical narratives do not form in postmodern time, just as the common medium of events that we call history simply does not exist in postmodern narratives. In Robbe-Grillet's *Jealousy*, for example, the reader is confined to the present tense and thus to a continuous present that constantly erases past and future. No serenely neutral ("Nobody") narrator recollects, from an unspecific fictional future, a meaningful history of events. Gone are the linear coordinates that make possible the description of a stable objective world; pattern is always emerging and dissolving without certain foundation or even intelligible residue. The chief object of focus becomes the movement of reader consciousness or what might better be called the questionable subject-in-process. Whether or not such postmodern temporality supports anything like a "humanism of the present" of the sort Gilson attributes to medieval art, we can certainly say that postmodern narrative forces readers into a new kind of present: not the dematerialized present of historical time but what Nabokov calls the "Deliberate Present" of rhythmic time.

This fatal disappearance of historical values in postmodern writing has been taken by many as a tragedy for moral life. After all, without the power to compare ourselves across space and time, what becomes of the generic "human" solidarity with which we confront the material universe? Without consequences, what becomes of self-control or of power over circumstance? How can there be regularities or laws prevailing among events and persons when those events and persons are separated by essential difference or finitude and not merely by accident in the neutral, bridgeable media of time and space? These worries are not misplaced. The stakes are high. To the extent that we all plan and think in terms of "the future" and of generic "human" activity, we all depend on historical conventions; the broadly based disappearance of those conventions signals a change that is far from trivial.

Because such reactions are based on an assumption that the historical convention of temporality is the only possible one, they cannot allow either for the possible existence of other kinds of time or for the tenacity of historical conventions.[38] "History" as a category, like "time" and "space," as we have come to conceive of it over many centuries, is an instance of representation that we have almost completely naturalized; it mingles with the air we breathe. Habermas, for instance, assumes it throughout. Quite apart from whether his straw definitions of postmodernism hold water, he accepts apparently without question a view of history he finds rooted in the

---

[38] Robert S. Brumbaugh suggests in *Unreality and Time* that different professions have different time specifications (Albany: State University of New York Press, 1984), p. 140.

eighteenth century and, for all one can tell, in German philosophy.[39] The construction of history—the neutral, homogeneous temporal medium and the historical consciousness that constituted it—was, however, a Pan-European achievement and one traceable in much earlier philosophical usages than Hegel's, depending on whether Habermas would call Erasmus, say, a philosopher (see *Realism and Consensus*, pp. 24–37). The political consequences of these emphases, furthermore, include forms particular to other nations than Germany, perhaps conspicuously so, and are too important to be muddied with definitions whose cultural limitations remain unspecified.[40]

Good attempts to confront the political implications of postmodernism founder when they refer the postmodern problematic to "history," thereby restoring essence and foundation to the anti-essential and anti-foundational discourse of postmodernism. Nancy Fraser and Linda Nicholson, for instance, are concerned to discover conceptions of social criticism that do not rely on foundationalist thinking, and they find in "the large historical narrative" an intermediate possibility between "philosophical metanarrative" and the "local, *ad hoc*, and nontheoretical." Leaving aside for the moment whether or not there can be any such thing as the "nontheoretical," this "large historical narrative" is precisely the crux of the old problem and not of a new solution. One cannot oppose history to foundationalism because history *is* foundationalism.[41]

[39] Habermas's distinction between two "kinds" of postmodernism—"neoconservative" symptom of modernism's exhaustion and "anarchist" misunderstanding of modernism as inseparable from rationalism—is couched in essentialist terms that users would do well to note (*Discourse of Modernity*, pp. 3–5, also pp. 6, 16).

[40] Ranier Näigle argues that the Belief in History still controls German theory, specifically that Adorno and Jauss, and this is "the line that separates them from 'New French Theory' " (Naigle, "The Scene of the Other: Theodor Adorno's Negative Dialectic in the Context of Poststructuralism," in Jonathan Arac, ed., *Postmodernism and Politics* [Minneapolis: University of Minnesota Press, 1986], pp. 96–97). Still working "the concept of universal history," they have recourse to "little histories"; but these are not a solution of the problem of lost consensus because that problem includes more than the disappearance of local agreements about political agendas, economic ventures, or other secondary forms of consensus. The problem of consensus is the disappearance of the medium of historical time, which, like realistic space, is itself the ultimate act of consensus that enables the more local agreements (p. 99).

[41] Nancy Fraser and Linda J. Nicholson, "Social Criticism without Philosophy: An Encounter Between Feminism and Postmodernism," in Linda J. Nicholson, ed., *Feminism/Postmodernism* (New York: Routledge, 1990), p. 25. It is easier to formulate a problem than come up with the solution, as many volumes of the nineteenth century testify, especially when the manner of formulating the problem is part of the problem. For example, this essay, like several in this excellent volume, resorts to history and looks for models for postmodernism in, say, the contemporary city (mediations between strangers), historical self-reflexiveness, or undefined postmodern feminism. But model-seeking and historical thinking are themselves representational (history is a representation, a model is a representation), and thus the effort reinscribes the problem. A slightly different case of foundational confusion is Francis Fuka-

The problem of "legitimation" is real enough (possibly even including the term itself), and Lyotard by no means solves it with his passing reference to temporary contracts or with the various passages in *The Differend* that graze the question but do not go into it. What constrains the temporary contract? What prevents smallish social narratives and temporary constraints from developing large, ugly consequences? How can such consequences be perceived where, as in Lyotard, there is no social totality but just multiple concrete practices? As Nicholson and Fraser argue, such formulations have one major practical and political failing. Where "we cannot have and do not need a single, overarching theory of justice" but only "a 'justice of multiplicities,' " we lose the capacity to identify and criticize those "macrostructures of inequality and injustice which cut across the boundaries separating relatively discrete practices and institutions. There is no place in Lyotard's universe for critique of pervasive axes of dominance and subordination along lines like gender, race, and class" (*Feminism/Postmodernism*, p. 23). The problem with this spirited objection to Lyotard is that to accept postmodernism as a discursive definition is to accept redefinition of such problems, something that may seem to have some potential value given the fact that such problems have proved intractable in historical discourse and were perhaps constructed by it.

It still remains to be seen (or improvised) what implications postmodernism may have for what used to be called social justice; certainly it is not a foregone conclusion, as Fraser and Nicholson seem to assert, that postmodernism ignores the problem, even elides and (some other essays in the same collection hint) possibly even exists to finesse the problem of sexism just as it is reaching critical mass in historical terms (*whether* it is reaching critical mass is another question). One thing, however, seems certain: no effort to come to terms with social agendas will succeed without the recognition that history itself is a representational construction of the first order, and that new social construction cannot take place until history is denaturalized. The effort of this book is to forward that possibility by imagining, with the consistent help of postmodern writers, what an alternative temporality, a postmodern temporality, might be like, and what its implications might be for a now questionable subject-in-process, and in a context where the operative dualisms of Western culture are collapsed (see Part One, II). In most discussions of social agendas these conditions are not observed; instead the use of static, spatial metaphors and the elision of

yama's "The End of History?" which finds that the end of history accompanies the universal triumph of western liberalism; this makes little sense, considering that these are the very institutions most dependent upon historical conventions for their existence (*The National Interest* [Summer 1989]: 3–18).

temporality as an issue deflect an argument into wheel-spinning even where traction is near.[42]

The problem of social agendas is real; so are the problems of reconceiving accountability and responsibility and agency. Fraser and Nicholson formulate the crucial problem presented by postmodern theory as follows: "that many of the genres rejected by postmodernists are necessary for social criticism. For a phenomenon as pervasive and multifaceted as male dominance simply cannot be adequately grasped with the meager critical resources to which they would limit us" (p. 26). But the problems of textuality that postmodernism raises are not dismissable as "anomic relativism" nor solved by the assertion that postmodernism's "agentic" problematic is compatible with "individual agency." Is any "social theory" a solution to inequities when it is arguable that the episteme that produces the inequities is the same one that produces "social theory" or that the

[42] For example, Anna Yeatman claims that postmodernism preserves subjectivity, but in what form or manner? Is it postmodernly possible to oppose "individual" and "social" in order to say that the multivocality of societies is one thing, the pragmatics of (focused) individual agency another? If it is not necessary, in other words, to renounce subjective agency as we renounce the totalizing constructs of social discourse, what conception of subjective agency is at stake here—the one we have inherited from the seventeenth century or one reconstructed in postmodern terms unspecified here? "It is important to emphasize that if postmodernism means we have to abandon universalistic, general theories and, instead, to explore the multivocal worlds of different societies and cultures, this is *not* the same thing as abandoning the political-ethical project of working out the conditions for a universal pragmatics or individualized agency. The very orientation of postmodernism to the agentic quality and features of our sociocultural worlds underlines the significance of this political-ethical project" ("A Feminist Theory of Social Differentiation," in Nicholson, ed., *Feminism/Postmodernism*, p. 291). Maybe so; maybe not. I think Foucault is right that "the subject" as we know it has been the founding subject of historical and representational discourse only since the Renaissance and something that would have been Greek to the Greeks; its expulsion from the modern frame of reference *founds* that frame; and the dissolution of that frame involves the dissolution of that subject (or, what is more likely, the dissolution of that subject undermined the frame). In any case the link between history and that subject needs attention before it is possible to use terms like "dialogue" and "democracy" in the same breath with postmodernism. A reformation of subjectivity and a breakup of the neutral "time" of history have the most profound implications for the very political structures in question. It is not enough simply to favor "dialogically oriented modes of theorizing" (Yeatman, p. 294) and to assert the "democratic implications of postmodernism" as against the apparent implications of "anomic relativism" (p. 292). There may be ways. The historic link between democracy and slavery may be irrelevant or misleading. The repression of "herstory" in "history" that Yeatman herself mentions may not signal that history by definition does not include her story. But no ways can be found so long as we maintain our conventional usages of history in which relativism is always conceived in terms of totalization, in which "dialogue" implies subject positions no longer possible with the dissolution of the representational frame that founds them. Leaving temporality out of the conversation elides a distinctive feature of the modern (post-Renaissance) era, and arguably the most distinctive feature of the two-hundred-year era beginning (roughly) around 1776 when European and Anglo-American society demonstrably experimented with the social constructs being mentioned.

theory itself is the problem? If you're not part of the solution, as the sixties slogan went, you're part of the problem; one must not minimize the difficulty of this, the difficulty of really writing and acting anew.[43] And history is no solution. Its language is radioactive with the very problems for which we are seeking constructive new formulation. In fact, proposing a solution is less interesting to me than experimenting with new ways of conceiving the problem that extend attention in new directions and exercise attention in new ways. These have something to do with the reconstruction of time as rhythm, not history; something to do with networks instead of structures; something to do with a subject as process, not entity; something to do with the conception of personhood instead of individuality;[44] something to do with the powers of multilevel awareness and other improvisatory acts of attention that postmodern subjectivity constructs through participation in the manifold networks of language. The priority of language as a metaphor for systems has, among its advantages, the effect of validating nonhierarchical organization. A network differs from a structure because it is headless and footless; it has no "heart" or "center," no "origin" or "end" but instead, and like a language, only pattern repeating itself with exactitude, an "interminable pattern without any meaning" (*Hopscotch*, chap. 34).

The discourse of postmodernism, whatever its specific savor may be regarding this or that value, is hardly the cultural bonfire that some of its critics seem to fear, nor is it the reflex of unregenerate narcissism on the part of fancy but obscure prose stylists. Fostering new acts of attention in the interest of cultural renewal seems sufficiently serious work. By undermining history—that transcendental medium in which perspective is possible—postmodern fictions undermine the collective time we used to inhabit and force readers to attend to the time of reading activity, to the time of language and consciousness itself. Self-reflexive subjects-in-process are not necessarily inferior achievements to the impossibly stable Cartesian *cogito* and its version of identity. By attending always to the act of reading as well as to the so-called content of reading, consciousness becomes subject to different stresses and discovers different capabilities from those available in historical narrative. *Never* dialectical, teleological, transcendental, and, above all, never neutral, postmodern narrative time always includes without transcending the actual practice of reading as it takes place for this or that person.

[43] The greatest danger may be confusing optimism and theory with solutions and change. It is quite true that the old vocabulary of social "action" having failed us, the postmodern critique seems to provide insufficient new language for social agendas, a failure that at least partly informs the current political irresolution in the United States.

[44] For definition of personhood as distinct from individuality, and network as opposed to structure, see Elizabeth Ermarth, "On Having a Personal Voice," in Gayle Greene and Coppelia Kahn, eds., *Histories/A History: The Making of Feminist Criticism* (forthcoming).

Practically speaking, the debates about postmodernism come down to discussion about what, if anything, provides a reality principle for any construct. Postmodern writers and theorists do not deny the existence of the material world, about which, as Robbe-Grillet says, we can actually "know" very little; nor, so far as I know, does anyone familiar with the issue seriously deny the exclusiveness of discursive languages to which we necessarily resort in order to say anything "about" either the material or the discursive worlds—statements that inevitably are interpretations and, consequently, a pre-interpretation or an a priori formulation. But if discursive rules provide untranscendable constraints, what constrains the discursive rules? The question is haunted by the specters of holocausts which, in various national forms, have already demonstrated what appears to be no restraint. If anything can be justified in some Name, is there no way to choose between justifications? If every interpretation, every system, every set of laws is a closed inertial system and if there is no longer validity for any privileged position (floating intelligentsia, superego, or *cogito*, narrator, administrator, supreme court) from which to view them, how can a person or polis choose between (or even for that matter identify) this or that course except by chance?

Chance may have more to do with it than the various forms of rationalism allow, as the surrealists asserted when they pronounced in favor of "objective chance." But leaving chance aside for a later chapter, the general question here is what are the grounds, if any, for restraint? The phrase "individual or collective restraint" seems to urge itself here, as if the very question about restraint belongs to the discourse in question, the one in which distinctions between "individual" and "collective" make any sense. I gather from the writing of novelists (what used to be called "literary" writing in the discourse that removes such writing from the realm of practical necessity) that postmodern discourse collapses the distinctions between subject and object that sustain the Cartesian idea of "individual." It is in this context that the question of restraint must be asked.

This question has been answered in various ways. For example, Richard Rorty finds a satisfactory answer in "tradition," an answer that, his appreciation of *bricolage* notwithstanding, seems theoretically based in the nineteenth century because of its acceptance of the long-standing representational view of time as historical time. Fredric Jameson finds in postmodern *jouissance*, "generalized as a cultural style," an escape from alienation, which is to say, from a condition saturated with nostalgia for full presence. Both these discussions slip back toward the ground of historicism and modernism, the discourse of dialectics on the horizontal. But even at its most venturesome, the discourse of modernism remains a discourse of history, of self and other, of "human" defined as the still small voice that to survive— to find a place, a standing ground, a basis and justification for that little

changeling, the individual subject—must resist what Borges calls "amazement" and what Jameson (speaking for "the individual human body") calls
the "sublime."[45] The Cartesian subject stands squarely against amazement
and in favor of rationalizing denominators that create "distance."

The problem of constraint is sometimes conceived of as a problem of
community—for a writer perhaps a problem of audience—and ultimately
these are political matters, especially where political definition is as fundamentally textual as it is in the United States. But "community" is a weasel
word and can simply mean "segregation," as blacks, women, and the young
have reason to know. "Social" theory, in order to be something more than
another classical subterfuge, waits upon the issues postmodernism raises.[46]
Postmodern politics needs to retool for subjects-in-process, for "individuals" who are, to put Lyotard's term to different use, "temporary"; politics
may need to retool for that (Foucault's words) "boundless diversity, which
eludes specification and remains outside the concept, if not the resurgence
of repetition."[47] Politics may need to retool for (Nabokov's words) the
"continuum of a life," which, like each moment that comprises it, is "unprecedented and unrepeatable" and thus not meaningfully comprehended in
terms of "billions of Bills" or "Jills," and concerning which the worker need
take care "lest the entire report be choked up by the weeds of statistics and
waist-high generalizations" (*Ada*, p. 76). Improvisation, as a collective activity, meets Lyotard's postmodern specifications to an extent: it is limited,
local, and temporary. It is also *theoretically silent* and beyond negotiations
among "perspectives."[48]

[45] Richard Rorty, "Postmodernist Bourgeois Liberalism," in *Journal of Philosophy* 80, no.
10 (October 1983), pp. 583–89; Fredric Jameson, "Postmodernism, or the Cultural Logic
of Late Capitalism," in *The New Left Review* 146 (July–August 1984), pp. 53–92. Jameson's
restatement of the need for a "cognitive map" uses the metaphors of Renaissance exploration
and cartography, the "map," "compass," and "globe," and thereby invokes the common space
and time of the representational conventions current at least to modernism, along with some
nostalgia for that discourse common in uncomprehending treatments of postmodernism; the
"world space" he calls for, while it may be a desirable project, is a modernist, not a postmodernist agenda.

[46] In response to general objections that postmodernism lacks a "social" theory, I should
say that "social" as we use the term belongs to the nineteenth century and to classical notions
of identity and dynamics that are problematized in postmodernism; their relevance to the
postmodern condition remains to be shown. To the extent that "society" implies what Ilya
Prigogine calls "integrable systems" (*From Being to Becoming: Time and Complexity in the Physical Sciences* [San Francisco: W. H. Freeman & Co., 1980], p. 29), it has no place in postmodern writing, where there are no common media to permit such integration and where "society" is what language conserves and what changes with language.

[47] Foucault, "Theatrum Philosophicum," in *Language, Counter-Memory, and Practice: Selected Essays and Interviews*, trans. Donald F. Bouchard and Sherry Simon (Ithaca: Cornell
University Press, 1977), pp. 181–82.

[48] Lyotard uses the term "improvisation," but he uses it synonymously with "dialogical"
(*Postmodern Condition*, p. 307) as a model for the kind of "community of difference"—some-

Questions of restraint or constraint are really questions about common denominators and the advisability of doing without them. Without consensus available as a basis for conducting affairs, what is there but force? N. Katherine Hayles, in arguing for a premise of "constrained constructivism," characterizes the postmodern situation as one of simultaneous habitation in conflicting epistemes: "In what episteme do I live? Not in any single epistemology, but in a complex space characterized by multiple strata and marked by innumerable fissures."[49] In this condition, she argues, we must acknowledge constraints because, even though any epistemic formulation cannot be taken as a mirror of reality, for many practical, scientific, and sensory reasons "reality" is there all the same. In this she shares the view of Rorty, who writes of the need "to be in touch with a reality obscured by 'ideology' and disclosed by 'theory.' "[50] Barbara H. Smith complexifies this approach, though without basically changing it, when she argues that it is possible to have "value without truth value" and that "value judgments may themselves be considered commodities" and that "some of them are evidently *worth more* than others *in the relevant markets*" or, one might say, in the relevant series.[51]

These cases seem directed by a view that absolute relativism is not only

thing that at least in Mikhail Bakhtin's usage is certainly historical and thus unreconstructedly modern.

[49] Hayles on "constrained constructivism" in chap. 8 of *Chaos Bound*.

[50] Rorty summarizes what's at stake between Habermas and Lyotard as follows: Anything (like Lyotard's) abandoning the theoretical approach and its metanarratives would "be counted by Habermas as 'neoconservative,' because it drops the notions which have been used to justify the various reforms which have marked the history of the Western democracies since the Enlightenment, and which are still being used to criticize the socio-economic institutions of both the Free and the Communist worlds. Abandoning a standpoint which is, if not transcendental, at least 'universalistic,' seems to Habermas to betray the social hopes which have been central to liberal politics.

"So we find French critics of Habermas ready to abandon liberal politics in order to avoid universalistic philosophy, and Habermas trying to hang on to universalistic philosophy, with all its problems, in order to support liberal politics." ("Habermas and Lyotard on Postmodernity," pp. 171, 162).

Rorty puts stock in the "we" that founds community (p. 172), yet everywhere demonstrates the exclusions upon which that "we" has foundered. Between Lyotard and Habermas, Rorty "splits the difference" by seeing "the canonical sequence of philosophers from Descartes to Nietzsche as a distraction from the history of concrete [presumably pragmatic] social engineering which made the contemporary North Atlantic culture what it is now, with all its glories and all its dangers" (p. 173).

[51] Barbara Herrnstein Smith, "Value without Truth-Value," in John Fekete, ed., *Life After Postmodernism: Essays on Value and Culture* (New York: St. Martin's Press, 1987), pp. 9, 11.

According to Smith, even "claims to universal validity may themselves serve, and take on value as a function of, particular contingencies." This goes, she says, "for science, as for art, because a scientist is always a social being in that she has acquired her knowledge from others and from language, and considers the adequacy of her models or conclusions in terms of that language and those others."

objectionable but possible. But even when "reality" becomes "realities" (or "relevant series"), the formulation merely pluralizes the common denominators and multiplies the systems in which value judgments can be absolute ("my/our/their reality"). To say some values are "worth more" in some "markets" is an interesting hedge but a hedge nonetheless. Value judgments conceived in terms of "markets" instead of "truth" still acknowledge the constraint of something "out there" that exceeds all our measurements and remains self-identical, and this includes Lyotard's contestation, which implies a something-being-contested and thus begs the ultimate question. The term "reality" implies something stable and self-identical; both in physical science and in other languages, such a foundational usage is increasingly marginal. In the physical "reality," as described by Ilya Prigogine's and Isabelle Stengers's treatment of chaos as a phase of order, "reality" is in a constant process of fundamental redefinition, so that the term "fundamental" does not even really apply. Postmodern language dissolves foundational usage in similar ways. In what sense can we say that something that completely changes its identity is "real," in that customary sense of the word? "Real" is a foundational word by long usage, so that it does not seem an appropriate word for a process of redefinition that leaves nothing "the same." To give up the "reality" or "realities" that constrain behavior and inscribe value does not mean anarchic relativism in which "everything is permitted" and brute power rules; in fact, as some voices in postmodern writing suggest, it is precisely the faith in "reality" (including "the market") that permits everything in the pursuit of "truth." The failure of a totalizing absolute like historical time may raise the fear of total relativism, the fear that "everything is permitted" but, as Dostoevsky's Raskolnikov discovers, there is no such thing.

The fears of moral catastrophe that postmodernism raises in some are usually posited on classical assumptions and thus by definition foreclose on the discourse of postmodernism where loss of the terms "reality," "truth," and "man" is compensated by other gains. The fear of extinction is not far from this corner of anxiety. On the one hand, nobody denies the presence of conditions external to our descriptive and linguistic systems; nobody hopes for complete solipsism of the kind that some ascribe, completely wrongheadedly, to postmodernism and that would in any case only be possible in a classical system. On the other hand, a term like "reality"—and the insistence of finding a reality principle—increasingly looks unworkable and uninteresting in a situation that no longer sustains the (religious) faith in universal rational laws and that calls for new kinds of virtue.

The physical sciences provide clear examples of the changed condition under which the term "reality" seems to need translation: for example, "chaos theory" and especially the "dissipative structures" described by Prigogine. As he and Stengers express it, the second law of thermodynamics introduces a new vision of process ("a probability process") and a "new concept of matter" that introduce us to a new conception of order that is independent of the closures and finalities of classical dynamics and that permits us to see how "*nonequilibrium brings 'order out of chaos.'* "[52] Irreversibility on the cosmic scale—an implication that Einstein and others had sought to resist—does not imply universal entropic death as they had feared; on the contrary, the process that comes to an end—whether chemical or musical—turns out to be merely a phase (or "phrase"?) that becomes *translated* into a new phase: one that, because of the presence of contingency in the multilevel complex environment of life processes, cannot be predicted or controlled in any classical sense. A particular phase of the process *has* to end in order for the life process to continue. This sustaining translation, moreover, depends on chance: on the "amplification" of fluctuations at the "right moment" (p. 176) in a stochastic (probabilistic) process unsusceptible to determinist and mechanical definition. So, for example, a chemical system fluctuates to a point where it leaves a stationary state and shows "periodic" behavior as a system-in-process. The element of chance, which in a rationalistic system is a spoke in the wheel, in a probabilistic process is the source of life, of rhythm, of continuance in ever-new states and modes.[53] The more determinist laws appear limited, the more open the universe is to fluctuation and innovation (pp. 213–14).

This reconceptualization in the physical sciences has implications not only for Newtonian mechanics but also for other dynamic systems posited on Newtonian and humanistic principles. Without drawing facile political

---

[52] Ilya Prigogine and Isabelle Stengers, *Order out of Chaos: Man's New Dialogue with Nature* (*La Nouvelle Alliance*, 1979) (New York: Bantam, 1984), pp. 286–87.

[53] The self-transformation of chaos into order through chance conjunctions belongs to the shift away from classical science that has produced new concepts of time as something "internal" to systems (p. 209), new concepts of measurement that must take into account both measurer and measured, and even new conceptions of objectivity (Prigogine, *Being to Becoming*, pp. 217–18).

Prigogine and Stengers describe how chance converts itself into order in this memorable passage describing chemical clocks, where the chemical system, because of fluctuation, crosses a threshold where it leaves a stationary state and shows "periodic" behavior. "Suppose we have two kinds of molecules, 'red' and 'blue.' Because of the chaotic motion of the molecules, we would expect that at a given moment we would have more red molecules, say, in the left part of the vessel. Then a bit later more blue molecules would appear, and so on. The vessel would appear to us as 'violet,' with occasional irregular flashes of red or blue. However, this is *not* what happens with a chemical clock; here the system is all blue, then it abruptly changes its color to red, and then again to blue. Because all these changes occur at *regular* time intervals, we have a coherent process.

"Such a degree of order stemming from the activity of billions of molecules seems incredible, and indeed, if chemical clocks had not been observed, no one would believe that such a process is possible. To change color all at once, molecules must have a way to 'communicate.' The system has to act as a whole" (*Order out of Chaos,* p. 148). At a more complex level, it is a "mixture of necessity and chance" that "constitutes the history of the system" (p. 170).

analogies, it is obvious that the following description suggests new formulations for old problems like the roles of chance or of individual behavior; and in a probabilistic process these things must be considered in the
context of the "moment" of the system.

> A system far from equilibrium may be described as organized not because it
> realizes a plan alien to elementary activities, or transcending them, but, on the
> contrary, because the amplification of the microscopic fluctuation occurring at
> the "right moment" resulted in favoring one reaction path over a number of
> other equally possible paths. Under certain circumstances, therefore, the role
> played by individual behavior can be decisive. More generally, the "overall" be-
> havior cannot in general be taken as dominating in any way the elementary pro-
> cesses constituting it. Self-organization processes in far-from-equilibrium con-
> ditions correspond to a delicate interplay between chance and necessity, between
> fluctuations and deterministic laws. We expect that near a bifurcation, fluctua-
> tions or random elements would play an important role, while between bifurca-
> tions the deterministic aspects would become dominant. (*Order out of Chaos*, p.
> 176)

Individual behavior, in short, can be decisive *or* ineffectual, and it cannot
be predicted which, or when. While this description in no way denies the
existence of the universe, it does preclude assumption of a self-similar "reality" accessible to reason simply because time permanently alters the description, dramatically at some moments and minimally at others.

The implications of such new descriptions for social formulations are
immense. The simple idea that "chance" must be accommodated throws
logocentrism into a cocked hat. What if, for instance, *Homo sapiens* is the
production of a series of chance events that, as Stephen J. Gould suggests,
might very easily never have occurred? The message of the Burgess Shale
"not only reverses our general ideas about the source of pattern—it also
fills us with a new kind of amazement (also a *frisson* for the improbability
of the event)." We [*Homo sapiens*] "came *this close* (put your thumb about a
millimeter away from your index finger), thousands and thousands of
times, to erasure by the veering of history down another sensible channel.
Replay the tape a million times from a Burgess beginning, and I doubt that
anything like *Homo sapiens* would ever evolve again."[54] The contrast between classical and postmodern descriptions throws emphasis on the "carrying capacity" of the system rather than on individual motivation: a carrying capacity that is a function of how that system is exploited (*Order out
of Chaos*, pp. 196–204). A system that constructs media (time and space)
that continue to infinity has, if one can so express it, a carrying capacity not

---

[54] Stephen J. Gould, *Wonderful Life: The Burgess Shale and the Nature of History* (London,
Sydney, Auckland, Johannesburg: Hutchinson Radius, 1989), p. 289.

inconsistent with the idea of immortality (or at least certain substitutes), and in fact relativity theory alarmed some distinguished physicists on precisely these grounds.[55] The instability recognized by the scientific descriptions just mentioned puts an end to some hopes but engenders others. "Even small fluctuations may grow and change the overall structure. As a result individual activity is not doomed to insignificance. On the other hand, this is also a threat, since in our universe the security of stable, permanent rules seems gone forever" (p. 313). What social (that is, moral) implications this may have remains to be seen, but it is not clear that there is any greater threat of moral catastrophe in probabilistic social descriptions than has already been shown in logocentric ones.[56]

Postmodernism acknowledges not a single but multiple constraints. Unlike the discourse of modernism with its common denominators for extension to infinity, postmodern time and space are warped and made finite: not, as in the Middle Ages, by divine agency but by the play of chance and necessity in the processes of life themselves. These processes include a mortality that tends to remains unrecognized and unaccounted for in modern discourse, where representational values—realism in art and elsewhere—encourage us to forget finitude by distributing energy toward an infinite horizon.[57] Postmodern writing destroys the homogeneity of time just as

[55] The revolution in early twentieth-century physics "was regarded by many observers at the time, and since, as a move from continuity to discontinuity" and thus away from the immortality with which continuity, however illogically, had been associated. Discontinuity meant skepticism (Alex Keller, "Continuity and Discontinuity in Early Twentieth-Century Physics and Early Twentieth-Century Painting," in Martin Pollock, ed., *Common Denominators in Art and Science* [Aberdeen: Aberdeen University Press, 1983], pp. 97–106, esp. p. 103). See also Prigogine and Stengers: "Equilibrium structures . . . by definition . . . are inert at the global level. For this reason they are also 'immortal' " (*Order out of Chaos*, p. 127).

[56] Prigogine and Stengers summarize their discussion in *Order out of Chaos* in a way that emphasizes the radical nature of their enterprise: "Our vision of nature is undergoing a radical change toward the multiple, the temporal, the complex. . . . We were seeking general, all-embracing schemes that could be expressed in terms of eternal laws, but we have found time, events, evolving particles" (p. 292). And these discoveries create new practical problems (from engineering to astrophysics "the problem of time, of irreversibility" is now urgent: [p. 231]). Where modernity from Newton to Einstein linked the intelligible (rational) with the immutable (p. 294), the new science confronts mutability to the point of saying, in a Nabokovian phrase, "Time is construction" (p. 301).

But the practical and personal implications of all this are far from clear when it is still so easy to slip into locutions like "our time" (p. 301), or to speak of the "two cultures" as "two related aspects of reality" (p. 310), or still to speak of "what exists in time" and "what is outside of time" (p. 312). If we still retain the dualistic distinctions between "reality" and "aspects," between stasis and process, between "inside" and "outside" so familiar in Western metaphysics, we are not far along the new road in practice. It takes a lot, evidently, to demonstrate to scientists this main point that "there is no activity that is not time oriented" (p. 300), but the discussion leaves the ontological cliffhanger hanging.

[57] Thanks to Tom Vargish for advice on use of the terms "finite" and "bounded," which

dissipative structures do, leaving us to cope anew with finitude, including the fact of death left with no transcendence to mediate its hard, blunt edge.[58] Postmodern writing seeks to expand our possible "reality" by thwarting those habits that constrain the available languages. By emphasizing the limits, the finite differences between one discursive set and another, postmodern writing, like dissipative chemical structures, sets the definition of "reality" in motion and forecloses on old certainties at the same time that it offers new kinds of intervention. "Reality," as postmodern narratives show, never stays "the same"; it is not inert but interactive and thus continually constructed and reconstructed.

This awareness of finitude, of limit, is the basis of an entirely new aesthetic and provides the main restraint on construction that postmodernism respects. A postmodernist would never speak of "historical reality": not just because "reality" doesn't exist except as defined locally but also because "history" doesn't exist either, except as defined locally. This is a proposition that seems hardest to grasp for those who use totalizing theoretical language. There is not *a* history but at best histories, and this pluralization has implications just as radical for "time" as Jackson Pollock's work has for "space": time and space, that is, as both are conceived in the early modern era and still widely assumed even in supposedly radical critiques of discourse. The dissolution of neutral time and space, and with them the bracketing of empiricist and historical thinking as just one more construction, puts emphasis in quite different places than it has been for at least several centuries.

The challenge, and the excitement, of postmodern writing comes in learning to manage this power of self-reflexiveness and to perform its particular, discourse-revising experiments. Such reflexiveness, however, is always a matter of practice in postmodernism, a matter of the lifting of an actual hand, the exercising of an actual restraint in the course of this or that specific improvisation with the material and tools at hand. This is self-reflexion that does not provide a protected position for viewing—for being, say, a reader or an implied spectator of realistic art, or a distanced and "represented" member of a political collectivity. This self-reflexion goes

preserve an important distinction in physics and one that is useful to maintain here ("this suggestion of a finite but unbounded space is one of the greatest ideas about the nature of the world which has ever been conceived": Max Born, speaking of the general theory of general relativity, quoted by Mook and Vargish, *Inside Relativity*, p. 137).

[58] The behavior of chemical instabilities in dissipative structures "greatly modifies the very meaning of space and time. Much of geometry and physics is based on a simple concept of space and time, generally asssociated with Euclid and Galileo. In this view, time is homogeneous. Time translations may have no effect on physical events. The formation of a dissipative structure destroys the homogeneity of time" (Prigogine, *Being to Becoming*, pp. 103–4). It also destroys time's neutrality.

through every position; there are no special circumstances, no ivory tower of the mind.

For aid in imagining the opportunity postmodern writing presents, it is helpful to consult another literary example: the notion of time as a multi-dimensional web of plural realities that is a characteristic feature of Borges stories. "The Garden of the Forking Paths" outlines (in this it resembles Cortázar's "The Pursuer") a mortal competition between the time of history and project, on the one hand, and a new kind of time, an "invisible labyrinth," which is nothing other than a written text and in which rhythm and multivalence prevail. In "The Pursuer," as in most of Cortázar's Moebius trips, one often imagines an alternative reality from what he calls "this side." Borges situates us on "the other side" of history, in a situation where the historical series is not allowed to form or, when it does, encounters some eerily fatal contradiction.

"The Garden of the Forking Paths" was published during World War II; Borges's narrator is Yu Tsun, a Chinese working for German intelligence during World War I. In this context of total war the important values are strategic and involve things like "necessary information," strategic assassination, and "national security." Yu Tsun, on the eve of discovery and arrest, determines to convey an important name to the Germans the only way he can think of: getting that name into the newspapers by murdering someone with that name and then getting conspicuously caught. His victim, Stephen Albert, chosen arbitrarily because his last name fits the secret programs of a closed intelligence code, coincidentally turns out to be a scholar and an expert on the work of Ts'ui Pen, the assassin's grandfather and maker of the invisible labyrinth that is an alternative vision of time.

This alternative temporal conception is presented to Yu Tsun at the moment he prepares to kill Albert, and of course it is a vision that would make such assassination, and the entire logic that supports it, pointless:

> Differing from Newton and Schopenhauer [Albert says], your ancestor did not think of time as absolute and uniform. He believed in an infinite series of times, in a dizzily growing, ever spreading network of diverging, converging and parallel times. This web of time—the strands of which approach one another, bifurcate, intersect or ignore each other through the centuries—embraces every possibility. We do not exist in most of them.

At this the assassin momentarily senses the rhythmic pulse of invisible worlds that surround him and in which his projects are merely some possibilities among a myriad of alternatives. "Necessity" pales into choice.

> Once again I sensed the pullulation of which I have already spoken. It seemed to me that the dew-damp garden surrounding the house was infinitely saturated

with invisible people. All were Albert and myself, secretive, busy and multiform in other dimensions of time.

But the suicidal assassin shakes off this kinetic "pullulation," preferring to sacrifice another and himself (his pursuer, Richard Madden, is close at his heels) rather than to change his convention: "I lifted my eyes and the short nightmare disappeared. In the black and yellow garden there was only a single man" (*Ficciones*, pp. 100–101). The other world may surround him always, but Yu Tsun believes only in the pilgrimage: only in the single track of historical time where his act has no immediate or personal benefit but instead ones that are hypothetical (he scarcely believes in it anymore), prospective, and collective. He falls back on habit—it is hardly any longer a "choice"—and opts for a way of doing things as much as for a specific result. By force of habit and a vested "interest" that destroys him, he chooses the time of Newton and of the universal historian, not the forking, relativistic time of the Borgesian garden.

The reader, however, has a harder time of it. The story forces reader attention into play between alternate semantic systems, and that play is what constitutes rhythmic time. The echoes of those multiple systems shine through, pullulate in the transparent moment, and force a reader to be aware that at any point multiple turnings are possible. Reader attention alternates between contradictory possibilities, and the rhythms of this attention cannot be reduced to a statement. There is a window, then there is another, and the crossing between them brings one face to face with the virtual quality of existence and its immense possibilities. Albert the Western scholar and Ts'ui Pen, the Chinese ancestor, have the capacity we are cultivating as readers and that the German-Chinese spy Yu Tsun lacks because he is totally lost in the linear track and his project of controlling ("making") history. Yu Tsun chooses to stay on the representational train and to ignore "the pullulation." Postmodern narrative encourages new rhythms of attention by pluralizing voice and by sustaining contradiction, effects that account for the risibility that this narrative provokes when it produces the link that cannot be explained and blows up the Law with laughter.

In his essay on "Time and Description," Robbe-Grillet describes the temporal experiments in his *Jealousy* as part of an effort to construct with readers a practice not based on faith in a preexistent order (of Being or Meaning or Reality or Truth), a practice not geared to the production of readers as rationalizing, founding subjects, a practice above all not answerable to historical temporality.[59] What his readers construct is not a realistic

---

[59] Robbe-Grillet theorizes on the postmodern novelists' attempts to baffle the reader-as-historian in essays, written mainly in the 1950s and collected as *For a New Novel: Essays on Fiction* (*Pour un nouveau roman*, 1963), trans. by Richard Howard (New York: Grove Press,

image, which is to say, a secondary image of a primary and single ("the") world, an image whose main purpose after all would be to revalidate the reader as an individual Cartesian subject. What *Jealousy* constructs instead is a primary reality, a reality of language, and an opportunity to be a reader who is both accomplice and co-creator of whatever series and temporality exist and not merely a passive, detached observer-recipient watching events "in" time:

> It was absurd to suppose that in the novel *Jealousy* . . . there existed a clear and unambiguous order of events, one which was not that of the sentences of the book, as if I had diverted myself by mixing up a pre-established calendar the way one shuffles a deck of cards. The narrative was on the contrary made in such a way that any attempt to reconstruct an external chronology would lead, sooner or later, to a series of contradictions, hence to an impasse. And this not with the stupid intention of disconcerting the Academy, but precisely because there existed for me no possible order outside of that of the book. The latter was not a narrative mingled with a simple anecdote external to itself, but again the very unfolding of a story which had no other reality than that of the narrative, an occurrence which functioned nowhere else except in the mind of the invisible narrator, in other words of the writer, and of the reader. (*For a New Novel*, p. 154)

The innocent phrase "no other reality" points to the characteristic, always interesting, fabulous fact in postmodern narrative that there is no Elsewhere: there is no "Reality" of which the novel is a secondary reflection, no superior system to that actual process in which this reader of this story is engaged; there is, in short (and to use the relevant terms of philosophers since Nietzsche who have sought an escape from the impasses of Western metaphysics), no transcendence. The narrator of realism, along with the historical time that narrator literally maintains, dissolves in postmodern writing into the consciousness of reader-and-writer, or reader-as-writer: reader, in any case, as co-inventor of the fiction that is, at the same time, no longer distinct from "reality" but itself constitutes whatever there is of reality. Time has become reader's time, phenomenal time; in a word, time has become a function of position.[60]

1965); repr. Evanston: Northwestern University Press, 1989. This collection remains the best single theoretical explanation of postmodern narrative.

[60] In novels the medium of historical time collapses together with that nineteenth-century narrative strategy known as "the narrator": a strategy that supports and holds in place the convention of historical time. Robbe-Grillet's discussion of this narrator is hasty and often falls into conservative and romantic clichés about how the narrator's claims to objectivity are claims to being like "God" (for example, *For a New Novel*, pp. 138–39). But while he almost always oversimplifies the achievement of nineteenth-century narration, the inadequacy of his peripheral analyses should not blind us to the immense power and usefulness of his general description of postmodern narrative.

By making an accomplice of the reader, the postmodern writer insures that postmodern temporality is always finite and functional. The new novelist shifts the burden of narrative from apparently neutral representation—what could be called Consumer Fiction—to what I call (altering Thorstein Veblen) "Conspicuous Construction: construction work that each reader self-consciously (conspicuously) does as she or he reads."[61] Such readers do without "the" rationalizable, unitary historical world where one finds meaningful causal relationships between before and after, where the reader's role is one of passive consumption, as in "oh, yes, the world is like that," or—with more sinister overtones—"see how everything can be explained." For the reader of postmodern novels there simply is no "time" for this sort of thing in the sense of the "same" medium inhabited by all "in" which one can make those mutually informative measurements that produce everything from personal projects to social programs. Far from enlisting the reader's consciousness in voyages of discovery, postmodern narrative eschews new or other worlds and restrains consciousness to new acts of attention and discovery in the finite, specific, and exceedingly perishable present.

In discussing this reader present where linear, historical time does not pass, Robbe-Grillet describes a continuous *dual activity* of construction *and* deconstruction. Through this often contradictory movement of description the postmodern narrative replaces historical time with reader time—something that must be at least partially unique to each reader and each reading. Consequently that time is bounded, operating only for the duration of a single "play" of the text. This reader-and-text operates by "a double movement of creation and destruction" in which "the entire interest of" (that is, "man's place in") these pages no longer lies in "the thing described, but in the very movement of the description" (*For a New Novel*, p. 148). In other words, *things*—whether objects with invariant structures or subjects (characters and readers) with autonomous identities—disappear into *movement*, into activity that includes the reader as an essential element. The point of this account, which only sounds paradoxical, is that aesthetic experience is not virtual, it is actual experience; or, more accurately, *all experience is essentially aesthetic*, that is, *defined* and essentially *qualitative*. One might think that this is obvious, except that the historical conventions denying it have become second nature. It is true, of course, that every author requires a reader's inventive complicity to make the black marks on a page into meaning, but it is postmodern writers who require their readers to have that experience deliberately and critically rather than

[61] Elizabeth Ermarth, "Conspicuous Construction, or Kristeva, Nabokov, and the Antirealist Critique," *Novel* (Winter–Spring, 1988), pp. 330–39. Reprinted in *Why the Novel Matters: A Postmodern Perplex* (Bloomington: Indiana University Press, 1990), pp. 348–58.

passively or mechanically. Reading, like any other use of consciousness, is literally writing in the expanded sense of inscribing and reinscribing the languages or discourses of culture. Postmodern writing makes that activity visible.

The rationale for such dealings with readers is that this active coinvention has immensely practical results:

> These descriptions whose movement destroys all confidence in the things described, these heroes without naturalness as without identity, this present which constantly invents itself, as though in the course of the very writing, which repeats, doubles, modifies, denies itself, without ever accumulating in order to constitute a past—hence a "story," a "history" in the traditional sense of the word—all this can only invite the reader (or the spectator) to another mode of participation than the one to which he was accustomed. If he is sometimes led to condemn the works of his time, that is, those which most directly address him . . . this is solely because he persists in seeking a kind of communication which has long since ceased to be the one which is proposed to him.
>
> For, far from neglecting him, the author today proclaims his absolute need of the reader's cooperation, an active, conscious, *creative* assistance. What he asks of him is no longer to receive ready-made a world completed, full, closed upon itself, but on the contrary to participate in a creation, to invent in his turn the work—and the world—and thus to learn to invent his own life. (*For a New Novel*, pp. 155–56)

In postmodern narrative invention is no longer the discredited cousin of "reason" (that elaborate invention) but instead the main activity of conscious adult life. The trick is learning to invent well, something this new narrative makes a point of promoting.

Those inclined to dismiss the new novel and everything it stands for usually single out for special opprobrium its departure from historical conventions and its always implicit idea that "the past" is a function of consciousness. After all, in the past, as we all know, things happened in this way, not that, and the idea that our past is invented threatens the moral universe with total solipsism. This objection is important because it touches on the heart of the problem in postmodern narrative, and the answer to this objection is complex. In simple summary, this objection betrays a fear of substituting a false history for a true one, a fear that simply restates in another form precisely the historical conventions in question. The postmodern subversion of faith in "fact" (the very idea of "fact" is necessarily historical) goes far beyond any mere revision or substitution of one "history" for another; its subversion undermines the very confidence that one can or could ever isolate a single or a true track of history. From a postmodern situation, such assurance looks fairly similar to the assurance of those who have the inside track on the intentions of God. In any case, the requirement of reader complicity does not let the reader do whatever he or she likes with the writing in question; in fact, postmodern narrative is a very demanding discipline precisely because it requires new acts of attention.

It is true, however, that by making an accomplice of the reader the author does shift the burden of narrative away from representation of a unified and rationalizable, which is to say historical world where "after" and "before" have meaningful causal relationships and onto the kind of conspicuous construction I have just described. The dual activity of doing and undoing that Robbe-Grillet describes forces readers back onto their own rhythms of perception, something that lasts only so long as the reader-text is in play. Such experience is not something that can be summarized; when it is over, it is over, and to recover what is "in" it necessarily means rereading it, a reading that is never a mere repetition of a prior reading but always a reinvention. Such experience can be shared but only *as* experience, not as knowledge or truth. There is no such thing as capturing in excellent summary the essential "story." The postmodern reading experience does not turn into knowledge or information or, in other words, into capital. Postmodern novels simply refuse to accommodate those who, as André Breton says, want to use their minds "like a savings bank" (*Manifestoes*, p. 129). What the postmodern reader does instead is to keep fragile contradictions in play for a certain duration, and to conjugate in that Tender Interval whatever immortality it is possible to know.

Rhythm Section: Alain Robbe-Grillet's *Jealousy*

Jealousy may be the novel that comes closest to cinema because of its resolute refusal to slip into the past tense, the tense of history and of traditional narrative "meaning." *Jealousy* forces its reader continuously to assume the present, to put on what is otherwise so easily left aside: the actual, intimate, profound movement of attention *as it takes place*. By confining attention to a series of repetitions and variations, the novel confines us entirely to the present tense and, by so doing, it dissolves both the narrator (that surrogate-subject function of realistic narrative) and with it anything like historical time. Unable to slide magisterially between past and future, the reader must attend only to the present and to its changing anticipations and memories. The more we insist on reconstructing plot, the more *Jealousy* insists on the fruitlessness of such effort. Here there is no neutral medium and no common chronological clock in which "a" plot would be possible, not even the daily cycle inconsistently suggested by the changing shadow of a column.

Among its reflexive features, *Jealousy* contains a description of how *not* to write a novel, in other words, of how prior forms of the novel have trained readers to read by encouraging distanced interpretation and at the same time suppressing questions of value. The passage describes A . . . and Franck discussing a novel about Africa that they are both reading.

> They have never made the slightest judgment as to the novel's value, speaking instead of the scenes, events, and characters as if they were real: a place they might remember . . . people they might have known. . . . Their discussions have never touched on the verisimilitude, the coherence, or the quality of the narrative. On the other hand, they frequently blame the heroes for certain acts or characteristics, as they would in the case of mutual friends.
>
> They sometimes deplore the coincidences of the plot, saying that "things don't happen that way," and then they construct a different probable outcome starting from a new supposition, "if it weren't for that". . . . The variations are extremely numerous. . . .
>
> [Then] Franck sweeps away in a single gesture all the suppositions they had just constructed together. It's no use making up contrary possibilities, since things are the way they are; reality stays the same.[62]

If *Jealousy* were a novel like the one "about" Africa, we might ask the same kind of plot-and-character questions about it: is A . . . having an affair with Franck? Is her husband jealous and, if so, unnecessarily? What does A . . . look like, or Franck, or the veranda? But in *Jealousy* there are only "contrary possibilities"; reality *never* stays the same. Robbe-Grillet moves his readers much closer to questions of a kind that A . . . and Franck never ask about the African novel, such as what do we do when we read it? Is that valuable and if so why? What *is* its value? What is its order or its play? How is play sustained and order achieved?

The ahistorical sequence of the novel contains descriptions that are repeated with subtle variations throughout the text, and the reader attends primarily to the series of variations, including what appear to be contradictions that are irreducible and unproductive of any discernible "meaning." These attentions run backward and forward rhythmically in anticipation and recollection from any given point, and that point is always moving, dissolving into another configuration, another arrangement that varies or departs from the preceding one. A reader's memory of the "text" is unstable, and whatever a single reading establishes differs with each reader and each reading. Robbe-Grillet's readers learn what it feels like to inhabit a language (hence a "reality") where time is a function of position and, consequently, always finite and defined, not neutral and infinite.

In such time attention moves in ways unapproachable by linear metaphors. Memory runs simultaneous parallel movies, "distortion" is the norm. Attention loops out and returns in anthematic fashion rather than

---

[62] *Jealousy* (*La Jalousie*, 1957), in *Two Novels ("Jealousy" and "In the Labyrinth")*, trans. Richard Howard (New York: Grove Press, 1965), p. 75.

following any linear track. It is neither possible nor interesting to assume—as old-fashioned interpreters like A . . . and Franck do—that "reality is always the same." Because of this disestablishment of perspective and its rationalizations, because of its utter reliance on the interventions of readers and what they may happen to pick up, a postmodern novel like this one is not something that can be successfully summarized; it must be repeated. Such writing effectively undermines the lingering linear necessities of the written word.

Given this artistic agenda, Robbe-Grillet's interest in cinema is not surprising. As he says, the "paradoxical movement (to construct while destroying)" works best in film because film "knows only one grammatical mode: the present tense of the indicative. . . . It has often been repeated in recent years that time was the chief 'character' of the contemporary novel. . . . The same is obviously true of the cinema: every modern cinematographic work is a reflection on human memory, its uncertainties, its persistence, its dramas, etc." He describes *Last Year at Marienbad*, the film he made with Alain Resnais, as a "world without a past" (*For a New Novel*, pp. 151–52). This description, like the film itself, acknowledges the extent to which the past exists in our conscious experience as a function of present awareness, the extent to which cinematic time is an unstable dimension of perception rather than a neutral medium containing it.

In narrative such temporality trains attention directly on the experience of reading and the rhythms of constructive awareness; it does not, as in the "productive" novels of plot and character, train attention on any residues of that reading. Robbe-Grillet described the effect in his essay:

> Time seems to be cut off from its temporality. It no longer passes. It no longer completes anything. And this is doubtless what explains the disappointment which follows the reading of today's books, or the projection of today's films. . . . Not only do they claim no other reality than that of the reading, or of the performance, but further they always seem to be in the process of contesting, of jeopardizing themselves in proportion as they create themselves. Here space destroys time, and time sabotages space. Description makes no headway, contradicts itself, turns in circles. Moment denies continuity. (*For a New Novel*, p. 155)

This circling, contradictory sequence forces readers into new acts of attention by foreclosing on old ones. The process can even be fun. For example, while it is impossible to reconstruct anything like a linear plot from *Jealousy*, the book nevertheless succeeds admirably with attentive readers—and this includes well-disposed undergraduates who have never seen a novel like this in their lives but who enjoy this elegant, mysterious, and delightful book.

The most obvious feature of *Jealousy* is its systematic repetition of details and descriptions. A balustrade with peeling gray paint, the position of a shadow, a banana grove, a crouching man, the slow brushing of long, blue-black hair, the mark of a centipede smashed on the wall, a car, a table arrangement on a porch: descriptions of these things are each repeated almost exactly several or many times, each time with just a little variation so that it is neither exactly the same nor very different. For example, the text begins: "Now the shadow of the column—the column which supports the southwest corner of the roof—divides the corresponding corner of the veranda into two equal parts." This theme reappears rhythmically with slight variations, usually at the beginning of sections, clear through to the end of the text: a theme with variations that means nothing at all on first reading and that (perhaps something like music) persistently refuses to *mean* anything, but that persists nevertheless, accumulating a resonance over many readings.

Detail in *Jealousy* functions paratactically and as a building block for reader construction, not syntactically as a carrier of meaning; it precisely lacks any connotative or signifying function. With the shadow of the column, the black hair being brushed, the ice cubes containing bundles of needles, the blue letter paper, the sedan, the centipede, the sound of crickets, with all such details in *Jealousy* their impression is too definite to be realistic (speaking of Kafka, Robbe-Grillet he says that "nothing is more fantastic, ultimately, than precision" [*For a New Novel*, p. 165]). There is a kind of *hyperfocus* that leaves the intervening space and time untouched: space and time that, in realistic narrative, would be the crucial connecting medium making possible mediation between what that very time and space have separated or dispersed. When details or moments float in this way free from their customary responsibilities to be ciphers for some meaning (for a value that transcends or goes beyond the detail) and to be carriers for that rationalization of consciousness achieved in historical time (from being merely the means to a future end), then such details and moments assume a clarity and an importance entirely different from the value they have in historical narratives, where they characteristically lose their distinctness in a series. Here the detail or moment exists as a locus of play and has little or no vestige of the teleological urge of history. Postmodern readers, having relinquished the categories that they formerly used to sort particulars, now find particulars that retain their roughness, their color, their figural value, which is to say, their systemic function, their value relative to an entire figure, their function as signs.

Temporality in *Jealousy* exists as the play of reader consciousness across the patterns of the text: an accurate definition that is nevertheless far too abstract to do justice to the edge, precision, and specific savor of the details and rhythms of this postmodern narrative. A detail in this novel has value for a reader primarily in anticipation of variations in its arrangement. Variation is what we watch for as a familiar piece of scenery flashes by: in the modulated descriptions of the parked car, the veranda, the bringing of ice bucket and lamp, the centipede being crushed. These changes in what can, for the duration of the text, be identified as the "same" description (though not necessarily the "same" object or event) force readers to participate in the invention of the text in this sense: that they *attend primarily to shifts of proportion and arrangement*.

For example, the distinctive instance of repetition in *Jealousy* is that of the centipede being squashed on the wall. This description appears at least ten times, which is to say, it literally "happens" ten times. *These shifts are rhythmic without content*; they create anticipation, tension almost to vertigo; but they do not create meaning in any conventional sense having to do with the actions of individuals and the causes of events. There are accelerated repetitions, building gradually in length and variation from the first description until we reach the final one, a long, exaggerated or even, by comparison with the initial statement, distorted episode lasting several pages in which the centipede, initially a small insignificant detail, has assumed the size of a dinner plate and has a considerable impact.

This thematic development, besides acting as one basis for paratactic comparison and construction, also furthers the overall effort to scramble any chronological sense of time; for example, A . . . discovers on p. 64 "a centipede!" that was already squashed on p. 62; or, another example, the text situates the squashing of the centipede in one instance before (p. 78), but in another instance after (p. 81) the car trip to town. In each instance different details attract our attention, and as readers we find ourselves forgetting about "meanings" and "messages" and instead becoming absorbed in noticing minute variations and making complex discriminations of a now familiar arrangement.[63] The absence of any mechanism for rationalizing time into a neutral, homogeneous medium erases the possibility of representing discrete events or individual characters.

Such a sequence continually forces a reader to violate that long-standing Western article of faith, the principle of noncontradiction:

> The table is set for one person. A . . .'s place will have to be added.
>
> On the bare wall, the traces of the squashed centipede are still perfectly visible. Nothing has been done to clean off the stain, for fear of spoiling the handsome, dull finish, probably not washable. The table is set for three, according to the usual arrangement. (p. 78)

Well? Is the table set for one, or for three? Are these descriptions of two different occasions? Is some mad individual narrating this story? Such

---

[63] The longest description of the centipede-crushing episode appears toward the end (pp. 112–13), but the "event" happens many times (pp. 47, 59, 62, 64 [backward in time], 68, 78 [it precedes the trip], 81 [it follows the trip], 89 [with different details], 97).

questions are not answerable in this novel; they are questions that insist on the world of "same and different," "after and before," "normal" and "individual," and in *Jealousy* there is no sequence except the reader's sequence, no identities or events except those involved in reading the writing. There is nothing *but* this kind of sequence, this kind of description. Here are some other examples: first A . . . and Franck have "finished the book" about Africa (p. 74), and a few pages later they still "are reading" it (p. 79); one time Franck's car "is always having engine trouble" (p. 76); later it "never gives its owner any trouble" (p. 90), and still later it might "have had engine trouble again" (p. 108); finally, A . . . is both in bed and in town, a feat of multiple locations maintained merely by a shift of paragraph:

> The bedroom windows are closed. At this hour A . . . is not up yet.
>
> She left very early this morning, in order to have enough time to do her shopping. (p. 119)

The principle of noncontradiction, so deep in Western consciousness, initially may seem to require us to transcend these contradictions by reaching for a higher level of generalization: this is the classic historical way. But these details have no meaning either in themselves or in any referential frame; they have value for readers as *markers* with which to anticipate variation in their arrangement: that is what we watch for, and that is what is important in *Jealousy*. This new kind of textual event involves new practices—especially holding simultaneously in awareness what is putatively "contradictory" but nevertheless *there* as an event of consciousness. A reader can either close the book and give up or forget consistency along with its exclusions and begin to situate his or her awareness where the novel directs it.

In the sequence of *Jealousy*, in other words, contradictions are irreducible and render completely inaccessible the time of historical mediation. The discontinuities function as *warps* in time, rather like an M. C. Escher print with its peculiar warps between contradictory but neighboring optical arrangements. What creates the "warp" is "some kind of distraction," as one of my students astutely observed, thereby providing a decent basis for a new definition of art as Formalized Distraction or Deliberate Digression. Whatever its name, the postmodern narrative sequence is a continuous process of changing the logic context. This project is already familiar in the images of surrealism—Magritte's locomotive coming out of a fireplace—which simultaneously impose two contradictory "realities" so as to emphasize the arbitrariness, the *semiotic surplus* of each. In daily life this is not an unfamiliar experience, as Cortázar is fond of pointing out; the "warp" is

any moment when you perceive something weird—a spider in your shoe—
or when your philosophical discussion ends because you run out of beer.[64]

These focal warps in *Jealousy* between one short descriptive passage and
another resemble the breaks between frames in cinema; and the rhythmic
pausing of reader attention is a form of editorial rumination, a counterpart
of cutting in film. These are moments of immense power for readers willing to assume such power. They are moments when the narrative makes us
conscious of the proliferating possibilities of direction and order; compare
this with the reassuring coherence of a "Victorian" (this includes our contemporary detective) novel. The *disjunctiveness* between the plot "line" and
what is really going on makes it hard to ignore one's own constructive
imagination at work. Such sequences provide an opportunity to practice
consciously what Nabokov calls *multilevel thinking*: a habitual reflex of
thought for most of us, but not one heretofore widely valorized in the
rationalized medium of historical time. To take a cinematic example, the
disjunctiveness in *Last Year at Marienbad* requires viewers to attend simultaneously to two distinct tracks, sound and image. While the film's narrator
describes a shoe heel broken in a garden, the viewer is actually watching a
screen image of a table game with sticks. By the time the viewer actually
sees the shoe heel broken, it has already been described so the first sight is
already a recognition; and while the image of the broken shoe heel occupies the screen, the voice-over narrative is describing a later conversation.
This is *figura*—the art of figural rather than representational order—raised
to a very high level of complexity.

The kind of experimental activity this novel forces on readers is described directly in several passages where Robbe-Grillet conjures up visual
analogies for the kind of rhythmic attention readers of his novel must practice. The first describes the distorting influence of flaws in a windowpane,
an obvious emblem of the way in which the "I" in *Jealousy* renders neutral
perception impossible:

> The thick glass of the window nicks the body of the truck with a deep, rounded
> scallop behind the front wheel. Somewhat farther down, isolated from the prin-
> cipal mass by a strip of gravel, a half-circle of painted metal is reflected more than
> a foot and a half from its real location. This aberrant piece can also be moved
> about as the observer pleases, changing its shape as well as its dimensions. (p.
> 81)

A variation of this description concerns the view through the same distorting medium of a large black spot of oil on the ground:

[64] *Hopscotch*, chap. 99, for example; and paragraph three of "Blow-up" on those special
occasions: "when something weird happens, when you find a spider in your shoe or if you
take a breath and feel like a broken window, then you have to tell what's happening, tell it to
the guys at the office or to the doctor. Oh, doctor, every time I take a breath" (pp. 115–16).

It is easy to make this spot disappear, thanks to the flaws in the rough glass of the window; the blackened surface has merely to be brought into proximity with one of the flaws of the windowpane, by *successive experiments*. (p. 95; my italics)

Successive experiments by an observer—an excellent description, like Cortázar's "exploratory repetitions," of a postmodern reader's experience in novels by Robbe-Grillet, Cortázar, Nabokov, and their peers—and as such novels demonstrate, a mode capable of surprising amplification. Like Magritte and other surrealists, Robbe-Grillet uses the window with transparent glass to thematize the dissolving of representation. The picture as window on the world, the ideal of Alberti's *Della Pittura*, has remained for five centuries an emblem of faith in neutrality, a faith also sustained by historical narratives which, at least in England, have largely appeared since the Enlightenment as novels and not as more overtly political histories of the kind represented by John Foxe's *Book of Martyrs* or Edward Gibbon's history of empire.[65] Magritte, for example, in *Les Promenades de l'Euclide* (1955) shows a canvas standing on an easel beside a window with the "same" scene on both: a long road disappearing to infinity and a series of conic rooftops and other geometrical shapes. The canvas representation is the "same" as the scene beyond the window, and yet, as Magritte's subtle hint goes, *not* at all the same because to see is to invent, to construct, even to re-cognize a powerfully collective set of constructions. For a reader, or spectator, to see is "to participate in a creation, to invent in his turn the work—and the world—and thus to learn to invent his own life" (*For a New Novel*, p. 156).

Like Nabokov and Cortázar, Robbe-Grillet emphasizes the nonrational and life-sustaining quality of these "successive experiments." Conspicuously described in similar terms, the pattern of native songs, the pattern of insect flight, the pattern of writing left in traces on a blotter all are implicitly linked as comparable activities: circular, iterative patterning that is largely instinctive, experimental. Here is the description of "the song of the driver":

It is doubtless the same poem continuing. If the themes sometimes blur, they only recur somewhat later, all the more clearly, virtually identical. Yet these repetitions, these tiny variations, halts, regressions, can give rise to modifications—though barely perceptible—eventually moving quite far from the point of departure. (p. 84)

[65] Leone Battista Alberti, *Della Pittura* (1435–36), translated as *On Painting* by John R. Spencer (New Haven: Yale University Press, 1956). Foxe's history of martyrs (*The Acts and Monuments of the Church*, 1563) was propaganda for the English Protestant church; Gibbon's better-known history considers sweeping causalities in the thousand-year fall of the Roman Empire (*Decline and Fall of the Roman Empire*, 1776–87).

This description of a pattern-making activity resembles the one on another page describing insect orbits around a night lamp:

> Other creatures similar to this one have already fallen on the table; they wander there, tracing uncertain paths with many detours and problematical goals. . . . One of them returns to the swarm of flying bodies.
>
> . . . The whorls which it described are also probably among the more capricious; they include loops, garlands, sudden ascents and brutal falls, changes of direction, abrupt retracings. (p. 107)

Another variation of such patterning is evident in the traces of writing (many activities in the novel are likened to writing):

> Inside the writing-case, the green blotter is covered with fragments of handwriting in black ink: tiny lines, arcs, crosses, loops, etc. . . . ; no complete letter can be made out, even in a mirror. (p. 114)

Like the song of the driver, *Jealousy* itself consists of "virtually identical" repetitions which, "though barely perceptible," nevertheless have enough variation to carry the reader "quite far from the point of departure." Important change, it appears, occurs minutely and repetitively, and has little to do with the classical idea of "event" and "cause." This patterning, as the passages linking insect activity with writing suggest, has little to do with "meaning" in any conventional sense. The traces of script on the blotter signify no particular message: only the activity or event of writing itself. "There is no message," as Cortázar puts it, "only messengers, and that is the message, just as love is the one who loves" (*Hopscotch*, chap. 79). The allusions between insect activity and writing only reinforce that point, and call attention to the ways in which *Jealousy* itself aspires to activity instead of meaning, "tracing uncertain paths with many detours and problematical goals . . . changes of direction, abrupt retracings." Finally, the mark on the wall of the squashed centipede, which looks somewhat like a partly effaced question mark, echoes these emblems of delicate tracings and retracings, rhythmically patterned and partly effaced.

This novel describes and enacts many variations of these thematic repetitions that together make for a complex and delicate reading experience. It is above all the variation, often minute variation in those repetitions that gives excitement, definition, interest to the description and to the experience of reading. Robbe-Grillet suggests the nature of mere repetition with another insect metaphor, the sound of crickets. Nightfall in *Jealousy* is accompanied by the sound of thousands of crickets whose iterative but unvarying song is merely *noise*, an instance of repetition with no (or indiscernible) variation: "it is a continuous, ear-splitting sound *without variations* in which *nothing can be distinguished*" (p. 42; my italics). "Nothing can be distinguished" where there is merely repetition with no variation, and what interests Robbe-Grillet in *Jealousy* is precisely the primary construction of intelligibility. The successive experiments of *Jealousy* are adjustments motivated by an "obscure enterprise of form" that literally constitutes changeable and changing "reality." Time is nothing more, and nothing less, than a dimension of this construction.[66]

This resolute lack of meaning—that is, this unavailability of those questions about what and why, motive and event, cause and consequence, identity and change that rationalize time and consciousness in historical narrative—corresponds to the lack of a stable perspective from which to view events. *Jealousy* maintains no narrator acting as a temporal version of the implied spectator in single-point perspective. The prevailing consciousness in *Jealousy* is eerily close to our own and not attributable to some Other, either to a character or to the featureless "Nobody" narrator of historical narrative. Freed from the controlling teleologies of historical hindsight, the narrative can move without going anywhere.

The destabilizing effect of the present tense becomes especially clear when a past and future are restored to it by turning a description from its present into the past tense. Every moment then automatically has an implied future and consequently a potential teleology. Even the first paragraph develops a portentous air when reformatted as a narrated past: "The shadow of the column—the column which supported the southwest corner of the roof—divided the corresponding corner of the veranda into two equal parts." Even when nothing but tense changes, the emphasis shifts to the kind of perspective that implies a gap between then and now and, consequently, questions and information to fill the gap. Why is this corner important? Why is there such emphasis on geometrical precision? What happened at this site? Such questions point in the direction of individual perception, motivation, causality, meaning: questions that have been asked—and, worse, answered—by interpreters of this book, even in a few cases those who should know better.

The crux of such interpretations is that the narrator of *Jealousy* is a jealous husband obsessed with details about his wife and their neighbor and that this accounts for the disjointed nature of the text. We recall from a passage quoted earlier that Robbe-Grillet collapses distinction between the invisible narrator, the writer, and the reader (*For a New Novel*, p. 54). Such interpretation even has appeared in print, but I'll take as an example a more perishable instance from a classroom quiz where the writer is explaining the contradictoriness of the text as follows: "Because of his psychotic vi-

---

[66] For related discussions of chaos theory and noise theory see N. Katherine Hayles, *Chaos Bound*; James P. Cruchfield, J. Doyne Farmer, Norman H. Packard, and Roger S. Shaw, "Chaos," in *Scientific American* 255 (December 1986), pp. 46–57; and William Paulson, *The Noise of Culture: Literary Texts in a World of Information* (Ithaca: Cornell University Press, 1988).

sions, the narrator goes back to the episodes, metamorphoses them, multiplies them; that is why we do not have a sequence, a linear structure." This student, in fact a very good one, takes the dodge of attributing the entire text to a psychotic mind. However, if you take out the single word "psychotic," everything the student says is true of the text; you have simply deleted the negative evaluation. Why is "psychotic" necessary? Because it converts the novel back into a (meaningful) linear sequence; it restores the novel's "neutrality" by reestablishing the possibilities of historical cause and invariant identity. If we need to resolve contradiction, we assign the consciousness in the novel to "him" and make that gendered and individualized consciousness "crazy"; or, as Cortázar puts it, we prop him up with a crumb of time: a move not confined to literature. In short, everything resolves again into the narrative of the founding subject. We can call this kind of interpretation the Psychiatric Dodge, and it is applied to other postmodern novels besides *Jealousy*, for example, *Lolita* and *Blood Oranges*; it is a kind of reading that rationalizes and naturalizes the narrative sequences and thus takes the reader off the hook so far as inventing his or her own life is concerned.

Such efforts completely destroy what the book has so carefully established. As Rudolf Kuenzli says of related texts, "If we want to understand these texts, we have to overlook their style, ignore their contradictions, their incomprehensible 'concepts,' and reduce them to a definite meaning. Understanding these texts is always misunderstanding them."[67] The crushed centipede leaves a question mark on the wall, an interrogation remaining to the end both important and mysterious. The persistent mystery of that mark seems to me essential to the power of the novel, and to "explain" it as the "symptom" of a jealous husband is to trivialize the text. Like other postmodern narratives, this one is a parody, a very witty one, and the "plot-and-character" *Jealousy* constructed by anxious interpreters has nothing whatever to do with this language event embedded with traces of *undecidable* human emotion and undecidable influences. *Jealousy* is a language event that playfully deconstructs such readings at every step. In spite of the apparently atavistic need for such explanations, it is material that they ignore much of the available textual evidence and make the novel pretty boring reading.

There is indeed a third consciousness in the text of *Jealousy*, one obsessively close to what he or she observes and eerily close to the reader's own: why not (and as the student writer puts it) simply "the other who narrates and who also stands in the circle"? Such consciousness, an observer-turned-inventor, a questionable subject-in-process who finds a "reality" that "can be moved about as the observer pleases," depending upon what

[67] Rudolf Kuenzli, "Derridada," in *L'Esprit Créateur* 20, no. 1 (Summer 1980), p. 21.

initial position that observer takes, is no longer the Cartesian subject, no longer the "I" of the *cogito* that has sustained the pursuit of knowledge and power in the West for centuries. The original title of the novel, *La Jalousie*, which can be translated in English both as "jealousy" and as "venetian blind," carries an important double meaning about emotion as a grid for observation that is entirely lost in the English translation of the title as *Jealousy*.

But the main problem for interpreting this novel is not a single word or phrase; it is a reader's disposition. If what a reader really wants is a rationalization of the world, then he or she should stay away from Robbe-Grillet. However, if a reader wants to practice paying attention to the mechanism of a discourse, and to exercise from the root his or her power to imagine and to change the tools of thought, then he or she must attend to the making of patterns, to what Robbe-Grillet calls this "obscure enterprise of form" (*For a New Novel*, p. 142). This enterprise, which begins by forcing readers away from ready-made meanings, is calculated by Robbe-Grillet to show a reader what freedom of observation might really feel like. In his essay "A Future for the Novel" Robbe-Grillet writes: "Objectivity in the ordinary sense of the word—total impersonality of observation—is all too obviously an illusion. . . . But *freedom* of observation should be possible, and yet it is not. At every moment, a continuous fringe of culture (psychology, ethics, metaphysics, etc.) is added to things, giving them a less alien aspect, one that is more comprehensive, more reassuring. Sometimes the camouflage is complete" (p. 18). This "continuous fringe of culture" that filters observation through the grids of "psychology, ethics, metaphysics, etc." is what the surrealists sought to circumvent. These ready-made categories and language, these conventions are what Cortázar's Johnny Carter sees in the mirror when he looks for his own image but sees instead a stranger composed and held in place by those categories and that language.[68]

It is a major postmodern insight that our entire set of assumptions, our terms for possessing "reality," are not so much managed by us as they are maintained through us in ways we rarely even see. To use Derridean metaphors, we do not speak so much as we are spoken by our languages of appropriation and grasp. Such talk sounds like mere paradoxicalness to

---

[68] "The Pursuer," p. 216: "Last night I happened to look in this little mirror, and I swear, it was so terribly difficult I almost threw myself out of bed. Imagine that you're looking at yourself; that alone is enough to freeze you up for half an hour. In reality, this guy's not me, the first second I felt very clearly that he wasn't me. I took it by surprise, obliquely, and I knew it wasn't me. I felt that, and when something like that's felt. . . . But. . . . You've hardly felt and already another one comes, the words come. . . . No, not the words but what's in the words, a kind of glue, that slime. And the slime comes and covers you and convinces you that that's you in the mirror."

those accustomed to thinking of language as a tool to be picked up and put down, neutrally, like a hammer or a pencil. But to those prepared to grasp the postmodern point—that every move of language and consciousness reinscribes a whole set of prepared interpretations—it appears that the exquisiteness of style in novels by Robbe-Grillet, Nabokov, and their peers is no small matter of authorial quirk but instead a large matter of emancipation and resistance. The discourse of Historical Truth and Objectivity, as a discourse that speaks us, simply does not speak nearly enough for a postmodern writer like Robbe-Grillet. It is a question of liberation. The discourse of truth, history, and objectivity brings with it a whole set of conventions—clock time, for example—that fix in place one particular definition of consciousness. The objection to those conventions is not that they exist but that they function as absolutes and thus obliterate the spontaneity, the freedom of perception, the surprise and play of life; they diminish the quality, the beauty, the savor given to life by an awareness of actual, unmediatable limit. For readers seeking plot and character (the old his-to-ho-rical rag), *Jealousy* is a nonevent. Most students who read this novel, in my experience, can and do suspend their interest in plot and character, which is to say, their interest in the rationalization of consciousness entailed by historical thinking; they seem to recognize in Robbe-Grillet what he claims to have put there: a realistic and intimate portrait of the actual activities of their consciousness and sensibility, and an offer of imaginative and conceptual freedom.

Reprise

The reaction against a novel like *Jealousy* must be attributable in part to the fear it generates of losing control of the world: a fear that has special psychiatric definition, no doubt, but that also seems quite practical. After all, no one wants to be like the character in Borges's story "Funes the Memorius," whose perception was so accurate that he could not think. "To think is to forget a difference, to generalize, to abstract. In the overly replete world of Funes there were nothing but details, almost contiguous details" (*Ficciones*, p. 155). Reading *Jealousy* is precisely an immersion in contiguous detail about which it is impossible to "think." This is not a small matter, but, and this is not a small matter either, there is much more to life and to consciousness than "thinking" as we have come to know it in Cartesian and empiricist terms. In a postmodern context such thinking looks like a disrupted practice severed from a vast range of powers including the intuitive, constructive, creative ones. Such "thinking," the kind that posits a mythical "neutrality" and takes no account of discourse or of the languages of cultural practice, is just what Joseph Conrad had in mind in *Heart of*

Darkness (1899) when he invented Kurtz, the man whom Marlow, that coinventive reader, says has "kicked the world to pieces."

As ideas, these are not news, but as ideas they are only half-baked. The difficult completion of the project Robbe-Grillet announces lies in practices that conform to these ideas, and that is much, much more difficult. Our "culture"—especially print culture—has elaborated a vocabulary, a language, and a set of intellectual, moral, emotional tools that block the power to make and do and hence block "the cause of freedom." The cultural formation in question—the culture of print and humanism—has a vast and hyperelaborated, not to mention a "sacralized" (Foucault's word) quality; nevertheless it has received a series of shocks significant enough to redirect us from what might be called a "disciplinary sleep" to a more wakeful attitude. These shocks to the system of belief in history, in a generic "human" identity, in the transcendence of "mind" over "facts" and "information"—these shocks include a range of achievements from Einstein's General Theory of Relativity (theoretical physics) to analytic cubism (painting) to world war (politics) to those semiotic theories of language and culture elaborated by (to name only a few) Saussure, Lévi-Strauss, Foucault, Kristeva, and Cixous (largely academic), and, last but not least, film media (everywhere). What postmodern narrative achieves is a feat of written language—as distinct from the languages of political action or visual experience—that reorganizes conceptual apparatus in keeping with these deep cultural reformations. It is "new" because the world is, and that is why students who don't "understand" Robbe-Grillet still find reading him pleasurable and even, once they stop clinging to old forms and worn-out cassettes that preserve nothing but false confidence, important and influential.

The style of presentation in all postmodern narrative is, like *Jealousy*, paratactic rather than syntactic; it moves forward by moving sideways. Emphasizing what is parallel and synchronically patterned rather than what is linear and progressive, parataxis is a technique popular with medieval poets and another instance of affinities between the discourses that lie outside the boundaries of the modern, that is, the boundaries of what might be called the culture of the Renaissance. Paratactic narrative moves against the linearity of language and—this is its chief power—in several directions at once. Unlike the syntactic style, which depends for its meaning on limiting the available value of a word in any arrangement, paratactic style thrives by multiplying the valences of every word and by making every arrangement a palimpsest rather than a statement, rather as poetry does when it draws together a rhythmic unit by means of repeated sound or rhythm.

The distinction I have made between historical and rhythmic time, between syntactic and paratactic sequences, between plot and pattern, between representational and figural values, draws deeply on feminist theory and echoes Julia Kristeva's distinction between the symbolic and the semiotic dispositions of language.[69] Postmodern narrative language involves parallel courses, urgent iterative pattern, arrangement and rearrangement of elements; this language remains distinct from the historical development of character or action that too often have been taken to be the chief validation for literature. The high points of postmodern awareness are those where readers must recognize the play of discourse, its poetry, its semiotic disposition: the very things that historical novels depreciate in favor of character development, plot, meaning. Postmodern narrative does not "produce" a result because any product or "message" is trivial in comparison with the activity of reading construction, an activity that postmodern narrative maintains as its focus and that postmodern writers can make very rich. Postmodern narrative, in short, calls our attention *not* to fictions of origins and ends but to the process of consciousness itself as it constructs and deconstructs such fictions and, most importantly, as it enables readers to perform those new acts of attention required by a writing that is going nowhere because it has already arrived.

[69] "From One Identity to An Other," in *Desire in Language*, pp. 124–47, esp. pp. 133–34. Part Three of the present book deals most directly with these affinities between feminism and postmodern narrative writing.

Part Two

Multilevel Thinking

Multilevel thinking: you look at a person and
you see him as clearly as if he were fashioned of
glass and you were the glass blower, while at
the same time without in the least impinging
upon that clarity you notice some trifle on the
side—such as the similarity of the telephone
receiver's shadow to a huge, slightly crushed
ant, and (all this simultaneously) the
convergence is joined by a third thought—the
memory of a sunny evening at a Russian small
railway station; i.e., images having no rational
connection with the conversation you are
carrying on while your mind runs around the
outside of your own words and along the inside
of those of your interlocutor.

    —Vladimir Nabokov, *The Gift*

THE DISJUNCTIVE SEQUENCE "line" of a postmodern narrative deflects readers' attention onto their own constructive imagination at work and thus into the kind of multilevel thinking Nabokov describes in the above epigraph. Paratactical postmodern sequences never hold digressive consciousness on a track as dialectical thinking does; instead, these sequences direct attention simultaneously in several different, perhaps even contradictory directions.[1] Multilevel thinking thus holds out the possibility of

---

[1] In physical science, instead of keeping to the classical idea of "integrable systems" and the single prediction trajectories belonging to them, one must speak instead of "*ensembles* of world lines" in a "non-equilibrium world" (Prigogine, *Being to Becoming*, pp. 20, 29, and 84).

An especially evocative instance of multilevel awareness is the description by Prigogine and Stengers of this comment by Neils Bohr made to Werner Heisenberg during a visit at Kronberg Castle: "Isn't it strange how this castle changes as soon as one imagines that Hamlet lived here? As scientists we believe that a castle consists only of stones, and admire the way the architect put them together. The stones, the green roof with its patina, the wood carvings in the church, constitute the whole castle. None of this should be changed by the fact that Hamlet lived here, and yet it is changed completely. Suddenly the walls and the ramparts speak a different language. . . . All we really know about Hamlet is that his name appears in a thirteenth-century chronicle. . . . But everyone knows the questions Shakespeare had him ask,

reimagining "the past" not only by pluralizing it but by releasing it from the dialectical and linear relationships to which it is constrained by historical narrative. In this, postmodern novels accommodate, perhaps even more fully than realistic novels, the actual workings of rarely linear consciousness. Robbe-Grillet's claim that the new novel is even more realistic than the old realism has considerable validity, so long as we don't understand him to mean that the new novel mirrors anything. The convention of realism does not pluralize the syntaxes of perception, only individual acts of perception; postmodern narrative pluralizes the very syntaxes of perception in order to bring back into a reader's present awareness all the "action" involved in following the perpetual play of its differential sequences. The play of difference that in *Middlemarch* eventually is recovered, closed, reduced to common denominators of time and consciousness, in *Jealousy* remains open, perpetual, always renewed by new readings, new readers, new acts of attention.

The collapse of depth, and the representational conventions that support it, is the prerequisite for multilevel thinking, which cannot thrive in a medium that is homogenized and neutralized. It is one or the other, as a comparison between kinds of cinema vividly shows. Compare, for example, a postmodern film like *Last Year at Marienbad* with more conventional narrative movies like those made by John Ford or George Lucas. *Marienbad* is composed of commonplace social rituals or games managed like musical themes in a context of extreme artifice: for example, the win/lose game, the courtship game, the same/different game (same-or-different person, event, day, clothes), and, above all, the past/present game. The actors are like mannequins whose interest to us lies in their visual arrangement; motion is kept to a minimum (they are often frozen in mid-gesture); there is no eye contact between them. The characters have no depth either—no fear to overcome, no virtue to defend. Much like the narrative present of *Jealousy*, the moving camera of *Marienbad* returns again and again, like a memory, to the static structures and details of these games, making of them new structures each time they are re-cognized. Each variant elaborates some details and drops others. For example, a bedroom scene accumulates more and then more detail with each repetition; the tracking through the baroque rooms picks up different things each time or picks them up in different order. Viewers must keep several things going at once—both the perception of each succeeding present sound-and-image pattern and memories of preceding repetitions and their relationship with the present

---

the human depths he was made to reveal, and so he too had to have a place on earth, here in Kronberg" (*Order out of Chaos*, pp. 292–93). Even though words like "fact," "human," and "everyone" create certain well-known theoretical wrinkles, still this statement makes tangible that elastic, multilevel awareness that precludes the rationalizations (and totalizations) of modernity and opens opportunity for postmodernism.

arrangement. The camera entails for viewers an inescapable exercise of multilevel attention. By emphasizing the disjunctiveness between things, concentrating instead on their arrangement in "themes" that are purely visual and that resist any discursive "meaning," the Resnais camera collapses depth.

Marienbad, in short, does *not* give us a representational window like Ford and Lucas do: *Star Wars* being, after all, just the same old western, only in the sky. They claim all space and all time as an arena for the mutually related actions of good and bad; they depend on the elements of plot and character that have been with us since Aristotle. They are the logical extension of that technique practiced by Leonardo in the *Last Supper* (c. 1495–98) fresco, a connection that only sounds remote; the convention that links them is fundamentally the same. The realistic medium extends a simple act to infinity. Leonardo's wall literally extends the sight lines and the space of the refectory room in Santa Maria delle Grazie where the monks ate their meals. At its painted high table Jesus is raising his finger to tell the assembled diners that one of them will betray him, and the realistic "window" that the wall creates links the two worlds of here and there, now and then, and it links the two groups of diners in one and the "same" world. This realistic effect has similar, if smaller, éclat in the wide-reaching connections between bad guys and good guys or between extraterrestrials and us so familiar from our conventional entertainment. The realistic cameras of Ford or Lucas maintain realistic "depth" by constantly emphasizing the connections between widely separated things, things that are identifiable in the first place because they exist in the conventions of time and space where separation is essential to the developing unity.

Marienbad, by contrast, is more like a painting by Wassily Kandinsky: a matter of arrangement, which is to say, a matter of proportion, balance, relationship. If you "close in" on or focus on its "meaning," you lose its value just as, in an Escher print, you lose the achievement when you try to make it "work" according to a single perspective. This postmodern camera works entirely differently from the panning, distance-gathering cameras of Ford or Lucas that delight in "original" compositions. Resnais's stylized camera frame maintains relatively constant compositions despite changing details: for example, the camera almost always confines people to half the frame and sometimes moves when the characters do in order to maintain that balance. This camera keeps the screen divided, sometimes into a tripartite arrangement not unlike medieval painting. It confines human figures to the left or right or bottom half only (or to the sides, leaving an open center (or vice versa, for example, at the end).[2] In this context, the

[2] Thanks to Michael Press for his thought-provoking observations about the details of stylization in Resnais's frame.

"background" comes forward; depth disappears. Only when depth disappears, and with it dialectics and history, can multilevel thinking come into play.

The great predecessor for these postmodern experiments is surrealism. At first primarily an influence in the visual arts and cinema, surrealism has also assisted in the transformation of narrative and the way it deconstructs historical temporality, making the act of reconstructing time the very subject of art. The classic film of surrealism is Luis Buñuel's *Un Chien Andalou* (in collaboration with Salvador Dali, 1928). In all the motives of this film we find exact precursors of postmodern narrative style as practiced by Robbe-Grillet, Cortázar, and Nabokov: the use of spectators and time notations to poke fun at the bourgeois fetish of clock time; the emphasis on theme (themes of ants, hands, accidents, messengers) as pure pattern not message; the unforgettable opening image of an eye sliced by a razor that simultaneously proclaims its artificiality (it immediately follows an image with the same pattern, the moon sliced by a cloud) and announces the film's intention to play around with the viewer's way of seeing.

Buñuel continued illustratively to practice this style in late masterpieces like *That Obscure Object of Desire* (1977), with its paratactic developments on money, servants, terrorism, food, burlap sacks (the unseen burden), and the refrain "she's gone, sir"; and with its witty treatment of the wealthy bourgeois, Mateo (played to innocent perfection by Fernando Rey), who literally sees nothing but what he desires to see. The innocence of this Mateo resembles the awful unreflexiveness of certain related narrative figures, like Hawkes's Cyril in *Blood Oranges*, or Borges's "Borges" in *The Aleph*, or Nabokov's Humbert Humbert in *Lolita*—he is oblivious to total changes in the appearance of his beloved (played by two different actresses), and he is oblivious as well to the political terrorists acting out all around him versions of his own obsession, of all kinds including that represented by his obsessive "love" relationship. It is just such unreflexiveness that postmodern narrative cures in readers by enforcing in their attention the paratactic temporal convention that derails the linear, univocal narrative logic characteristic of such antiheroes. In both these films Buñuel's style of organization is paratactic, and its goal is redefining the very tools of thought: both surrealist goals that, like much else in surrealism, have continued to survive and flourish. While surrealism technically was a between-the-wars phenomenon of the arts located in Europe and chiefly Paris, it, in effect, was like a powerful hand passing over the media of representation. Its interdisciplinary quality and broad social agendas were just two indications of its revolutionary potential and two reasons for its continuing importance.

Section I: Surrealism and the Crisis of the Object

In 1924 and again in 1930 André Breton published his two *Manifestoes of Surrealism*, which brilliantly summarize the surrealist agendas and cast light on that all-important crisis he announced, "the crisis of the object."[3] Although the surrealist "movement," like cubism and other "schools," was created by academic recollection in tranquillity and was not the property of a simple or single group, still there was a more or less immediate set of people who knew one another, knew of one another, or shared in common a large and revisionist view of Western culture and its formations, including (but not exclusive to) those of art. The group's members included writers (Jean Cocteau, Louis Aragon), playwrights (Eugene Ionesco and other so-called dramatists of the absurd), filmmakers (Luis Buñuel), photographers (Man Ray and a host of others), painters (René Magritte, Max Ernst, Marcel Duchamp, Yves Tanguy, Joan Miró, and Salvador Dali). In his manifestoes as in his personal influence Breton condensed into expression some aspirations of this varied group of writers, artists, and intellectuals.

While Breton was not the only surrealist, his *Manifestoes* are a unique quarry of phrases and agendas that echo down through the narratives of postmodernism. Again and again in postmodern narratives the themes of surrealism appear: to restore language's power to shock and to upset the smooth logical mechanism of the sentence; to restore the "voices" that will derail logic and to step "beyond" the doors to the "other side" of reason; to revive inspiration by short-circuiting the rational desire to make "sense"; to rediscover that language is an unmotivated, sublime "gift," not an informational pointer, and that as such language is the only site of meaningful change; to break the syntaxes of things by providing multiple contexts, as in dreams or anagrams or collage, so that the arbitrariness of habitual systems and syntaxes becomes evident (*Manifestoes*, pp. 152, 161–63, 169), and so does the heterogeneity of a world that confounds the intolerable "dreams of reason."[4]

---

[3] "The Crisis of the Object" (1936), in *Surrealism and Painting* (1965), trans. Simon Watson Taylor (New York: Harper & Row, 1972), pp. 275–81.

[4] While this is not the place to discuss links between surrealism and the Latin American "boom," it is important to note the affinities between the two, as distinct from the Anglo-American response to such views as the following from Octavio Paz and Antonio Machado concerning the terror of reason.

"Modern man likes to pretend that his thinking is wide-awake. But this wide-awake thinking has led us into the mazes of a nightmare in which the torture chambers are endlessly repeated in the mirrors of reason. When we emerge, perhaps, we will realize that we have been dreaming with our eyes open, and that the dreams of reason are intolerable. And then, perhaps, we will begin to dream once more with our eyes closed" (Paz, *The Labyrinth of*

Surrealism, like dada but perhaps more optimistically, based its agendas on an unalterable hostility to all rationalism, especially modern positivist forms of it in everything from personal attitudes to politics and science. Breton summarizes this opposition to what he calls "the realist attitude":

> The realist attitude, inspired by positivism, from Saint Thomas to Anatole France, clearly seems to me to be hostile to any intellectual or moral advancement. I loathe it, for it is made up of mediocrity, hate, and dull conceit. It is this attitude which today gives birth to these ridiculous books, these insulting plays. It constantly feeds on and derives strength from the newspapers and stultifies both science and art by assiduously flattering the lowest of tastes; clarity bordering on stupidity, a dog's life. (p. 6)

For surrealists the critique of realism constituted a positive search for new creative power at the basis of all activity, a search that undertakes to discredit first of all the very word "reality" because it belongs to the attitude Breton despises. "The realist attitude," which in effect is an entire discourse or system of "knowing," depreciates the imaginative, constructed quality of conventions and instead elevates them to a status beyond invention, construction, or reformation: a critique with obvious similarities to more recent French theoretical efforts.

Breton advocates doing everything possible to get around, get past, or otherwise subvert the system of logical mechanisms that passes for knowledge, and to subvert the very distinction between "virtual" and "real." "There is no reality in painting," he writes, and this is because painting, like everything else human, is invented, virtual, constructed, made up (*Surrealism and Painting*, p. 28). Man is *Homo fabricans*, not *Homo sapiens*; consequently we must learn to perceive not "reality" but the mechanisms by which we constitute a reality, especially the mechanisms of language. Much rides on this ability to perceive the mechanisms in which we would otherwise blindly participate, and this formulation of the challenge remains constant through postmodern writing. As Kafka's Gregor Samsa learns in "The Metamorphosis," as Borges's Dahlman learns in "The South," and as Western Europe might have learned by the mid-1930s, inattention to mechanisms can be fatal. Surrealist art produces the crisis of the object in order to denaturalize it so as to restore a viewer's awareness of the artificial,

---

Solitude: Life and Thought in Mexico [*El Laberinto de la Soledad*, 1959], trans. Lysander Kemp [New York: Grove Press, 1961], p. 212).

"The other does not exist: this is rational faith, the incurable belief of human reason. Identity = reality, as if, in the end, everything must necessarily and absolutely be *one and the same*. But the *other* refuses to disappear; it subsists, it persists; it is the hard bone on which reason breaks its teeth. Abel Martin, with a poetic faith as human as rational faith, believed in *the other*, in 'the essential Heterogeneity of being,' in what might be called the incurable *otherness* from which *oneness* must always suffer" (Antonio Machado, cited in Paz, *Labyrinth*, p. 5).

enculturated qualities of perception that the "realist attitude" sought to mask.

An object is put in crisis by radically pluralizing the context in which we must perceive it, specifically by removing it from the contexts where we conventionally perceive it and placing it in surprising ones. This is tantamount to the production of crisis in the convention of realism, where the "object" is recognizable as such mainly because of the formulating system that rationalizes sight.[5] Surrealism throws such rationalization into question and reveals the constructedness of "objects." The Comte de Lautréamont's famous juxtaposition of umbrella and sewing machine on a dissecting table is a classic surrealist image; Meret Oppenheim's fur-lined teacup is another. In the work of Magritte there are many classic examples, one of which, *Time Transfixed*, was discussed in Part One. Another example is his painting entitled *Personal Values* (1952), which shows a realistically detailed bedroom containing familiar articles: a bed, a comb, a glass, a closet with mirrored doors, a shaving brush, a rug, a bar of soap. The otherwise perfectly maintained conventions of realism, however, are deranged by the fact that the toilet articles are gigantic, drawn to a completely different scale from the rest of the room. Magritte combines two entirely incompatible "realistic" grids to unsettle conventional perception, an effect furthered by the pictorial fact that the room appears to float in the air, its transparent walls open to blue sky and clouds. In such paintings appearances are faithfully reconstructed but *relations are altered*. The painter simultaneously employs the single-point perspective of conventional realism and violates the conventions associated with those spatial norms, especially the convention of proportional unanimity; his objects are weightless, they cast no shadow, their size is determined by their importance in personal experience, not their position in a neutral space. Such a painting puts us at some threshold where secondary figuration, a figuration that Kristeva would call "heterogeneous to meaning," makes semantic bridges from ordinary meaning to figural value: in short, a threshold where we can confront the formulating principles of so-called normal or natural perception. It is this "normal" perception that is in fact alienated because it constrains objects to preformulated and narrowly conceived functions. The job of the surrealist is to liberate perception from a naturalness that is really the height of artificial constraint (*Surrealism and Painting*, pp. 269ff. and 401–3).

---

[5] On this interdependence of time and objects, Einstein offers a helpful angle. To the question of an interviewer in New York in 1921, can you explain relativity in a few sentences, he answered: " 'If you will not take the answer too seriously, and consider it only as a kind of joke, then I can explain it as follows,' he said. 'It was formerly believed that if all material things disappeared out of the universe, time and space would be left. According to the relativity theory, however, time and space disappear together with the things" (Clark, *Einstein*, chap. 14, p. 469).

This estrangement of objects from their "normal" order calls attention *to* that order *and* to its arbitrariness. The final consequence of this estrangement is the disappearance of what we once took to be "the object" into a function of the systems in which it appears. As it appears simultaneously in *multiple* systems, "the object" is in crisis because its solid identity can no longer be established. One cannot resort to the crude proof of kicking the stone to verify its presence because we are not talking about an exclusively material world but rather a world of cultural formations where all objects are given identity. The surreal fact is that alternatives exist, and alternatives of the most fundamental sort. The surrealist effect is thus a sort of ongoing contradiction, the purpose of which is not to seize or grasp some "reality" but to spur association; the surrealist image does not result from premeditation or encourage it but, on the contrary, it generates an *activity*, a process, where the worst thing (in Breton's word) is to lose your "impetus" (*Manifestoes*, p. 33). This nonlogical, psychic activity is for Breton the source of creativity and life affirmation: a source suppressed by the "reality" models from Augustine to American science and liberated by the pluralizing of syntaxes. "It is, as it were, from the fortuitous juxtaposition of the two terms that a particular light has sprung, *the light of the image*, to which we are infinitely sensitive" (*Manifestoes*, p. 37). There is something almost hallucinogenic in the activity sponsored by surrealism, something like an opening of the doors to consciousness, but in a way that emphasizes what is permanent and socially viable as well as temporal and personally delightful.

The Italian surrealist Giorgio de Chirico describes the estrangement and uncanniness of surrealism in terms that could stand as a specification of my opening epigraph, "the other world surrounds us always and is not at all at the end of some pilgrimage":

> We experience the most unforgettable movements when certain aspects of the world, whose existence we completely ignore, suddenly confront us with the revelation of mysteries lying all the time within our reach and which we cannot see because we are too short-sighted, and cannot feel because our senses are inadequately developed. Their dead voices speak to us from near-by, but they sound like voices from another planet.[6]

This surrealist estrangement, like phenomenological "reduction" or bracketing, suspends habitual relations with the world in order to amplify its other "voices": voices that we "discover" but that are also our own; voices that constitute "the world" both because our perception is intentional and

[6] Quoted in Herbert Read, *Concise History of Modern Painting*, p. 121. Note the combination of romantic perception (nostalgia of the infinite, arbitrary limitation of sensibility) and modernist estrangement (sudden confrontation of suppressed elements).

also because what we perceive is intentionality. One could say that surrealism, like phenomenology and postmodern narrative, shows the objectivity of subjectivity, except to say this collapses the dualism that gives importance to these terms in the first place. By showing the strange side of familiar things and by provoking sudden confrontations with suppressed elements, surrealists sought to produce a discursive crisis that would permit the mind to call up the profound possibilities of memory and imagination long suppressed by unexamined rationalist habits.

In postmodern narrative the effort at estrangement moves simultaneously in two directions: one magnifying the subjectivity of perception, and the other, without in the least devaluing that subjectivity, diminishing to extinction any sense of mimetic connection between that subjectivity and the world that remains intact beyond and apart from it. A major technique for accomplishing this estrangement is distortion of scale so that perception must operate through one end of a telescope or the other, either magnifying or diminishing the image but never viewing it in a system of single-point perspective, that is, from what is called a "normal" distance. The objective, in Nabokov's words, is to find "a kind of delicate meeting place between imagination and knowledge, a point, arrived at by diminishing large things and enlarging small ones, that is intrinsically artistic."[7] There are many ways to achieve this effect, from Robbe-Grillet's contradictory sequences and logic-baffling repetitions to Cortázar's hopscotch structure and Moebius short-story sequences to Nabokov's digressive sentences and anagrams. But whatever the paratactic pattern, the accumulated values of these details and patterns are not meaningful in terms of plot or character but in terms of the figure, almost like musical themes: themes that act in the course of a narrative like a rhyme does in poetry, calling attention to pattern by punctuating it and, at the same time, giving special prominence to details of unique variants.

The details that belong to such sequences have a kind of eerie quality precisely because of their resistance to meaning. Nabokov's writing is a perfect case in point; it digresses off the syntactical track by increasing obsessive attention to a single detail—a pencil, a mosquito, or a kind of bird. Focus on the detail—and "the detail is all" (*Ada*, p. 77)—brackets the textual event from any "normal" context, that is, from any context of assumptions in which we habitually perceive it, and sets apart one angle, one aspect, one detail, giving it multiple or potentially multiple resonance. This style preserves and amplifies the concreteness, the specific importance of a detail or a moment and works in the opposite direction from the historical methodologies whose causalities undermine that concreteness and specificity. Paratactic narrative structure gives incremental value through the

---

[7] *Speak Memory: An Autobiography Revisited* (New York: Capricorn Books, 1970), p. 167.

course of a text to such details as they are thematically repeated and varied. This style produces an hallucinatory precision of the kind Robbe-Grillet finds in Kakfa's style, where descriptions have a kind of resistant intensity that is so precise as to be fantastic ("nothing is more fantastic than precision") and that has nothing to do with the profound meanings attributed to Kafka by his admirers.[8] The same could be said of Robbe-Grillet's own descriptions, or those of Cortázar, Nabokov, Hawkes, Duras, García Márquez, and Borges. Nothing is more fantastic than their precision, nothing more intense and meaningless than their detail. Such details are intensely valuable in the moment for thematic construction but not particularly easy to remember because they submit to no generalizing power.

Examples of such haullucinatory detail are hard to cite briefly because so much depends on the sequences in which they appear, but two examples from the first sentences of Borges's "Death and the Compass" might be illustrative. In each, the details in question are conspicuously located and intensely, strikingly meaningless. The first paragraph begins with this sentence: "Of the many problems which exercised the daring perspicacity of Lönnrot none was so strange—so harshly strange, we may say—as the staggered series of bloody acts which culminated at the villa of Triste-le-Roy, amid the boundless odor of the eucalypti." And the second paragraph begins, "The first crime occurred at the Hôtel du Nord—that high prism that dominates the estuary whose waters are the colors of the desert." Details like "the boundless odor of the eucalypti" or "the estuary whose waters are the colors of the desert" have an exquisiteness that abruptly shifts attention from the conventional concerns of plot and character with which both sentences open. The detail is intense, irrelevant, unsystematic, and ungeneralizable; to be strange and surprising, in fact, is exactly their function, their value, in a story dominated by the failures of rationalizing consciousness. These failures are manifested in Lönnrot, the detective who is fatally trapped by his own propensity to seek reasons, causes, and symmetries. Lönnrot skips the details in favor of the search for deep structures and causalities; like Dahlman in "The South," he is "inattentive to the mechanism"; he prefers "daring perspicacity" and interesting symmetries to the operations of chance. He also finds these habits fatal.

[8] "The hallucinatory effect derives from their extraordinary clarity and not from mystery or mist. Nothing is more fantastic, ultimately, than precision. Perhaps Kafka's staircases lead *elsewhere*, but they are *there*, and we look at them, step by step, following the detail of the banisters and the risers. Perhaps his gray walls hide something, but it is on them that the memory lingers, on their cracked whitewash, their crevices. Even what the hero is searching for vanishes before the obstinacy of his search" (*For a New Novel*, pp. 164–65).

Foucault, in a book that pays homage to surrealism, says that the more accurate the detail, the more profound the deception (*This Is not a Pipe: With Illustrations and Letters by René Magritte* [1973], trans. James Harkness [Berkeley: University of California Press, 1982], p. 62).

The reader of this story, on the other hand, is prevented from immersion in Lönnrot's fatal exercise of reasoning power because this reasoning is mocked along the way by the digressive narrative sequence and its burgeoning, riveting irrelevancies. These sustain the parody, the laughter, and the life-affirming "noise" that surrounds Lönnrot's determined linear progress toward resolution, a resolution that, he is rather surprised to find, is his own death. While Lönnrot (and many another postmodern narrator) gets lost in his plot, the reader gets savingly distracted by the details, which defy the effort to reduce them to meanings. This digressiveness, while it differs locally from Robbe-Grillet's paratactic repetitions or Nabokov's thematic voices or Cortázar's twists of linear logic, nevertheless sustains a similar process for readers: it derails rationalizing impulses in favor of a textured and complex process of multilevel awareness.

Nowhere is the difference between modern (historical) and postmodern (rhythmic) narrative systems plainer than in their use of detail. In realistic narratives, details generally have transcendental value, that is, they represent something other than themselves (economic, social, psychic conditions; causes, probabilities, identities, actions); the differences between details are significant only if they produce the similitudes, the "sameness" or "identity" between one instance and another that constitutes what we take to be "meaning," in other words, they are quantitatively significant in a range of character and plot development where meaning depends on the cumulative products of time as they emerge from and override their details. In contrast, postmodern narrative offers readers no portable property in this sense but instead a cumulative experience of differentiation and discrimination that preserves the detail and becomes unexpectedly complex and rich without becoming information.

This crisis of objects and objectivity may seem an impoverishment from the point of view that values knowledge primarily as a means of control and projection; it is precisely these habits that surrealism seeks to disable. From another point of view, however, these crises produce a new humility in the face of the world and a new interest in the possibilities of construction. "The world," as Robbe-Grillet puts it, "is neither significant nor absurd. It *is*, quite simply." Consequently art's job is to make us perceive that unassimilable quality of the world: to experience "the shock of this stubborn reality we were pretending to have mastered. Around us, defying the noisy pack of our animistic or protective adjectives, things *are there*. Their surfaces are distinct and smooth, *intact*, neither suspiciously brilliant nor transparent. All our literature has not succeeded in eroding their smallest corner, in flattening their slightest curve" (*For a New Novel*, p. 19). The perception that Nabokov describes as "intrinsically artistic" becomes the model of all perception, not the marginal province it has been culturally for at least several centuries. Every construction from painting to polis—

what Cortázar in *Hopscotch* calls our "scripture, literature, picture, sculpture, agriculture, pisciculture, all the tures in this world" (chap. 73)—entails this "intrinsically artistic" operation, this obscure enterprise of form.

The estrangement entailed by postmodern narrative thus calls attention with every word to the constructedness of what often conventionally has been treated as "natural." Some, like the sensible rationalist, find this perception unwelcome, and postmodern novelists get a certain amount of hilarity out of anticipating the rationalist refusal. An already familiar example is good old Bruno, in Cortázar's story "The Pursuer," who, when Johnny Carter gets down on his knees in the Café de Flore, is terrified at the "horror" he perceives in this loss of ordinary convention. But estrangement works even on Bruno. Shocked out of his comfort, suddenly Bruno understands "the loving attitude some painters have for chairs, any one of the chairs in the Flore suddenly seemed to me a miraculous object, a flower, a perfume, the perfect instrument of order and uprightness for men in their city" (*Blow-Up*, p. 205). If Bruno could maintain this perception of the world's miraculousness, he might be closer to that authenticity Heidegger calls *Dasein* but, as it is, Bruno needs constantly to be surprised out of his cover-ups and flights from death. When one is surprised, says Heidegger as if in the same mood as Breton, one glimpses Being-in-itself, something that happens when conventions of reference or assignment (one's "referential totality") are disrupted.[9]

The point of estrangement from habit is not to promulgate any particular conclusions so much as it is to make evident discursive boundaries. Once again the link between postmodern narrative and contemporary theory comes into view. Contemporary theory is a form of guerrilla activity that seeks to subvert what is stable rather than to provide a new stability: and this not with the silly intention of disconcerting the establishment but in order to bracket habit and to raise into conscious exercise that construct-

---

[9] "Uncanniness is the basic kind of Being-in-the-world." *Being and Time*, p. 322 (II.2.57); pp. 104–7 (I.3.16).

Estrangement that does not recognize itself as such Heidegger calls "idle talk": "Idle talk, which closes things off in the way we have designated, is the kind of Being which belongs to Dasein's understanding when that understanding has been uprooted. . . . To be uprooted in this manner is a possibility-of-Being only for an entity whose disclosedness is constituted by discourse as characterized by understanding and states-of-mind—that is to say, for an entity whose disclosedness, in such an ontologically constitutive state, *is* its 'there', its 'in-the-world'. . . . When curiosity has become free, however, it concerns itself with seeing, not in order to understand what is seen (that is, to come into a Being towards it) but *just* in order to see . . . a kind of knowing, but just in order to have known. . . . Curiosity is everywhere and nowhere. . . . Curiosity, for which nothing is closed off, and idle talk, for which there is nothing that is not understood, provide themselves (that is, the Dasein which is in this manner [dem so seienden Dasein]) with the guarantee of a 'life' which, supposedly, is genuinely 'lively' " (*Being and Time*, pp. 214, 216–17; I.5.35–36).

ing activity that otherwise goes on *unconsciously*. In this search for the springs of discourse, especially the search for the point of discursive contradiction or breakdown, the point is not simply to destroy habitual practice; the point is to make a deliberate action of what has heretofore been automatic, a political agenda in contemporary theory (I'm thinking of Foucault, Derrida, and what has been called French feminism) that is too often missed by its interpreters. This is what Foucault and Gilles Deleuze mean when they say the purpose of theory is to sap power, and that "theory is by nature opposed to power"; they mean that theory does not put an end to construction by arriving at Truth but instead continues, much as postmodern novels do, by a constant action of construction and destruction that keeps perception radically pluralized and thinking multilevel.[10] Intellectuals have power to the extent that they give voice to what is taken for granted, say Foucault and Deleuze, because the explicit formulation of what has been unstated subverts automatic reinscription and reenforcement of discursive habits. Theory, because it relies self-consciously on hypothesis, always implies plural views, and so theory pluralizes the application of power.

The most subversive theory is the one that resists the habit of Western knowledge to totalize, to go for first and final cause. In Western epistemology, for example, the structure of induction and deduction (it does not matter which is first) implies that theory must somehow be adequate to practice, or that practice must conform to theory. The postmodern idea of theory as a guerrilla tactic—if you haven't got one, make one up—flies in the face of this structure and this centuries-old discursive habit. The practice of postmodern theory, clearly, like the practices encouraged by postmodern narrative, requires a fine sense of play and a total willingness to live without discursive sleep: not, certainly, an easy discipline.

The methods appropriate for provoking estrangement are those that exploit chance, experiment, surprise: in Breton's phrase, any form of "fortuitous juxtaposition" (*Surrealism and Painting*, pp. 36ff.). *Collage* was a favorite surrealist method because it took material objects out of conventional contexts and brought them together in an arrangement that was new but at the same time linked by means of this very amputation with plural contexts that retained a ghostly presence in the collage image. Such methods create for the spectator (again in Breton's words) a "problem of *objective chance*, or in other words that sort of chance that shows man, in a way that is still very mysterious, a necessity that escapes him, even though he experiences it as a vital necessity. This still almost unexplored region of

[10] Foucault, "Intellectuals and Power," in *Language, Counter-Memory, and Practice*, p. 208. By "radically" pluralized I mean pluralized as discourse and not pluralized within a single discourse that mediates pluralities (the latter is the usual usage of the term "pluralism").

objective chance at this juncture is, I believe, the region in which it is most worth our while to carry on our research" ("The Surrealist Situation of the Object" [1935], in *Manifestoes of Surrealism*, p. 268). It is a short step from this to Foucault's injunction that "we must accept the introduction of chance as a category in the production of events," and to the postmodern practice of writing that organizes what were once called elements so as to call attention to their other contexts.[11]

Such chance is far from mere randomness; an example of its necessity is a gestalt image, one which is both of two entirely separate images—a duck and/or a rabbit; a face and/or a vase—depending on the perspective or grid assumed by the viewer. Such a double image is the result of what Dali calls the "paranoiac process": paranoiac, presumably, because of the anxiety it produces in those who wish to remain comfortable in their habits. These chance encounters, like the encounter on an operating table of a sewing machine and an umbrella, take a "ready-made reality, whose naive purpose seems to have been fixed once and for all (an umbrella)" and puts it out of its element; it escapes its naive purpose; consequently, its "identity" becomes something problematic and mysterious.[12] Postmodern narratives maintain this surrealist emphasis on the concrete detail liberated by chance connections from "normal" (that is, unexamined) discursive syntaxes. In narrative this means that chance never develops into the kind of coincidence that supports the historical or even the providential effect in realistic narrative. The temporal superposition of details in rhythmic as opposed to linear patterns has the same effect in narrative as collage and other forms of superposition in painting: they flatten the medium—the time and space of art. Depth, that sine qua non of realistic and historical narrative, and with it "the object," disappear into arrangement, into figure.

Postmodern narrative inherits another positive emphasis of surrealism, its essential optimism about the human psyche and emphasis on *eros* in its large sense of life affirmation in the face of death. This positive emphasis cannot be mentioned often enough as long as the guerrilla activities of postmodernism are mistaken for anarchic self-indulgences. When Breton defines surrealism as "psychic automatism" (a "definition" offered at least partly tongue in cheek considering the surrealist position on conventional forms of definition), he opposes that energy to the controls of reason, mo-

[11] Foucault, *Archaeology of Knowledge*, p. 231; and see Gregory L. Ulmer on Derrida's *différence* (the *gram* of *Grammatologie*) as a kind of collage in "The Object of Post-Criticism," in Hal Foster, ed., *The Anti-Aesthetic*, pp. 84–88, 96–97. On cosmic theories that incorporate chance see Stephen W. Hawking, *A Brief History of Time: From the Big Bang to Black Holes* (New York: Bantam, 1988).

[12] Dali, quoted in "Surrealist Situation of the Object" (1935), *Manifestoes of Surrealism*, pp. 274–75. Dali describes the surrealist image as one that promotes *"the fortuitous meeting of two distant realities on an inappropriate plane."* It creates *"a systematic bewildering."*

rality, and order and he emphasizes the "play" of association as against the "interested" mechanisms for solving the problems of life. For Breton "automatic writing and the description of dreams represent" products of psychic activity "as far removed as possible from the desire to make sense, as free as possible of any ideas of responsibility which are always prone to act as brakes." The point of all this effort to circumvent reason is to liberate those powers admired by the metaphysicians on Tlön, the powers of awe, wonder, and for Breton above all the power of love. The techniques of surrealism are, Breton says in an important footnote, our means "of casting light upon the unrevealed and yet revealable portion of our being wherein all beauty, all love, all virtue that we scarcely recognize in ourselves, shine with great intensity. . . . [A]t the present time there are great expectations for certain techniques of pure deception whose application to art and life will result in fixing the attention, not any longer on what is real, or on the imaginary, but, how shall I express it, *on the other side of reality*." Breton seems always to trust in the creative quality of the unrepressed unconscious and in its positive energy as a source.[13]

It is important to note that Breton does not speak of the unconscious in terms of psychological "origins," an idea that participates in the desire to "make sense" of what is essentially nonrational (*Manifestoes*, pp. 162–63). Breton, while he was still a medical student, took an interest in Freud's work before shifting his field of study from medicine to writing. He valued especially Freud's endeavor to uncover psychic powers by suspending certain habits, but he was decidedly not a Freudian. In his emphasis on dreams, on the uncanny, or what is outside "normal" or "rational" states Breton is less mechanical than Freud and more intelligent about the creative impulses. Breton insisted on seeing *no separation between the real and the dream*, a position that implies that the very idea of psychology, a logic of the psyche, is worse than useless. Dream work and waking work belong in the same continuum of consciousness, a view epitomized by the poet who, just before retiring to sleep at night, put on his door a sign that announced, "The Poet Is Working" (*Manifestoes*, p. 14). Breton sought to rescue the realm of dreams from the "parenthesis" of the night to which positivism had relegated it.

[13] *Manifestoes of Surrealism*, p. 162. Breton's (partly tongue-in-cheek) definitions of surrealism appear in the "First Manifesto" (1924) as follows:

"SURREALISM, n. Psychic automatism in its pure state, by which one proposes to express—verbally, by means of the written word, or in any other manner—the actual functioning of thought. Dictated by thought in the absence of any control exercised by reason, exempt from any aesthetic or moral concern.

"ENCYCLOPEDIA. *Philosophy*. Surrealism is based on the belief in the superior reality of certain forms of previously neglected associations, in the omnipotence of dream, in the disinterested play of thought. It tends to ruin once and for all all other psychic mechanisms and to substitute itself for them in solving all the principal problems of life" (pp. 25–26).

The surrealist attack on convention was radical but not primarily negative; it was a search for a more positive basis on which to organize social
and personal life. Anna Balakian puts it this way:

> For if Dada was bent on destruction, surrealism was in search of the power of
> creation. In a world in which abstract idealism had become intolerable, and oth-
> erworldly transcendence unacceptable, the artists used the object, as the poet
> used the word, for a means to personal freedom and for the transfiguration of
> the universe.
>
> The apocryphal aspect of the universe in a Tanguy painting is more relevant
> to our time than the angels of Raphael, for it conveys in succinct eloquence mod-
> ern man's current obsession: to extricate himself from the established order of
> earthbound measurements and to discover a new relationship between his moral
> self and the infinite reality with which he considers himself in daily contact.[14]

A Tanguy painting, characteristically relieved of the laws of gravity and
location, is a good example of how the change in syntax necessitates
changes in the definition of "things." As the artist uses the object, so the
poet can use the word, and Breton could see and articulate the implications
for language of this new method, especially its insistent connection between language and the largest human aspirations. His revision of language, of discourse was intended as a means to revive life, love, and inspiration from the failing world of war and economic collapse. In fact, what
he calls "love" remains the one requirement for surrealist activity or for
anything else worth doing.

> I have always believed that to give up love, whether or not it be done under some
> ideological pretext, is one of the few unatonable crimes that a man possessed of
> some degree of intelligence can commit in the course of his life. A certain man,
> who sees himself as a revolutionary, would like to convince us that love is im-
> possible in a bourgeois society; some other pretends to devote himself to a cause
> [perhaps even his work] more jealous than love itself: the truth is that . . . who-
> soever fails . . . in this respect . . . how, I ask, can he speak *humanly*? [Love is]
> the site of ideal occultation of all thought. . . . Odious control does not work all
> that well. The person you love lives. (pp. 180n–81)

The emphasis on love is far from treacle; it is, rather, an emphasis on the
erotic in the largest sense: on what is life-affirming and creative, on what
confronts death in all its forms, including especially the death entailed by
living on automatic, hampered by an unperceived discourse, co-opted by
"this ridiculous illusion of happiness and *understanding* which, to its ever-
lasting glory, the nineteenth century denounced" (*Manifestoes*, pp. 152–
53).

[14] Anna Balakian, *Surrealism: The Road to the Absolute*. (New York: Dutton, 1970), p. 208.

This emphasis on *eros*—on love conceived in the largest sense as life affirmation and creativity—is crucial to the endeavor of postmodern narrative. In order to grasp its importance we must begin by bracketing our own conventional language, which inexorably betrays us into a trivial interpretation of terms like "eros" and "erotic" or "pleasure" and "satisfaction." Whatever contributes to the impression that such things as eros and pleasure are somehow unsavory contributes, Breton was bold to imply, to every form of violence against life, by which he meant a range of things that today might include heedless pollution of the ecosystem or "policies" that turn governments into purveyors of weapons and drugs or the complex varieties of domestic violence beginning with the contempt for women that is still widely shared among both sexes. The scandals of such large-scale madness, surrealists insisted, can only be addressed by changing the most fundamental practices, which is why the problem of social action is, as Breton called it, *"the problem of human expression in all its forms"* (*Manifestoes*, p. 151).

Breton's formidable accomplishment in the *Manifestoes* was to put into words exactly how it is that art addresses practical problems: how it is, for example, that a painter like Joan Miró addresses the real problems of social action more directly than any governmental agent. A familiar of surrealists in the 1930s and still a major influence, Miró exercises in the viewer new instruments of thought and perception: specifically he exercises the power of improvisational construction. His pictorial space is not neutral, rationalized, or homogenized but dense, rhythmic, charged; it does not encourage detachment. His space is warped by irrational, singing pressures; it is in the large sense erotic. He takes the most conventional images— letters of the alphabet or geometrical or representational forms—and gives them a new amplitude. Jacques Dupin nimbly describes Miró's space: "It is a space alive with the ambiguous brushing of fear and desire, a dizzying space that provokes wild eruption of lines which carry the nocturnal world within them." Emptiness is explored by dots, marks; lines "oscillate, intertwine, bunch into knots, break apart"; letters, words, numbers are as important in their placement as in their meaning "or lack of meaning." This power of improvisational construction substitutes itself for those once inspired by pictorial realism: the powers of detachment, generalization, mutually informative measurement, cumulative effect, iconic meaning, and, above all, collective agreement. Miró's defiance of this spatial rationalization makes a difference at the very root of perception. In the best surrealist manner it stirs up and surprises the sleepy habitué. This capability, one that I am calling "erotic," is the power that Breton calls "love."[15]

[15] Jacques Dupin, "The Birth of Signs," in *Joan Miró: A Retrospective* (New York: Solomon R. Guggenheim Museum, and New Haven: Yale University Press, 1987), pp. 33–40.

The emphasis on *language* in surrealism as the key to political and social change is an emphasis that retains its utmost value in postmodernism. In the "Second Manifesto" Breton explicitly designates language itself as the locus of action and of change, a move that anticipates the discourse analysis of subsequent decades. Changing one's language necessarily precedes any effective political or social action because every *practice* is a construction, an invention, a mode of imagining, a system of expression. Any practice can be corrected, but only by altering the mechanisms whereby, quite apart from any "individual" intention, any action is produced. Breton's statement of this commitment is worth quoting at length:

> The problem of social action, I would like to repeat and to stress this point, is only one of the form of a more general problem which Surrealism set out to deal with, and that is *the problem of human expression in all its forms*. Whoever speaks of expression speaks of language first and foremost. It should therefore come as no surprise to anyone to see Surrealism almost exclusively concerned with the question of language. . . . People pretend not to pay too much attention to the fact that the logical mechanism of the sentence alone reveals itself to be increasingly powerless to provoke the emotive shock in man which really makes his life meaningful. By comparison, the products of this spontaneous, or *more* spontaneous, direct or *more* direct, activity, such as those which Surrealism offer him in ever-increasing numbers in the form of books, paintings, and films, are products which he himself looked at dumbfounded at first, but which he now surrounds himself with, and begins, more or less timidly, to rely on to shake up his settled ways of thinking. . . . Let us not be afraid to make a law of this insalubrity. It must never be said that we did not do everything within our power to annihilate this ridiculous illusion of happiness and *understanding* which, to its everlasting glory, the nineteenth century denounced. (*Manifestoes*, pp. 151–53)

"This ridiculous illusion of happiness and *understanding*" is what surrealism attacks: the positivist illusion that the world can be appropriated and grasped. Language is the key to foiling this illusion because the illusion rests on the view that language is a representation of a "reality" external to it, whereas, in Cortázar's words, "language means residence in a reality"; "and that's why the writer has to set language on fire. . . . Not words as such any more, because that's less important, but rather the total structure of language, of discourse" (*Hopscotch*, chap. 99). Although Cortázar did not think surrealism went far enough, still the purpose of surrealism's relentless spontaneity is radical: it goes to the root, to language, to foil forever the forces repressing the unconscious from violent eruption into the social machine. From the point of view of the social machine, this is naturally a frightful prospect until it becomes evident that stasis invites dissolution. From the point of view of repressed life, it is a necessity.

In writing, the techniques of estrangement apply shocks to the logical mechanism of the sentence, that same mechanism Kristeva calls the "thetic" or "symbolic" disposition of language, by which she means the sentence's power of production, especially the production of meaning. Breton sought to shock the logical mechanism of the sentence with the same techniques employed by surrealist painting: by pluralizing its contexts with collage, juxtaposition, distortion. Breton's own style, especially in the "First Manifesto," has a vigor and a spontaneity of impression quite unlike the ordinary rationalizing and objectifying prose. His prose (that of Nabokov and Cixous could be described the same way) reads like the trace of consciousness at the moment awareness first takes shape; it has a manifest rhythm, a breathless, risk-taking speed and capacity to include anything and everything without resorting to invidious classification and without losing point or power.

The emphasis on language—both as literal linguistic exercise (the use of this word not that and this structure not that), and also language as discourse (a system of differential functions)—tends to collapse the (positivist) distinction between what is personal and what is social, and to detach what is personal from ossified notions of the individual. The result goes to the heart of the Cartesian *cogito* and its autonomous individual *subject*, but, far from depreciating the agency of persons, surrealism puts new emphasis on the necessary link between social and personal reformation. The surrealist seeks the revision of social practices at home in the quotidian—we can scarcely even call them individual—structures of experience that provide the matrix for all cultural formations. For example, if you want to avoid World War III, to save the rain forests, or to abolish apartheid, the way is not merely to oppose existing structures—an action that generally reinforces them. The way is to modify those general habits of mind and practice that make possibilities of world war, environmental disaster, and apartheid in the first place. "Nothing can be denounced," says Cortázar, "if the denouncing is done within the system that belongs to the thing denounced. Writing against capitalism with the mental baggage and the vocabulary that comes out of capitalism is a waste of time" (*Hopscotch*, chap. 99). Without such effort, the implication runs, no real change in the "realist attitude" is possible.

While the activities of surrealism theoretically extended to all forms of "language" and to all forms of "text" in the postmodern senses of those words, the surrealist movement per se is known chiefly for its pictorial achievements and not for narratives like Breton's *Soluble Fish*. Nevertheless, the surrealist ambition to shock the logical mechanism of the sentence survives in the work of postmodern novelists who have moved on to deconstruct what Foucault calls the "founding subject" of Western metaphysics. Along with the surrealist object, the postmodern subject loses its discreteness and its simple location and metamorphoses into a differential function of systems.

Section II: Humanism and the Crisis of the Subject

Lurking in the surrealist crisis of the object is a crisis of a different kind, a crisis of subjectivity, and an "object" of a different kind, the mind itself. Surrealism sought to estrange the human mind from its own conventional systems of grasping and fixing so-called reality in univocal postures and "meanings," a process that would reveal the arbitrariness, the fictionality of those meanings. This reformation of perception that produces the crisis of the object extends, as the surrealists knew full well, far beyond objects like apples or oranges to the most important "object" of the modern period, the individual mind. The thinking subject since Descartes has supported metaphysics with the familiar founding declaration, *cogito ergo sum*. This subject is the same individual "perspective" that appeared as a rationalization in the Renaissance and was separated out of worldly systems in order to found them. This subject, evident as the implied spectator of realistic, which is to say, single-point perspective, painting, manifestly vanishes in painting at the turn of this century. It is this implied subject, the subject of the Cartesian *cogito*, that postmodern narrative in its turn disperses into a fractured, multi-identical version of subjectivity consistent with the other discursive reformations of the postmodern aesthetic. In the postmodern matrix the modern rationalizations of sight and of consciousness disappear into other discursive formations. With the reformulation of modern "space," the self-identical thinking subject, like any other object, loses its discreteness and simple location and metamorphoses into a differential function of systems.

Postmodern writing, extending the work of surrealism, calls into question the very process that establishes and is established by the founding subject in the first place. The postmodern novel has a certain family resemblance to the drama that consisted of an invasion of the audience by actors. This theater of "happenings" attempted to break down, to violate the sacred boundary line between art and audience, between "in here" and "out there," a gesture akin to that made by novelists who refuse to allow their readers to assume a passive detachment from "reality" as they read. The subject as spectator, as autonomous identity, as free-floating windowless monad, as the "I" of "I think, therefore I am," disappears into a phenomenological definition of the reading "event" that dissolves the boundary between subject and object that was so important to modern epistemology. When the subject and object lose their discreteness and become indistinguishable functions of a multidimensional "event," the object known as "the subject" properly ceases to exist. This leaves aside the whole question of whether such an individual subject, even in historical discourse, ever really existed or whether it was always an *intersubjective* definition without constant individuality (this argument is made in "The Narrator as Nobody," Chap. 3 of *Realism and Consensus*). The linked denial of time and subjectivity is an old argument, at least since Hume, but postmodernism gives it new weight and extension.[16]

Robbe-Grillet's novel *Jealousy*, to take an example already used, is an almost pure instance of a new subjectivity in process. Its narrative perspective no longer maintains either historical, causal, linear time or a stable, separate, distanced position for the reader, who, waiting passively for a good tale, finds herself or himself yanked into the story and made its main subject. The rhythmic distractions of this novel, the repetitions without point, the constant encounter with contradiction all force the reader to consider himself or herself in the very act of inventing meaning, to consider the play of the mind with its own self. No longer "safe" from implication in this world of invention and unstable definition, the reader must participate in the making of never neutral and always contestable interpretations. Whereas a primarily symbolic modern narrative like *Middlemarch* or *Le Rouge et le Noir*—whose language is thetic, conclusive, and productive— both implies and confirms a subject, a primarily semiotic postmodern narrative operates reflexively in the opposite direction to destroy and undermine the stable, individual subject and its univocal meanings. In other words, whatever is heterogeneous to or other than meaning—for example, most of *Jealousy*—puts the subject in crisis. Postmodern narrative confronts a reader with the necessity of experiencing this undoing, with the task of undoing his or her own stable subject, with the opportunity of learning new kinds of confidence and power. This pluralization complicates the definition of "the subject" considerably but certainly under no circumstances does away with it; postmodern subjectivity becomes multilevel, not dispersed. While we search for appropriate terminology for the subjectivity thus reconstituted, we might use Kristeva's phrase "questionable-subject-in-process," so long as we remember that "process" is plural. Subjectivity exists in processes not apart from them and copes with multilevel processes simultaneously.

A pictorial comparison between realism and cubism helps to show the difference between the multilevel subjectivity implied by postmodern art and the single subject implied by representational conventions. The im-

---

[16] Borges revives this argument in his "New Refutation of Time," in *Personal Anthology*, esp. pp. 50, 52, 59: "And, if time is mental process, how can myriads of men, or even two distinct men, share it at all?" (p. 50). "I do not know yet, the ethics of the system I have here outlined. I do not know if they exist" (p. 52). Borges goes so far as to deny succession: "I deny, in a high number of instances, the existence of succession" (p. 50).

plied spectator of realistic painting, like the fixed Cartesian subject, orients the system of pictorial relationships from (that is its point) a single perspective. This subject not only can, it must occupy only one place at a time. The narrative analogue of this implied spectator is the realistic modern narrator, a form of pure human consciousness unencumbered by individual limitation and capable of moving from one location to another in such a way as to maintain the rationalization of time—its confinement to a linear and developmental relationship between a carefully delineated past, present, and future.

By contrast, a cubist painting presents multiple perspectives simultaneously, fracturing "space" and literally requiring any single spectator to be in several different places at once. Such ontological diversification may be somatically impossible, but in terms of consciousness it is quite usual to be aware of several things simultaneously. Postmodern writing in one sense is just writing that catches up to ordinary practice where consciousness never operates in a single ambit. By creating unresolvable contradictions between one moment of awareness and another, postmodern narrative maintains multiple perspectives that produce a crisis in the temporal system of rationalizing perspective because the multiplicity is irreducible. Immersion in such unavoidable contradiction makes it impossible for readers to locate either an object or a subject as they are classically defined. The reader finds substituted for those classical delineations a process, a rhythm, a primary experience that is over when it is over, leaving none of the residues of realistic narrative, none of the information about human experience that is the nineteenth-century narrative version of portable property. Time that is not neutralized, not historical but rhythmic, cannot support modern conceptions of personality and, while narrative maintains the presence of subjectivity, any implied spectator has a fractured existence of a sort not far from that of the medieval spectator described by Johan Huizinga.[17] Because postmodernism sees subject positions as given by discourse, and because discourse is never single at any moment but instead multiple and pluralized, any subject position is always contested between languages simultaneously to the point that postmodern subjectivity can be defined as a site of contest between subject positions.

To many this postmodern crisis of subjectivity appears profoundly threatening because it involves the explicit disappearance or end of a specific humanist definition of "man." Postmodernism, in short, is resisted in the name of humanism. As Foucault notes, this reaction has claimed to be

---

[17] Huizinga characterizes the spectator position of medieval painting as follows: "there is not point of view at which the spectator is supposed to stand," and so the viewer must be imagined as stationed in front of whatever surface is presented, which is to say simultaneously in several different places at once (*Realism and Consensus*, pp. 8–10; and Johan Huizinga, *The Waning of the Middle Ages*, trans. F. Hopman [London: Edward Arnold and Co., 1937], pp. 255–56).

motivated by a candid effort to preserve the freedom of "movement, spontaneity, and internal dynamism" implied by phrases like "continuous history," "teleology," and "endless causality"; however, and on the contrary, it is motivated by a fearful and unacknowledged effort to preserve against erosion the fundamental faith in the individual subject and its "human" consciousness or, in other words (again Foucault), the "powers of a constituent consciousness, since it was really they that were in question" (*Archaeology of Knowledge*, p. 203). But to give up individuality is not necessarily to give up subjectivity, as *Jealousy* shows. There is a third person present in *Jealousy*: we the readers, with our always obsessive attention. But this consciousness is neither precisely individual nor precisely collective in the old terms; it is the creature of the language, not vice versa; in English it is not even gendered. For those unwilling to accept this gambit, the only way to individualize and gender it is to assume without much evidence that "it" is "the author" or a masked character. Whatever the implications of this reformation of consciousness and redefinition of human subjectivity, it belongs with that reformation that makes time, like consciousness, a dimension of events rather than discrete events in themselves. These related changes are what prompt Cortázar to substitute for the old Cartesian "I think, therefore I am" a new dictum, "I swing, therefore I am" (*Hopscotch*, chap. 16).

Their new air of *fictionality in no way depreciates the value of those meanings that human subjectivity constructs*; on the contrary, their value may increase with their tenuousness, with their hint of mortality. What is more, the mutation of the Cartesian subject, in effect a pluralization of subjectivity, is a definition of conscious experience that seems entirely in keeping with the experience of those whose lives are increasingly pluralized and who, in making frequent transitions from one context to another, are intensely aware of the arbitrariness of even the most intimate "subject" definitions (for example, "I am" means one thing when "I am" at home, another at work, another when "I" speak Italian or French). This subjective state of affairs, in fact, is not altogether new and surprising. Nietzsche was not alone in noticing that "the subject" was a "little changeling," and so were other, similar identities like "the atom" and "the Kantian 'thing-in-itself' " (*Genealogy of Morals*, First Essay, sect. 13). What has changed in the discursive description of "reality" is that the subject-in-process and its characteristic multilevel thinking have become more important. This change, incidentally, goes far beyond any possiblity of "dialogic" relationship of the sort Bakhtin theorizes because his term "dialogic" (*dia-logos*) implies the kind of temporal common ground that historical models sustain. "Dialogics" is a fundamentally representational word.[18]

---

[18] Mikhail Bakhtin, *The Dialogic Imagination: Four Essays*, trans. Caryl Emerson and Michael Holquist (Austin: University of Texas Press, 1981).

When subject and object forego their oppositional self-definition (we note even in their disappearance how subject and object declare their symbiosis),[19] what do we have in place of this old alternating duo? What we have is something like a Moebius relationship where subjectivity, being all there is humanly speaking, is wholly objective. Or we might say that the only objectivity is total subjectivity. To say that all structures are constructs is to say that they are the inventions of human imagination, and hence fabrications or art, both terms that formerly signaled "marginal" or "trivial." Art and fabrication were exported from cultural (often to cosmic) discourse, often for the same reason that the subjective consciousness was exported from the "objective" picture: in order to act as the foundations for an entire rationalist order. By using fiction-making as the model of consciousness, the postmodern novelist undermines those foundations.

This new subjective reality that cannot be separated from its engagements is what Heidegger calls *Dasein*, being-in-the-world, a formulation that suggests the important postmodern recognition that the Cartesian conception of subjectivity was of a subject-*not*-in-the-world or a subject-*not*-in-process. Heidegger, and in his wake many other writers (the trace of Heidegger runs through postmodern writing), collapses the distinction between subject and object so that subjectivity becomes, paradoxically, the only true objectivity. "If the 'subject' gets conceived ontologically as an existing Dasein whose Being is grounded in temporality, then one must say that the world is 'subjective'. But in that case, this 'subjective' world, as one that is temporally transcendent, is 'more Objective' than any possible 'Object' " ("The Temporal Problem of the Transcendence of the World," in *Being and Time*, p. 418; II.4[c]). Why, as Robbe-Grillet asks, should this be grounds for pessimism? Is it so distressing to learn that one's view is *only* one's view, or that every project is an invention? "Obviously I am concerned, in any case, only with the world as *my point of view* orients it; I shall never know any other. The relative subjectivity of my sense of sight serves me precisely to define *my situation in the world*. I simply keep myself from helping to make this situation a servitude" (*For a New Novel*, p. 74). Far from threatening terminal narcissism, the postmodern situation of consciousness throws emphasis on the negotiation between one system, one

[19] The symbiosis of subject and object is one of the interesting games of classical systems. As realism perhaps inadvertently shows, the articulation of an object position is precisely an articulation of a subject position. For example, what is being contested between science and humanities is not so much descriptions of objects as kinds of subject positions that those descriptions establish.

For a clear explication of the symbiotic relation between subject and object in classical physics, for a thoughtful statement concerning the problem of holism in postmodern writing, and for discussion of the "field concept" as characteristic of postclassical physics (including Niels Bohr's remark, "We are suspended in language"), see Hayles, *The Cosmic Web*, pp. 52–53, 58, and the introductory chapter.

inertial frame, one "identity," and another. We no longer require an "objective" world to guarantee—like some sort of bank for intersubjective transactions—the relations between one consciousness and another, or to guarantee an identity between illusions. There is *only* subjectivity; there are *only* illusions. And every illusion, because it has no permanently objectifying frame, constitutes reality and hence is totally "objective" for its duration. The postmodern event comes in negotiating the transitions from one moment to another.

Heidegger's rigorous refusal to accept the Cartesian *cogito* makes possible a reconception of subjectivity that still echoes through theoretical writing, especially in discourse analysis, and through art from cubism (for example, Braque, who, with others, invited Heidegger to France) to Robbe-Grillet. Unlike the Cartesian self so congenial to empiricism, Heidegger's "self" is always situated; there is no such thing, he claims, as "a bare subject without a world" (*Being and Time*, p. 152; I.4.25). Being (*Dasein*) is always, literally, being *there*, that is, being somewhere in particular. There is no other kind of existence and no possibility, humanly speaking, of any escape from *Dasein* altogether into some transcendence from which any "objectivity" could be verified. Although there is a difference between authentic and inauthentic being, there is *no* being independent of human and social, which is to say, mortal and moral existence. His words—always allowing for the Heideggerian style—remain evocative: "*Authentic Being-one's-Self* does not rest upon an exceptional condition of the subject, a condition that has been detached from the 'they'; *it is rather an existentiell modification of the 'they'—of the 'they' as an essential existentiale.*" Consequently, there is always an ontological gap between the authentic self and the " 'I,' which maintains itself throughout its manifold Experiences" (p. 168). The new existential condition of any self is what Heidegger calls the "they": an entity that is at once real and potent and, at the same time, is "nobody" (not individual). "The 'nobody', is by no means nothing at all" (p. 166), but—and this is crucial—this "they" is *less than* "the world" so that there is always a margin of mystery surrounding every human explanation, even the most complete. What is "Other" belongs to the mystery of the world, especially the human world; our proper attitude toward it is wonder, not "understanding," and our proper behavior toward it is respect, not aggression. Postmodern narrative focuses attention on this ephemeral frame of consciousness. What we know beyond this ephemeral moment is not a world of forms, or divine clockmakers, or transcendental Presence. All we can possibly know is another frame of consciousness.[20]

---

[20] Heidegger's "self" thus hovers between an "I" and an "authentic Self," depending upon what posture it takes toward the rest of the universe: either treating it as something "ready-at-hand" (i.e., something with the status of tools) or treating it as something "present-at-hand" (i.e., what is here but Other) (*Being and Time*, I.4.27). Obviously there are cases where

Emphasizing subjectivity to this extent has nothing to do with certain forms of idealism in which one can deny that rocks, stones, and trees have existence independent of consciousness; and it is helpful to remember that the philosopher who famously did so, Bishop Berkeley, did so primarily in order to prove the existence of absolute consciousness. What is being denied, from Heidegger to postmodern narrative, is precisely the existence of absolute consciousness. Consciousness, like Einsteinian time, is a matter of measurement and has no way of knowing whether or not any absolute time or consciousness exists. There is no consciousness independent of situation, but at the same time the links between consciousness and situation lack essentialist value. Consciousness is tied to the world and is saturated with meaning, but there is no *essential* link between those meanings and the world. Our meanings are our own, the province of human imagination. Whatever the material world of nature may "be"—something only science can know and only in limited ways—*it* contains no meanings, our metaphors notwithstanding.[21] We necessarily approach the world in language, which means that we always approach it through a complex system of transactions that distorts as it measures. Subjective consciousness thus always partially constitutes the reality it observes, which means that the subjectivity can no longer be identifiable as separate from that reality. No longer removed from the reality that it then represents, reproduces, grasps, alters, or controls, the postmodern consciousness exists only *systemically*, dispersed in its creations.

But what about "the problem of social action," as Breton calls it? What about the social construction of the subject? What becomes of intersubjective agreements when the responsible, causally located, individual subject disappears, leaving only a trace? How can we recognize the social construction of the subject when we focus on specific sites of activity? These questions are such big ones in the postmodern context that any answers must be exploratory, but there are certain things that can be said about the New World of subjectivity for those unaccustomed to living there. What has come to an end in postmodernism is not subjectivity but a particular form of it. One does not cease being conscious by ceasing to be a Cartesian subject, nor do moral, which is to say social, problems disappear. Social life requires mediation; as Iris Young puts it, "temporal and spatial dis-

---

it is appropriate to treat things as tools, but this posture gets to be a bad habit of the sort Robbe-Grillet condemns. It is worth mentioning, as Breton sometimes does, that ideas quite similar to these, although with different emphases on the social "nobody" and its relation to the material world, already had been thought in the nineteenth century, and in this case particularly in Germany.

[21] See, for example, Robbe-Grillet, *For a New Novel*, p. 71. This effort to detach human awareness from essence is an achievement of the nineteenth century (Ludwig Andreas Feuerbach, for example), the implications of which are still being imagined.

tancing are basic to social processes," and, consequently, "a society of immediacy is impossible." Young hopes for a social life without "that specific process of mediation [she calls it alienation] in which the actions of some serve the ends of others without reciprocation and without being explicit, and this requires coercion and domination."[22] The postmodern condition may be an even more likely context than the modernist condition for realizing this aspiration, although most of the terms would change.

For some centuries in the West ideas of social life and individual agency have depended on a particular form of mediation that postmodernism erases: a form of mediation based on a separation or dissociation between the material and the transcendent. This dissociation includes uneasy relationships like those between "self" and "other" or "idea" and "object" or "word" and "thing." The linguistic model so often invoked in postmodern writing reconstitutes subjectivity as difference, or rather as a differential process. Young, for example, highlights the contrast between the conventional opposition of ideal and particular on the one hand and the "irreducible particularity of entities" on the other: "Difference means the irreducible particularity of entities, which makes it impossible to reduce them to commonness or bring them into unity without remainder. Such particularity derives from the contextuality of existence; the being of a thing and what is said about it is a function of its contextual relation to other things."[23] This irreducible contextuality that remains inaccessible to the transcendental dualisms of historical thinking and its language has potentially radical implications both for subjectivity and for language. In postmodern writing one is always aware that there is nothing more mediate than consciousness or language, but that, at the same time, there is nothing more material.

The agreements that constitute historical time and its version of subjectivity, the "consensus" of realism, have obvious social and political manifestations viewed in postmodern terms. Lyotard, for example, calls such consensus a "terrorist" apparatus because of its repression of strong new statements. "The stronger the 'move,' the more likely it is to be denied the minimum consensus, precisely because it changes the rules of the game upon which consensus had been based." This description applies particularly well to academia, where the increasingly attenuated, even adventitious game seems to require repetition, not adventure ("Adapt your aspirations

[22] Iris Marion Young, "The Ideal of Community and the Politics of Difference," in Linda Nicholson, ed., *Feminism and Postmodernism* (New York: Routledge, 1990), p. 315.

[23] She speaks, for example, of Theodor Adorno (*Negative Dialectics* [New York: Continuum Publishing Co., 1973], esp. Part II, pp. 134–21), who "contrasts the logic of identity with entities in their particularity, which for him also means their materiality. Idealism, which Adorno thinks exhibits the logic of identity, withdraws from such particularity and constructs unreal essences" (Young, in "Ideal of Community," p. 304).

to our ends—or else" [*The Post-modern Condition*, pp. 63–65]). Lyotard's postmodernism requires recognition of the heteromorphous, "a renunciation of terror," and a "quest for parology" (p. 66), as well as avoidance of Habermas (p. 65). Every rule must be established locally "in other words, agreed on by its present players and subject to eventual cancellation," and every contract is temporary.

Unfortunately, Lyotard, at least in *The Post-modern Condition* and even *The Differend*, falls short of imagining the media in which these arrangements take place. He speaks uncritically of these postmodern transactions as taking place in "space and time" (p. 61), those ultimate forms of modernist consensus; and even more problematically, Lyotard in this instance oddly begs the question of language.[24] Yet for postmodernism language is the ultimate local problem and the site of the practical solution. Lyotard's own language, for instance, keeps devolving into metaphors inimical to his subject: for example, militaristic metaphors of the kind he uses to make the questionable claim that Braque and Picasso "attack" Cézanne's objects (p. 79)—a peculiar description for the respect those two twentieth-century painters had for their great and enabling precursor—and to make his final call to arms: "Let us wage war on totality" and "save the honor of the name" (p. 82). Where have we heard this before?

The postmodern problem of political and social discourse requires the construction of new forms of mediation, beginning always with language: not language as "moves" or as a metaphor for discourse but language as the words we speak and write, the formulations in which we find our voices and make those voices heard. It is difficult, as Attali says, to conceptualize, and this partly because the postmodern alternative is not theoretical in the old sense, or rather its theory and practice are not dissociated. Take improvisation, for example. The peculiar postmodern narrative arrangement, as in *Jealousy*, where many paratactic voices play at varying frequencies through the course of a text, certainly is a mediate arrangement, but it is never a unified field except temporarily and with a reader's unique partici-

---

[24] One entail of his apparent exclusion of certain kinds of postmodern writing is that he seems to make points that were made decades ago by other writers; for instance, Robbe-Grillet said nearly thirty years ago much of what Lyotard says about modernist nostalgia for the sublime (*The Postmodern Condition*, p. 81); and Breton anticipated fully his critique of consensus. Given the agendas of postmodernism, such omissions cannot be justified with disciplinary reasons (e.g., Lyotard is a philosopher, not a poet). If the strong "move" is local, it is also a situated and not a disciplinary move. When Lyotard defines imagination as "this capacity to articulate what used to be separate" and includes cybernetic capability (p. 52), he limits considerably his presentation of postmodernism; happy cybernetics, as Cortázar calls it, hardly accounts for the linguistic consciousness of postmodernism. Is the grammatological system local? Does creative invention lie somewhere between it and particular speech acts? Lyotard's *The Differend*, a much more ambitious effort to imagine the linguistic revolution implied by postmodernism, is discussed below in Part Three.

pation. This subjectivity in improvisation is something like the wager that Attali articulates in describing his political economy of "composition."

> Composition belongs to a political economy that it is difficult to conceptualize: production melds with consumption, and violence is not channeled into an object, but invested in the act of doing, a substitute for the stockpiling of labor that simulates sacrifice. . . . The wager of the economy of composition, then, is that social coherence is possible when each person assumes violence and the imaginary individually, through the pleasure of doing.
>
> Composition liberates time so that it can be lived, not stockpiled. *It is thus measured by the magnitude of the time lived by [persons], which takes the place of time stockpiled in commodities.* (pp. 144–45)

Yes, this does mean "bringing an end to repetition, transforming the world into an art form and life into a shifting pleasure" (p. 147), and this has the most radical implications for disciplines, occupations, and the range of endeavors as they have been distributed by modern discourse: something that can seem an opportunity as much as an apocalypse.

For example, both the artist's and the reader's situations change in postmodern writing from what they were in the era of representational conventions. It is no longer thinkable to produce books that, as Nabokov says, "mirror reality" or that give the reader a "good laugh" or "that make one think"; "it is only your healthy second-rater who seems to the grateful reader to be a wise old friend, nicely developing the reader's own notions of life."[25] The postmodern artist seeks out the actual act of construction and forces readers to explore the fiction-making consciousness itself. "The author today," Robbe-Grillet writes, "proclaims his absolute need of the reader's cooperation, an active, conscious, *creative assistance*. What he asks of him is no longer to receive ready-made a world completed, full, closed upon itself, but on the contrary to participate in a creation, to invent in his turn the work—and the world—and thus to learn to invent his own life" (*For a New Novel*, p. 156). Instead of tricking readers into a suspension of disbelief ("Why must one 'disarm' the reader? Is he dangerous?" [*Gift*, p. 23]), the postmodern novelist attempts to bring to the level of consciousness the imaginative process itself as it takes place in language. Perhaps the reader *is* dangerous to himself and others when he cheerfully wields without knowing it a whole language, a whole discourse of prefabricated formulation. "Give me," says Nabokov, "the creative reader" (*Gogol*, p. 140). Cortázar echoes the thought in various ways: when his Horacio fulminates against being a "spectator" in his life (*Hopscotch*, chap. 90), and when Morelli the writer denounces the passive reader, "the type that doesn't want any problems but rather solutions, or false and alien problems that will

[25] Nabokov, *Nikolai Gogol* (1944) (New York: New Directions, 1961), p. 140.

allow him to suffer comfortably seated in his chair, without compromising himself in the drama that should also be his" (chap. 99). Nabokov captures the condition to be avoided in his early novel, *Despair*, when his "abstractly personal" Hermann ("Hell shall never parole Hermann") is such a spectator that he ends up watching himself make love to his wife from an armchair in the next room. A postmodern novelist wants less disengaged readers, those armed with a capacity for self-reflexiveness, not straying off into transcendence or the history of this or that object.[26]

To heighten in this way one's awareness of language transactions is substantially to alter one's moral condition because writing and reading no longer easily replicate ready-made views and a ready-made world. By forcing readers to read and write creatively, postmodern novelists attempt to preempt the automatic reflex of unquestioned, preexisting interpretations, received truths, and conventionalities. Although as readers we still interpret what we find in the book, we are kept constantly aware that we are creating (have created) what we find. The play of the mind with its own self, a pronounced and often objected-to quality of postmodern fiction, has the effect not of reconfirming the individual mind in its pleasures and prejudices but, on the contrary, such play sustains at each step a questioning of those reinscriptions. In the deconstructive effort inherited from surrealism, such play of the mind with its own self is essential to the reconstruction of the world.[27]

Deliberate artists like Robbe-Grillet, Cortázar, and Nabokov thus carry on their exploration at the site of a crisis in modern epistemology. The visions they make available have profound resonance for every field of activity. Nothing is safe from *Homo fabricans*. The act of reading, for example, is not epiphenomenal in postmodern narrative because there is nothing to be epiphenomenal *to*; there is only the act itself, which is an actual happening, an event of consciousness, an act of imagination that is not secondary to reality but constitutive of it. Reading itself is a primary act, an act of creation, anything but a virtual activity to be casually treated "as if" it were real. The implied warning in this writerly posture, as Cortázar makes clear in "Continuity of Parks," is that readers should watch out what they do with their minds; the text they read—and the conception of "text" expands along with the conception of writing to include the whole range of imaginative activity—literally constitutes immediate reality for the reader. Writing, it turns out, is not a neutral transparency but an intervention. The style is not a means to an end; it is the end itself because it is a primary act of construction. It is the writing, "the *écriture*, and it alone

---

[26] Nabokov, *Despair* (1932) (New York: G. P. Putnam's Sons, 1966), pp. 59, ix, 22–23.

[27] Misunderstanding this difference—and it is every reader's option to misappropriate the postmodern novelist's challenge—often leads to quite bizarre interpretations of postmodern novels; *Lolita* seems to have been especially favored.

which is 'responsible' . . . for the work of art contains nothing," its "form is invention and not formula," in other words, not a brilliantly colored envelope for ready-made ideas of reality (*For a New Novel*, pp. 30–32, 44–45, 47).

The joint crisis of object and subject belongs to that larger crisis of historical conventions discussed in Part One and to the crisis of that humanism which those conventions support. What vanishes in postmodern narrative is the "narrator," which is to say, that "Nobody" power of consciousness that maintains historical time and its "distances", that maintains perspective, objectivity, verifiability, neutrality, and, above all, the rationalization of consciousness supporting those common denominators like "human" understanding and "human" nature that Western culture has developed over several centuries. Postmodern subjectivity, dispersed in system, inhabits a temporality that is not historical but rhythmic, not infinite but defined, not neutral but warped by interest, by the play of systems, by the negotiations between moments of identity. This postmodern redefinition of subjectivity literally wipes out any possibility of historical time, that is, the time of linear causality, because there is no longer an infinite collection of discrete subjects who can "agree" on past, present, and future "facts" and thus constitute the "same" (that is, historical) time. This ontological dependence between individual consciousness and historical time is a factor obscured by Cartesian models but essential to the historical convention nevertheless. The temporal rationalization of consciousness that we call "history" exists where the individual perspective locks together with others (potentially all others) into a common temporal medium, thereby creating a "neutrality" in which mutually informative measurements can be made between widely separated instances or events, and invariant qualities of "objects" thus constituted can be "discovered."[28] These temporal agreements, analogous to the agreements of single-point perspective, create a communicating flow between past and future, where the emergent "human" forms made available by this historical medium have the same status for the so-called human sciences that analogous forms have in botany, anatomy, or projective geometry. This historical medium that connects one time with another in a universal neutrality has its primary guarantees in the autonomous, individual consciousness that constitutes it. Practically though paradoxically speaking, historical time and historical consciousness are one and the same medium, and when you lose the one, you lose the other. Given the investment of Western culture in the constructs of modern, which is to say post-Renaissance, culture—so much depends upon its still "self-evident" truths—it is no wonder that postmodern challenges raise hackles and create anxiety. It was the agreements between subjects that

[28] This rationalization is discussed in *Realism and Consensus*, pp. 1–99, esp. pp. 40–55, and above, Part I, section one.

composed and sustained the common neutral medium of history in the first place, so the crisis of this subject literally dissolves the basis of history.[29]

These disappearances (of the Cartesian subject and its historical temporality) belong to a general dissolution of anthropocentric habits in postmodern narrative. In his important essay on "Nature, Humanism and Tragedy," Robbe-Grillet explains the disabilities of this habit—what he calls "habitual" humanism—and few texts join more directly than this essay the postmodern argument over humanism. (It is interesting to compare Robbe-Grillet's with Gyorg Lukács's critique of modernism: both so similar in their analyses and so opposite in the conclusions they draw.)[30] The disappearance of the human subject and its historical temporality frankly and deliberately undermines humanism and, with it, many of our accepted definitions of freedom, honor, political action, individual identity, and the like. Robbe-Grillet's essay explains the terms of this rejection. Responding to the reaction against novels like *Jealousy*, he states his objection to the cultural habit of seeing everything in terms of "human" nature, "human" experience, "human" weakness:

[29] Foucault expresses a similar thought this way: "Continuous history is the indispensable correlative of the founding function of the subject: the guarantee that everything that has eluded him may be restored to him; the certainty that time will disperse nothing without restoring it in a reconstituted unity. . . . In various forms, this theme has played a constant role since the nineteenth century: to preserve, against all decentrings [sic], the sovereignty of the subject, and the twin figures of anthropology and humanism." Foucault demonstrates the tremendous gravitational pull of this long-established social discourse (it is much older than the nineteenth century) on even the most vigorous attempts to revise it, for example, on the decenterings of Marx or Nietzsche, which only inspired searches for total history and for origins ("Introduction," *Archaeology of Knowledge*, pp. 11–14).

The dissolution of the subject takes many forms because there are many surrogates of this subject in representational writing. Foucault's discussion of the founding subject includes important extensions such as "the author" to which textual interpretation can be referred, thus not so much explaining the text or the writing as validating and reinscribing in yet another version that founding subject ("The Discourse on Language" [also called "The Order of Discourse"], appended to *Archaeology of Knowledge*, see esp. pp. 221–22). Another important variant of this subject is "the narrator," which is often individualized in the same way (this entirely distorts the narrator function in the text), and referred, as if for its interpretive bottom line, to "the author" as historical subject. It would be interesting to speculate on political and other variants.

[30] Lukács sees "man" as the "focal point" of all "content" and hence of all "form"; he values Homer, Thomas Mann, and Maxim Gorky for being "realist" about "man" and rejects Heidegger, Kafka, Musil, James Joyce, Sören Kierkegaard, surrealism, and expressionism as disintegrative both of "man" and (consequently) of "art." Antirealism is antisocial; art is representation or nothing, therefore Homer is representational ("The Ideology of Modernism," in *Realism in Our Time: Literature and the Class Struggle*, trans. John and Mande Necker [New York: Harper and Row, 1971]). Marxism, which "has a grasp of the main lines of human development and recognizes its laws," especially the law that "history moves forward," is the ally of classicism. "It is not by chance that the great Marxists were jealous guardians of our classical heritage in their aesthetics as well as in other spheres" ("Preface," in *Studies in European Realism* [1948] [New York: Grosset and Dunlap, 1964]).

If I say, "The world is man," I shall always gain absolution; while if I say, "Things are things, and man is only man," I am immediately charged with a crime against humanity.

The crime is in the assertion that there exists something in the world which is not man, which makes no sign to him, which has nothing in common with him. The crime, above all, according to this view, is to remark this separation, this distance, without attempting to effect the slightest sublimation of it.

He is attacked, in other words, in the name of "the *humanist* point of view, according to which it is not enough to show man where he is: it must further be proclaimed that man is everywhere" (*For a New Novel*, pp. 52–53). Robbe-Grillet traces this projection of man into the universe back to "Greco-Christian civilization":

A common nature, once again, must be the eternal answer to the *single question* of our Greco-Christian civilization; the Sphinx is before me, questions me, I need not even try to understand the terms of the riddle being asked, there is only one answer possible, only one answer to everything: man.

This will not do.

. . . Man looks at the world, and the world does not look back at him. Man sees things and discovers, now, that he can escape the metaphysical pact others had once concluded for him, and thereby escape servitude and terror. (p. 58)

The "terror" of humanism—a point worth pondering in an era of international terrorism—lies in the inevitable abysses of meaning characteristic of a universe where the answer to every question is "man." It is a terrorism similar to Lyotard's consensus, which excludes everything that is not itself. The servitude lies in the wearying necessity of *being* projected everywhere all the time. Postmodern narrative takes up at the end of that "human" hegemony.[31]

The discourse of humanism that eventually made consciousness coextensive with time put on the individual subject a demand and a strain that theoretically inspire heroic achievement but that Robbe-Grillet finds paralyzing. The structure of experience on which he focuses attention is that of "tragedy," something he sees as a method of fixing the individual subject in a posture of perpetual failure and loss.

---

[31] For those who have temporarily mislaid recollection of the riddle of the sphinx (to which Oedipus correctly answered, "man"), it went like this: what walks on four legs in the morning, two legs at noon, and three legs at night?

Before the eighteenth century the term "human" is rare, the term "humane" carrying both meanings, which split into two words early in the eighteenth century, one with the original spelling, "humane," limited to the sense of sympathetic behavior toward others (first OED listing, 1533), and another with the new spelling, "human," meaning having attributes or qualities distinctive of man (first OED listing, 1727). In the seventeenth century "humane" carries and mixes both meanings and tends to align with a distinction between human and supernatural beings.

Tragedy may be defined, here, as an attempt to "recover" the distance which exists between man and things. . . . Tragedy therefore appears as the last invention of humanism to permit nothing to escape: since the correspondence between man and things has finally been denounced, the humanist saves his empire by immediately instituting a new form of solidarity, the divorce itself becoming a major path to redemption. . . . For tragedy involves neither a true acceptance nor a true rejection. It is the sublimation of a difference.

Let us retrace, as an example, the functioning of "solitude." I call out. No one answers me. Instead of concluding that there is no one there—which could be a pure and simple observation, dated and localized in space and time—I decide to act as if there *were* someone there, but someone who, for one reason or another, will not answer. The silence which follows my outcry is henceforth no longer a *true* silence; it is charged with a content, a meaning, a depth, a soul. . . . Henceforth nothing will matter except this false void and the problems it raises for me. (p. 60)

The tragic mode always posits a universe filled with (if unacknowledged) consciousness, meaning, and interpretation: presences that may not reveal themselves as such but that are posited nevertheless by the narrative structure. In nineteenth-century novels this structure of consciousness presiding over every detail of the universe becomes explicit in the form of the Nobody (not personal, not individual) narrator whose presence is a formal feat of the first order even if that narrator never utters a single opinion in a personal voice but remains only a reflex of the historical past tense. The universe that is conceived as saturated with consciousness and hence with meaning is a congenial place for common denominators like "human" nature to form and for enterprises like global exploration and colonization.

Rather than acknowledge any limit of consciousness and of human extension, this tragic humanism purports to recover "meaning" from what might otherwise appear to be entirely without it. The lack of an answer from the universe, once it is taken as a refusal, has the insidious effect of validating suffering at the expense of achievement. Tragic humanism is inescapably a discourse of distance, separation, cleavage. Wherever you find these,

there is the possibility of experiencing them as suffering, then of raising this suffering to the height of a sublime necessity. A path toward a metaphysical Beyond, this pseudo-necessity is at the same time the closed door to a realistic future. Tragedy, if it consoles us today, forbids any solider conquest tomorrow. Under the appearance of a perpetual motion, it actually petrified the universe in a sonorous malediction. There can no longer be any question of seeking some remedy for our misfortune, once tragedy convinces us to love it. (p. 61)

"Habitual" humanism, that is, requires that we lodge our hearts in the abyss and endure the terror and servitude entailed by forms of self-definition that demand perpetual alienation. In order to feel my "human" heart, in order to know that I have one, I must be in pain. It is a peculiar maneuver: we fit into the universe by not fitting in, by being inadequate, by enduring loss. In this discourse the subject, the "I," can exist only in exile: across an abyss from the wholeness, the unity, the oneness that "I" posit and desire in order to make sure that it is always elsewhere.

Tragedy, in short, is a loss that confers a meaning so grand that it is sufficient compensation for the loss. Tragedy is a totalizing system because "it is impossible to regard a tragedy from two points of view," as E. M. Forster says in *A Passage to India*,[32] a novel that suggests to the horrified Western mind that there is no unity either in man or in his media of time and space. And with time and space divided, one can no longer have two points of view on the "same" thing. Tragedy is a syntactical structure par excellence. As such it is more than a privileged literary convention of Western literature; it is an entire mode of recognition and perception—"the tragic sense of life"—that the literary convention validates and reinscribes.

It is worth considering how much the word "tragic" has become a journalistic staple, a cultural buzz word that helps to naturalize suffering and loss and thus to keep alive certain political, practical, and social agendas. For example, it's a "tragedy" that an airplane goes down, that a man murders his family, that Santa Claus passes over poor or homeless children. These events may not be *King Lear* but they are "tragic" in the same way: first of all because they are not—we must believe they are not—pointless, meaningless chance or the result of unpreventable cruelty. Here history—the meaningful lapse of time—comes into play as a support of the tragic. In a "tragedy," at least, the loss confers some meaning and, consequently, some gain. Does King Lear, before he dies, recognize what has happened to him? Well then, he has affirmed the possibility of transcending the mindless misery that briefly controlled him, and we the audience participate in that transcendence. But *does* he recognize what has happened to him? If the answer were "no"—and a good case can be made for such a reading—then we have a rather different spectacle: one where a lifelong habit precipitates, finally, a fatal carelessness succeeded by betrayal, grief, and death without relief, without hope, without redemption. The "tragic" reading makes a virtue, a "natural" condition, even a necessity of what might be chance, mere cruelty, or unredeemed loss.[33]

---

[32] New York: Harcourt Brace, 1924, p. 165.

[33] Roland Barthes summarizes in part this important argument in a passage Robbe-Grillet quotes as the epigraph to his essay: "Tragedy is merely a means of 'recovering' human misery, of subsuming and thereby justifying it in the form of a necessity, a wisdom, or a purification: to refuse this recuperation and to investigate the techniques of not treacherously succumbing to it (nothing is more insidious than tragedy) is today a necessary enterprise" (*For a New Novel*, p. 49).

In rejecting the humanist definition of subjectivity and accepting the multilevel powers of consciousness as they are distributed in postmodern narrations, the reader Robbe-Grillet imagines ("man today") gives up the perpetual vertigo of living in a universe where it is necessary to reach for infinity in order to discover meaning and thus ground an "identity."

> And man today (or tomorrow) no longer experiences this absence of significa-
> tion as a lack, or as a laceration. Confronting such a void, he henceforth feels no
> dizziness. His heart no longer needs an abyss in which to lodge.
> For if he rejects communion, he also rejects tragedy. (pp. 58–59)

According to this interpretation, the disappearance in postmodern narrative of the "individual subject" and of its history signals an effort to liberate
attention from ready-made perception and to make possible new terms for
new times. It scarcely signals a loss of interest in human realities; on the
contrary, it signals a new emphasis on them. In "New Novel, New Man,"
Robbe-Grillet puts as plainly as possible the interest of postmodern narrative (he calls it "the new novel") in circumventing the rationalizations of
historical time and its notion of individuality:

> *The New Novel is interested only in man and in his situation in the world.* . . .
> For what is at issue here is an experience of life, not reassuring—and at the
> same time despairing—schemas which try to limit the damages and to assign a
> conventional order to our existence, to our passions. Why seek to reconstruct the
> time of clocks in a narrative which is concerned only with human time? It is not
> wiser to think of our own memory, which is *never* chronological? Why persist in
> discovering what an individual's name is in a novel which does not supply it? . . .
> Which brings us to the major question: does our life have a meaning? What is
> it? What is man's place on earth? We see at once why Balzacian objects were so
> reassuring: they belonged to a world of which man was the master. . . . Not
> much of this is left today. . . . The significations of the world around us are no
> more than partial, provisional, even contradictory, and always contested. How
> could the work of art claim to illustrate a signification known in advance, what-
> ever it might be? (pp. 137–41)

The experiments of postmodern narrative are attempts to make room for
human powers that have been kept under house arrest by traditions favoring the rationalization of human experience, or, in Breton's more potent
words, "this ridiculous illusion of happiness and understanding." The
shrinking of rational man makes room for values heretofore unavailable in
our narrative conventions: room for the human being who can feel, who
can dream, who can invent a world, room above all for a new sense of
proportion unconstricted by the compass of rationalist considerations alone.
    What postmodernism implies for humanism is an open and important

question; we have nothing like adequate preparation for answering it. Postmodern writing certainly is antihumanistic in the sense that it subverts history and its subject, but its agendas have traditions reaching from the philological revolution of the Renaissance to nineteenth-century attempts at dispensing with transcendence and its teleological tic. In addition, the term "humanism" means widely different things. If humanism is synonymous with Judeo-Christian morality, causality, and historical time as these were constructed between (roughly) 1500 and 1900, then perhaps humanism is in deep trouble, but I am not persuaded that either the problem or so-called crisis has yet been fully conceived. If humanism can be defined in philological terms, and there is, to say the least, a certain precedent for this, if it involves care for textuality and language, attention to difference between textual moments, an expanded sense of language and a model for each human system in all its complex multivalence, then perhaps humanism is only just finding its own demystified way. In any case, the current postmodern and antihumanistic emphasis on semiosis does move us well beyond the usual models of personal project and collective action; it does move beyond complacencies and disputes the privilege of representational language. This emphasis would naturally seem most irritating to those who identify themselves by means of privileged positions based on hidden hierarchies and teleologies, but their irritation is not about the end of morality or humanism; it is about the end of hegemony.

In postmodern writing, the unsettling of meaning and subject is not inconsistent with social and moral function. The crises where postmodern effort is located are, as Kristeva says, "inherent in the signifying function and, consequently, in sociality." This is scarcely a world-denying remark. The author of *Lolita* shows that crime is not just a legal matter and that what has been denied a certain girl-child is the right to her own imagination. The fortunate rhythms of postmodern writing constitute an enormous literary and linguistic effort to construct conventions where various motives can coexist without finality and defeat.

To summarize: postmodern subjectivity is without a subject because it is without an object; the subject is dispersed in the world it observes, except for the world of rocks, stones, and trees, which is, humanly speaking, unsusceptible to meaning, however accessible it may be to science. As soon as we speak of a "human" world, we speak of subjectivity as the objectively central fact. The postmodern novelist attempts to prevent our habitual flight from that subjectivity into some putatively (and functionally impossible) objective state by finding ways to avoid making that subjectivity a servitude. Not aiming at total objectivity, which would be a functionally dehumanized picture of things, and aiming instead "*only at a total subjectivity*," the postmodern writer, in Robbe-Grillet's view, must seek to free objects from the signification and from the putatively "objective" status they sustained in the nineteenth-century novel. To achieve this, the postmodern writer must invalidate the convention that sustains these significations and objectifications, the convention of historical time and its preeminent, all-encompassing narrative consciousness. Robbe-Grillet's *Jealousy*, Nabokov's *Ada*, and Cortázar's *Hopscotch* are narratives that depend on the conscious participation of readers and that thus are governed by "the least neutral" consciousness, one always subject to the rhythms and distortions of subjective perception, and one "*always* engaged . . . in an emotional adventure of the most obsessive kind" (*For a New Novel*, p. 138). In one light it is possible to see that these writers have simply made clearer a corollary of the old empiricist and Cartesian discourse: specifically, that subjectivity rationalized is no longer subjectivity but becomes instead and by definition part of "objectivity," perhaps even part of "nature" and "history." In the postmodern novel subjectivity remains unrationalized and so subjectivity parts company with individuality. This new narrative engages willing readers at the level of language and consciousness in an adventure of subjectivity without servitude.

Rhythm Section: Julio Cortázar's *Hopscotch*

For those who have not yet read *Hopscotch*, a brief description of the situation will be helpful. The novel contains 155 chapters (although this is debatable, like any other rational structure in Cortázar), and these chapters can be read in any order. The first fifty-six chapters (they account for two-thirds of the novel's length) are divided into two unequal sections entitled "From the Other Side" (chaps. 1–36, almost half the novel) and "From This Side" (chaps. 37–56). The first section involves various relatively recognizable places and personae—Horacio Oliveira, Paris, Big Bill Broonzey—and ends under a Paris bridge where Horacio's quest to escape dialectics and individuality ends in the embrace of a *clocharde*. The second section involves Horacio (only tenuously "the same"), Argentina, and what appear to be old friends and conventional ways, and it ends with Horacio on the same quest, seeking a way through the (representational) window and into the (hopscotch) game on the other side. The remaining third of the book, entitled "From Diverse Sides" (chaps. 56–155), is composed of mostly short chapters varying in length from several lines to several pages and entirely unsystematically invoking voices and details of the first two parts.

There are many ways to read *Hopscotch*, but, as the author's "Table of Instructions" suggests, "chiefly two":

The first can be read in a normal fashion and it ends with Chapter 56, at the close of which there are three garish little stars which stand for the words *The End*. Consequently, the reader may ignore what follows with a clean conscience.

The second should be read by beginning with Chapter 73 and then following the sequence indicated at the end of each chapter. In case of confusion or forgetfulness, one need only consult the following list:

73 – 1 – 2 – 116 . . . . (etcetera)

While the second, or hopscotch, reading can vary extensively depending on what series a reader constructs, all hopscotch readings have one thing in common—a self-conscious, active participation by readers; by contrast, the "normal" reading is consecutive and essentially passive and ends about two-thirds of the way through the novel. Depending on the choices made by readers, *Hopscotch* is an infinitely alterable series. The effect of this is to splinter reader consciousness. The very reading experience itself entails a choice of sequence, even a "normal" one. Each reading produces a different series, a different combination, a different "conjugation," a different text: one that is not "the same" as other readings, whether the text differs between readers or between readings by "the same" reader (it's a tribute to Cortázar's effect that one begins to wonder what in this context a phrase like "the same" could possibly mean). Readers thus learn to recognize as they read this novel that the order, in this case a series, determines identity and that, for practical purposes, order varies infinitely.

The two readings suggested by Cortázar, one consecutive and the other hopscotch, produce profound differences in the identity and status of events. Read straight through, for example, chapters 9 through 17 or 18 deal with a single event: a meeting of a group of friends who loosely call themselves "The Club" and who, when they get together, listen to music, drink beer, and have philosophical discussions. In this first way of reading, "The Club" meeting is a unified event. Read hopscotch, however, these chapters are widely separated, which means that the "event" becomes "events." This effect reverses that of realistic conventions, where what is widely dispersed proves to have a hidden connection; here what appears to be single, identifiable as "the same," becomes dispersed, multiplied. Read hopscotch, the single meeting becomes pluralized meetings; a discrete and unique event becomes an iterative, rhythmic element. Moreover, this way of reading involves constant recognition of the subjective and constructed nature of identities like "event" and "person" because "event" more obviously refers to events of consciousness. Whatever hopscotch series is chosen, so long as it is not the merely arithmetical series from 1 to 100, it splinters the identities ordinarily known as "character" and "plot," transforming each into a multiple and multilevel arrangement.

Read consecutively, the novel, at least the first fifty-six chapters, partially resembles a regular historical narrative, where the "same" characters reappear in different discrete "events"; but read hopscotch, there is no possibility of historical time, with its linear relation between past and future. Time, as La Maga explains to Rocamadour, "is like a bug that just keeps on walking" (chap. 32, p. 186); or it is something someone else keeps for you, as in the chapter where a line of irate Parisians outside the telephone booth attempt to keep Horacio to his allotted six minutes (chap. 100, pp. 450–53). But except as the basis for laughter, historical time, dialectical time, past-and-future time is something that a hopscotch reading explodes, along with the idea that time can be understood.

> I think about those objects, those boxes, those utensils that sometimes would turn up in storerooms, kitchens, or hidden spots, *and whose use no one can explain any more*. The vanity of believing that we understand the works of time: it buries its dead and keeps the keys. Only in dreams, in poetry, in play—lighting a candle, walking with it along the corridor—do we sometimes arrive at what we were before we were this thing that, who knows, we are. (chap. 105)

For a hopscotch reader there is in this reading experience no linear or rationalized time (except in Horacio's hang-ups): no medium that recovers everything, leaving no debris, no lost or forgotten identities, no projection that removes all sense of quality from the moment by dematerializing it with great expectations. The temporality experienced by a reader is one infinitely specified by distinction, by difference, one where every arrangement has a partial and mysterious quality, one equal to the complex irrationality of what we live and dream.

There is another difference between the two ways of reading that has much to do with the entire project of this novel. Read straight through, the linear transitions from one to an "other" side are sadder, more absolute, more imbued with a sense of loss. But read hopscotch—constructed in what might be called a multilinear way—the transitions take place all the time, back and forth, from one "residence" and "reality" to another, and back again. Nothing is permanently lost. Whatever has been encountered may be encountered again; it remains constantly available and accessible to choice. It is a lighter, more buoyant novel where one takes pleasure in, rather than feeling chagrin at, the interstices in "reality," the gaps between one "side" and another. Read hopscotch, the novel is a mandala (*Mandala* was the novel's original title): each chapter leads to all the others, depending on one's power to meditate through its forms; every point leads to every other, and "beginning" or "end" are just accidents of attention.

Readers thus are confronted with the possibility of pluralized identity whether or not they undertake the novel hopscotch fashion; the two different readings mean two different readers, not necessarily *in seriatim* but as constant potentials. Subjectivity or consciousness, that is, can be experienced in more than one way, depending on what series is chosen, and the presence of two implies a potential series of different readings and readers, even for "the same" person tackling the novel two or three times in different ways. *The series determines the identity*, and this fact, which operates surreptitiously in nineteenth-century novels, is brought home repeatedly to any reader of Cortázar's novel.[34]

Horacio Oliveira personalizes the large problems of discourse that *Hopscotch* poses for readers because he moves from one identity to another and then back again. In chapter 56 Horacio balances in an open window, a hopscotch game on the pavement outside and the institution for "straightening out" consciousness inside. This moment that marks "the end" of the consecutive reader's novel is also the moment that epitomizes Horacio's vacillation, caught in the window, unwilling or unable to return to reason and hesitating to become a hopscotch player. The window, as the surrealist painter Magritte was fond of showing, is a pictorial emblem for the unified subject, the implied spectator of realist ("window-on-the-world") art. (Such windows also occur in Nabokov, for example, in *The Defense* and *Transparent Things*.) To lean out the window, to jump into the hopscotch game, is to give up clinging to that convention and to that form of identity. Horacio leans toward the liminal threshold of another kind of existence than that of "same" and "different," of "identity" and "other," of "this side" and the "other side." It is the potential beginning of multilevel consciousness, the beginning of "diverse sides." It is "paff, the end" of a psychic, not a somatic, identity; the end of my me, "miserable treasure." On the painful, institutional side of the window Horacio is a contradictory (that is, "sick") subject; on the other side of that final window is the hopscotch game, an instrument of meditation, an emblem of play.

For Horacio the effort to retrain habit for a hopscotch world literally takes him to the brink of "self" destruction. In chapter 56 Horacio sets up his "territory" between the mad rationalizations of an insane asylum and the magical world of the hopscotch and La Maga. His territory has the poignance of being set up within a larger institutional territory as a kind of fortress where he barricades himself with imaginary weapons like a web of threads, a "heftpistole," and a helping of "rulemans"[35] in a last-ditch effort

---

[34] Foucault discusses the importance for discourse analysis of differentiating kinds of series in the "Discourse on Language" (also known as "The Order of Discourse") appended to *Archaeology of Knowledge*.

[35] The word "rulemans" is meaningless to readers initially but, taken for granted by Horacio and the inmate with the malignant green eyes, soon begins to develop hands and feet of its own and a whole context evolves around it. In any given group everybody imagines these miraculous objects differently: for some they are small things, about "this long" (gesturing with two fingers) with round things in it; for others, they are like banana peels with round

to consolidate his ego, his self, his boundary definition against the threat of leaning out of it and going "paff, the end." At "The End"—just before the asterisks—Horacio may at last be approaching the moment when he becomes capable of play, the moment when he learns that life, like language, is not engineering but bricolage, the moment when he accepts the multiform exactitude, the semiotic surplus of his world.

How hard it is for Horacio, even with an "other" life potentially at hand, to give up being a subject; how hard it is to give up the notion that somatic singleness, that is, discrete physical identity, applies to the multilevel, paralogical powers of conscious life. The effort requires the utmost discipline and courage.

> Man is the animal who asks. The day when we will really learn how to ask there will be a dialogue. Right now questions sweep us away from the answers. What *epiphany* can we expect if we are drowning in the falsest of freedoms, the Judeo-Christian dialectic? We need a real *Novuum Organum*, we have to open our windows up wide and throw everything out into the street, but above all we also have to throw out the window and ourselves along with it. It is either a case of death or a continuing flight. We have to do it, in some way or another we have to do it. To have the strength to plunge into the midst of parties and crown the head of the dazzling lady of the house with a beautiful green frog, a gift of the night, and suffer without horror the vengeance of her lackeys. (chap. 147)

We have to throw the window out the window and our "selves" along with the rest of our representational baggage. Why? Not in order to put a complete end to "human" life, certainly. On the contrary, the motive for this effort is to expand the arena for life by putting an end to the dialectical model of experience and its "continuing flight" from what is actual, precise, concrete. What is required is even more than the difficult act of will and courage required to sacrifice habit and to suffer the vengeance of lackeys. Beyond these is required the sacrifice of one's "self" that is entailed by changing one's language, one's "residence in reality." The "individual subject" finds itself in the mid-twentieth century "in the midst of the crisis and complete breakup of the classic idea of Homo sapiens" (chap. 99): this is Morelli's problem as a novelist, and this is the source of Horacio's endless practical problems with living. He is stuck in a parodic quest for the "other side" of his habits—his categories, his language, his pieties—but the form of his questioning only returns him to his prison. He has no trouble adopting unconventional behavior; he does not fear the vengeance of lackeys, but his insuperable difficulty is escaping from his "language," from the

---

things in them; for still others a cylinder as in children's building blocks. For Horacio and his accomplice with the malignant green eyes, the rulemans are part of the defense of "the territory"; and a territory, with its inevitable spatial correlatives, is the protected space that Horacio constructs and maintains with such magical instruments and tools as his rulemans.

emotional and intellectual and plain unconscious baggage that comes with language and that trains him, literally keeps him from straying off the track.

For Horacio the insuperable problem of his "language" is dialectics: the dialectics that creates history and that creates the "self" (these are discussed above in Part One, I). The point here is the many ways that dialectical thinking blocks the exercise of multilevel thinking. Horacio is fully aware of the moment that dissolves dialectic and identity and yet he is incapable of finding a new way. He *knows* what he has to do, but he doesn't know how to *do* it because the new way is not a matter of thought in the familiar, dialectical sense. There is in *Hopscotch* a reiteration of his baffled efforts that suggests stalemate. Only once does the reader encounter Horacio enjoying the happiness (it is not so much happiness as it is undialectical *relief*) of being completely *in* the experience of the moment, and though it is a most unlikely moment (chap. 23), the determining factor is that he stops making the kind of calculations, oppositions, and rejections that only reinscribe what he's trying to escape, the Judeo-Christian dialectic, falsest of freedoms. Horacio is a modern-day version of another Horacio, the legendary Roman who single-handedly held off his enemy at a bridge while his comrades escaped and then saved himself by jumping into the Tiber. Cortázar's Horacio has a trickier enemy, his own "language," and he can't save himself (that is, lose himself) because he can't jump. "Language means residence in a reality" (chap. 99). How does one jump out *that* window? This is the battle for a modern-day Horacio.

The identity in play (questionable-subject-in-process) that Horacio reaches toward—what might be called the hopscotch alternative—is a possibility that the novel invites the reader to explore. It is an identity epitomized by La Maga, Cortázar's magic person, who improvises and digresses as a matter of course. Where Horacio constantly chews over his contradictions, La Maga accepts hers; where he insists on rationalizing what is arbitrary, she knows how to make a medium of arbitrariness and an art of accident. She knows how to improvise; she knows how to preserve the game. Her success has nothing to do with being "happy," the dialectical word Horacio applies to her; her way is not easy or carefree. But her way has all the richness and pleasure and complex value that Horacio's, with its thousand devices of deflection and postponement, almost completely lacks. Horacio leans out of the window, seeking "that terrible sweet instant" where he can cross the threshold from one territory into another, straining to put his *cogito* or his consciousness-as-self out the window onto the hopscotch on the pavement below, "paff, the end." For a magician like La Maga, or perhaps the accomplished reader-player, "that terrible sweet instant" potentially *is every moment*. It doesn't bother La Maga that when the instant is over, it is over; only an idiot like Horacio would run after it and try to store it, or preserve it, or build a treasury with it either here or in heaven.

The reader's choice, like Horacio's, lies between two essentially different ways of being-in-the-text (reading—as postmodern narrative never tires of reminding us—because residence in a language is essentially an acceptance, however provisional, of one form of being-in-the-world). On the one hand, a "normal" reader accepts a dialectical temporality and a subjectivity disengaged from present experience by a continuous reflex toward tomorrow and yesterday, toward what is Beyond, toward some version of heaven. On the other hand, a hopscotch reader accepts a temporality without dialectical alibi or founding *cogito*: a time in instants and a multilevel subjectivity with which to improvise provisional arrangements. As Breton and the surrealists did, *Hopscotch* offers the improvisational alternative as a means to explore those mysterious rhythms of creative life that are marginalized and suppressed by dialectical inventions. This novel encourages hopscotch readers not to make Horacio's mistake. Its multilevel arrangement focuses our attention on the obscure enterprise of form involved in the creation or reformulation of language, and, like surrealist art, emphasizes the accidental, the aleatory, the chance encounter. To read the novel "hopscotch" fashion means that a reader must consent to being a split subject, one whose reading experience is relatively independent of "normal" sequences, although a considerate author provides a list of numbers "in case of confusion or forgetfulness."

Multilevel thinking is what hopscotch readers must practice; one of Cortázar's narrative voices calls it "paravision." Wandering along the Quai des Célestins, a narrative voice that calls itself "I" (we cannot tell who it is merely from the fact that "I" is wandering around Paris), this "I" picks up some dry leaves and puts them on a lampshade at home:

> I keep on thinking about all the leaves I will not see, the gatherer of dry leaves, about so many things that there must be in the air and which these eyes will not see. . . . There must be lamps everywhere, there must be leaves that I will never see.
>
> . . . I think about those exceptional states in which for one instant leaves and invisible lamps are imagined, are felt in an air outside of space. It's very simple, every exaltation or depression pushes me towards a state suitable for
>
> I will call them paravisions
>
> That is to say (that's the worst of it, saying it) an instantaneous aptitude for going out, so that suddenly I can grasp myself from outside, or from inside but on a different plane. . . .
>
> It doesn't last, two steps along the street, the time needed for taking a deep breath. . . .

and in that instant I know *what I am* because I know exactly *what I am not* (what I therefore ignore astutely). . . . I see what I am not. . . .

It's a little like this: there are lines in the air next to your head, next to your glance

zones for the detention of your eyes, your smell, your taste,

that is to say you're going around with your limits *outside*. (chap. 84, pp. 405–6)

I see what I am not. Paravision, like paralogic and parody, brings into view both what is present and what is absent: a negative definition of identity. Such consciousness—multilevel or paravisionary—revises the very conception of "identity," which in this context gets determined functionally and differentially and is therefore always on the brink of a change.

As a feat of personal recognition, this paravisionary power shows its most subversive potential. How to be an "I" that recognizes itself primarily by recognizing what is "not I" rather than fixing an identity by denying it? How to "be" when identity is defined negatively? Doesn't this mean that identity, like any other arrangement, is more an accident of perception or sequence than it is a stable entity like an ego or an object?

It's so very strange to be able to be in three places at once, but that's just what's happening to me this afternoon, it must be the influence of Morelli. Yes, yes, now I'm going to tell you about it. In four places at once, now that I think of it. I'm getting close to ubiquity, and going crazy is just one step away. (chap. 84)

How safe can it be to be in four places at once? Multilevel thinking, or paravision, may seem but one step away from "going crazy," but the activity these terms describe is a perfectly familiar one even for logophilic Western readers, although an activity depreciated and marginalized in the dialectical discourse of identity-and-other, same-and-different. Multilevel thinking, paravisionary awareness, ontology of ubiquity: such practices go only so far until they are stopped by "the defenses of wakefulness, oh pretty words, oh language" (chap. 57, pp. 353–54). It is the language, the discourse, the controlling habits as automatic as "native" speech, that puts on the brakes for Horacio, however self-reflexive his mind may get: "people like him and so many others . . . got into the worst paradox, the one of reaching the border of otherness perhaps and not being able to cross over" (chap. 22). Horacio winds up getting lost again in linear time and its identity instead of getting the swing that conjugates identity as one dimension of a pattern. The reader, however, is constantly reminded that a rationalist definition of what is "sane" or "normal" is itself a completely "crazy" standard by various measures in *Hopscotch*. Cortázar likes to explode that norm with laughter.

The problem of "language" in *Hopscotch* is postmodern in the sense that it extends beyond nouns and verbs to entire systems of "discourse" that inscribe through a range of social experience certain powerful (that is, unspoken) assumptions or preconditions that block certain questions, certain solutions and enable others. Thus, broadly conceived, every problem is a problem of "writing," and, as the normative voice in *Hopscotch* affirms, the "writer" may choose his or her invention:

> Everything is writing, that is to say, a fable. But what good can we get from the truth that pacifies an honest property owner? Our possible truth must be an *invention*, that is to say, scripture, literature, picture, sculpture, agriculture, pisciculture, all the tures in this world. Values, tures, sainthood, a ture, society, a ture, love, pure ture, beauty, a ture of tures. . . . Why surrender to Great Habit? One can choose his ture, his invention, that is to say, the screw or the toy car. . . . An invented fire burns in us, an incandescent ture, a whatsis of the race. . . . We burn within our work, fabulous mortal honor, high challenge of the phoenix. (chap. 73)

This, and the rest of chapter 73 (the designated first chapter for a hopscotch reader), affirms the same connection that the surrealists made between personal habit and the quality of an entire cultural discourse. We make what we seem to "find": we invent it, even at the level of blind acceptance. As participants and co-creators, we can be more or less lazy, more or less courageous, but in reading *Hopscotch* we cannot escape the necessity to invent.

Multilevel thinking depends in *Hopscotch*, as elsewhere, on a paratactic deployment of details where value intensifies as it is disconnected from meaning. "Green," for example, is such a detail: green sweater, green linoleum, green candles, green smoke, green fetish doll, malignant green eyes. "Green" does not signify envy, it does not symbolize a "green world," in fact it does not signify or symbolize at all; instead, it simply is a constant in a series of repetitions with variation. The "point" of this paratactic series, as I have argued in the case of Robbe-Grillet, lies with a reader's accomplishment of (using Nabokov's words) a certain "mysterious mental maneuver needed to pass from one state of being to another,"[36] and not at all with any "meaning" to be distilled from the text.

Possessing only rudimentary syntactical value, such emphatically paratactic detail is amplified by reiteration until it gains an importance far in excess of its meaning. Because of this and related techniques Cortázar's writing conveys a sense of the importance of *things*. Clearly indebted to surrealist images, his details have a characteristic capacity to float free of any particular system of rationalization: the color of Parisian night, the

[36] Nabokov, *Transparent Things* (New York: McGraw-Hill, 1972), penultimate sentence (p. 104).

miraculous chair in the Café de Flore, *mate*, lipstick, windows, a lyric, a Gauloise—these aren't characterizing or scenic details; they aren't allegorical or symbolic ones either. Their point lies in their ability to elude such explanatory systems. Neither are they "objective correlatives"; they evoke no feeling ostensibly common to all because the case differs with each reader. Their contextless intensity, their overdetermined contextuality varies for each reading and each rhythm of attention.

Liberated from systems of meaning, Cortázar's detail captures as no commentary could the tactile, visceral, erotic quality of experience. Paratactically amplified, detail in *Hopscotch* burgeons out of proportion, becoming by turns surprising, funny, erotic, threatening. This emphatic use of detail, this repetition of each through different contexts, gives them an almost sacramental quality. *Mate*. Even for those without a shred of Latin American experience, *mate* in *Hopscotch* achieves such sacramental value because it ritually punctuates attention. All such repetitive details are baptized with value precisely *because* they cannot be assigned a meaning. Each iteration becomes an obscure recognition, becomes a satisfaction, becomes (like the golden screw for the villagers in chap. 73) "peace."

Multilevel thinking not only entails a rearrangement of subjectivity, it rearranges relations between present and past from what they were in historical temporality. When the past is no longer part of a dialectic, it is not destroyed but it does exist more as a function of what is present. Postmodern subjectivity, as the reader of *Hopscotch* knows it, is a capacity to be aware of several things simultaneously, including the so-called past; the capacity for multilevel thinking includes the power to retain very precise memories. The past can be conceived in rhythmic time as a present potentiality, surrounding us always and not at all at the end of some pilgrimage. As one of the voices in the novel says:

> It occurs to me that this famous Yonder cannot be imagined as a future in time or in space. If we continue holding to Kantian categories, Morelli seems to say, we will never get out of this blind alley. . . . What we call reality, the true reality that we also call Yonder . . . is not something that is going to happen, a goal, the last step, the end of an evolution. No, it's something that's already here, in us. You can feel it, all you need is the courage to stick your hand into the darkness. (chap. 99, pp. 445–46)

Far from being a narcissistic emphasis on Me, Now, Me, Now, postmodern subjectivity combines the precision of sensation in the moment with the plural powers of multiple consciousness as each sensation triggers them anew in all their plenitude. Far from living without memory in the world, the multilevel subject has an increased access to what is called "past." The worst mistake, one Horacio seems prone to, is to think that in order to get rid of the falsest of freedoms, history and its dialectics, he must get rid of everything—a position still saturated with history and its dialectics.

The difference between the two kinds of reading sequence in *Hopscotch* etches vividly the difference between the historical and the postmodern or rhythmic relation to the past. When Horacio leans out of the window at the end of chapter 56, seeking "paff, the end" of his troublesome dialectical identity, this is for the hopscotch reader just one more moment in his range of moments that cross from one "side" to another side of the novel, of the Atlantic, and so on. For the consecutive reader it is quite a different matter; the end of chapter 56 in effect marks Horacio's disappearance from the novel. Even if this reader goes on to the "expendable chapters," their fragments and their voices seem disconnected from any of the cumulative meanings available in the first part. There is no reprise of the Horacio voice, no reappearance of familiar moments in a rhythmic pattern. When linear time puts an end to the univocal subject, it puts a permanent end to it; in fact, it can be said that linear time predicates such termination (just as the extinction of individuals is a condition of the survival of a species). In contrast, rhythmic time and the multilevel thinking it encourages keep a multilevel subject in play; "the end" of an arbitrary arrangement may arrive, but something else always begins. The problem of being-in-the-world, as Heidegger put it, is a problem of being in relation to death, but death can be (with one exception, usually is) encountered in less than absolutely final ways. Such moments of life or death are matters of habit, as the presence of alternative sequences in *Hopscotch* perpetually shows.

The detachment of subjectivity from historical time has enormous discursive implications, among them the redefinition of "time" and "subjectivity," and even mortality and immortality. And this redefinition is no mere mystification of material death. Death of the kind Horacio faces—jumping away from individual subjectivity of the kind held in place by "point of view" in favor of multilevel subjectivity—is one thing. The death of the child, Rocamadour—his name suggests his importance—is quite another. Rocamadour's death is a central, perhaps *the* central, "event" in *Hopscotch*. His loss is absolute and cannot be contained in a pattern stretching (like Bruno's time in "The Pursuer") from the zinc counter of the present into the Future. There is no Beyond, no Yonder, no Elsewhere. The fact of such absolute, *unmediatable* definition is rarely met in nineteenth-century narrative, but there is no escape from it in *Hopscotch* or in rhythmic time.[37] What is present, though, is made doubly valuable by the fact that when it is gone, it is gone. For those who cannot stand too much of this reality, and who need to blunt the perception and fall back on transcenden-

[37] Occasional exceptions like Hetty Sorrel in George Eliot's *Adam Bede* (1859) or Jude in Thomas Hardy's *Jude the Obscure* (1895) only confirm the point.

tal flight, there is always the recourse (as the novel puts it) to "vodka and Kantian categories, those tranquillizers against any too sharp coagulation of reality" (chap. 14). Without such tranquillizers, however, the hopscotch reader must sustain a new and *asyntactical* relation to particulars, including his or her own "self" and a different awareness of every limitation, including the ultimate material limitation. Postmodern narratives contain quite a number of syntactical accidents and quite a number of personae, often narrators, who survive their own deaths by accepting the "reality" of invention.

Accidents were a favorite device of surrealists for short-circuiting the force of habit. Properly, which is to say undialectically, speaking, every moment is an accident, a chance, an *hasard objectif* of the kind mentioned by Breton and so often encountered among the surprises of *Hopscotch*. The theme of accidents in Cortázar's novel is one of the ways he literalizes a metaphor in order to show the practical reality of invention, the invented nature of practical affairs. La Maga and Horacio never plan to meet in Paris; instead they deliberately set out to meet by accident, and they do, usually (and appropriately) on a bridge. This raises the question, can accidents be planned? Say I give up my habitual reliance on causalities, can I make an art form, that is, a deliberate construction, out of accident? *Hopscotch* raises the practical question, how does one translate such techniques into practical terms, especially in an eminently *social* world where questions of identity and language always involve other people?

This problem of social, which is essentially to say moral, considerations becomes crucial with the disappearance of historical causalities and their emphasis on controlled action. The question of the fate of morality is raised repeatedly and in infinitely various forms in hostile and/or uncomprehending readings of postmodern narrative, and the question is important. This novel supplies some terms in which—delicately—to consider possible answers to questions about the bases of morality and responsibility in asyntactical posthistorical time and with multilevel subjects-in-process. One passage in particular (ch. 22) leads readers from a scene of mechanical accidents and irreconcilable separation to a scene where relationships are reimagined as "delicate contacts, marvelous adjustments with the world" constituted simultaneously from several directions at once.

The so-called Expendable Chapters of *Hopscotch* often contain opinions of the novelist, Morelli, an author much admired by "The Club" composed of Horacio and his friends, although none of them has ever met him. Chapter 22 initiates an opportunity for their paths to cross Morelli's, something that they manage because of a moment of spontaneous interest in the anonymous life of someone they literally encounter by accident. This accident strangely and incidentally provides a fine metaphor for the kind of contacts that are possible in a world populated by multilevel subjects in rhythmic time.

Chapter 22 begins, quite anonymously, "Opinion had it that the old man had slipped," and it goes on to describe the traffic accident in which an old man is injured and taken to the hospital. The hopscotch reader soon learns from the Expendable Chapters that this old man is Morelli himself, something the sequential reader may never find out except by a superhuman feat of recall and inference. A voice, very like the Horacio voice, ponders the accident at the scene without yet knowing the identity of this old man.

> They carried him in the stretcher and spoke friendly, comforting words to him, *"Allez, pépère, c'est rien, çà!"* from the stretcher-bearer, a redhead who must have said the same thing to everybody. "A complete lack of communication," Oliveira thought. "It's not so much that we're alone, that's a well-known fact that any fool can plainly see. Being alone is basically being alone on a certain level in which other lonelinesses could communicate with us if that were the case. But bring on any conflict, an accident in the street or a declaration of war, provoke the brutal crossing of different levels, and a man who is perhaps an outstanding Sanskrit scholar or a quantum physicist becomes a *pépère* in the eyes of the stretcher-bearer who arrives on the scene. Edgar Allan Poe on a stretcher, Verlaine in the hands of a sawbones, Nerval and Artaud facing psychiatrists. What could that Italian Galen have known about Keats as he bled him and helped him die of hunger? . . . It was easy to remember all of those who had denounced the solitude of man among his fellows, the comedy of greetings the "Excuse me" when people met on the stairs. . . . Contacts made in action in tribes in work in bed on the ballfield were contacts between branches and leaves which reached out and caressed each other from tree to tree while the trunks stood there disdainfully and irreconcilably parallel. "*Underneath it all* we could be what we are on the surface," Oliveira thought, "but we would have to live in a different way. . . ." That true otherness made up of delicate contacts, marvelous adjustments with the world, could not be attained from just one point; the outstretched hand had to find response in another hand stretched out from the beyond, from the other part. (chap. 22)

The final metaphor can stand as a description of postmodern subjectivity in its social dimension and as a description of the kind of awareness offered to a hopscotch reader. Meetings like those "delicate contacts" between tree branches, like the accident itself, like the crossings of consciousness from moment to moment, like the surprise of a new threshold, and like those improvisations of the jazz musician, the collage artist, the postmodern writer: "delicate contacts, marvelous adjustments with the world" that cannot be attained from "just one point" but from a plurality of points that can be reached only rhythmically and without dialectics.

Like the mandala it so often invokes, *Hopscotch* itself is a device for meditation that is both symmetrical and meaningless. A hopscotch, a labyrinth, Paris, a mandala: another way of using consciousness that escapes preencoded habits like saying, "I love you," which very often means "picking out a woman and marrying her." The word creates the thing; "in general without the *verba* there isn't any *res*." But (a different voice objects) "Beatrice wasn't picked out, Juliet wasn't picked out. You don't pick out the rain that soaks you to the skin when you come out of a concert." Forget the words:

> Beat it, the pack of you, we have to think, what's called thinking, that is to say, feeling, locating yourself, and confronting yourself before you let pass the minutest main or subordinate clause. Paris is a center, you understand, a mandala though which one must pass without dialectics, a labyrinth where pragmatic formulas are of no use except to get lost in. Then a *cogito* which may be a kind of breathing Paris in, getting into it by letting it get into you, *pneuma* and not *logos*. Argentine big buddy, disembarking with the sufficiency of a three-by-five culture, wise in everything, up to date in everything, with acceptable good taste, good knowledge of the history of the human race, the periods of art . . . philosophical currents, political tensions . . . action and reflection, compromise and liberty, Piero della Francesca and Anton Webern . . . Fiat 1600, John XXIII. Wonderful, wonderful. (chap. 93)

"*Pneuma* and not *logos*." Living without getting lost in pragmatic formulas, without getting detained in the dialectic of planned action. With its arbitrary skipping around in a numerical sequence of chapters, its perpetual digression from familiar syntax to surprising experience and back again, *Hopscotch* brings into focus the rhythm of attention itself: the rhythms of consciousness and language at work in many, not just some, of their functions. It makes an art of digression, like walking the streets of Paris, that mandala in glass and stone. The new *cogito* is like breathing or like a heartbeat, not like thinking, *pneuma* not *logos*, a most intimate rhythm. In this way every moment is a "terribly sweet instant" where conscious life first is conjugated and then goes "paff, the end," to be succeeded by another, and another again. This delicate shift of equipoise initiates a profound reformation: a new definition of consciousness, and a new world of practice without transcendence, or depth, or history, or dialectics, or the "subject" and the "object." Pneumatic, not logocentric, like Robbe-Grillet's successive experiments, like the heartbeat of *Ada*, the redefinition of consciousness and subjectivity empowers that " 'swing' that puts discourse on the march" (chap. 99).

Part Three

Language and Time

> Before the work of art there is nothing—no
> certainty, no thesis, no message. To believe that
> the novelist "has something to say" and that he
> then looks for a way to say it represents the
> gravest of misconceptions. For it is precisely
> this "way," this manner of speaking, which
> constitutes his enterprise as a writer, an
> enterprise more obscure than any other, and
> which will later be the uncertain content of his
> book. Ultimately it is perhaps this uncertain
> content of an obscure enterprise of form which
> will best serve the cause of freedom. But who
> knows how long that will take?
> —Alain Robbe-Grillet, *For a New Novel*

THE CRISIS that puts an end to classically defined subjects and objects also produces a crisis of the referential sign. This means first and most simply that a sign cannot be conceived as a traveling pointer because there are no longer any simply located things to point *at*. In other words, a radical re-thinking of the nature of language, its functions and qualities, accompanies the radical postmodern questioning of representational agendas. The problem for postmodern writers is to balance our habitual (perhaps crippling) emphases on the linear, directional, rational and syntactic powers of language with a new linguistic emphasis on the digressive, aleatory, paratactic, and semiotic disposition of language, the one that flourishes in rhythmic time. The problem for postmodern writers, in short, is to restore the "play" of language at all levels of magnitude: from sentences to discursive boundaries. It is not a question of elevating play over meaning, as meaning was once emphasized at the expense of play; it is not a question of "revolution"—that modernist concept—but instead of retrieving into practice, into play, a dimension of language that has been repressed. The emphasis in postmodern narrative on the paratactic and semiotic value of language is thus primarily an act of restoration.

This act, however, does not leave "reality" unchanged. Postmodern writing collapses the representational dualisms that posit a "reality" separate from time, consciousness, and language. If time is no longer a neutral medium, a place of exchange between self-identical objects and subjects and "in" which language functions, then the language sequence—especially in the expanded theoretical sense of discourse—becomes the only site where temporality can be located and where consciousness can be said to exist. This symbiosis between consciousness and temporality, it is important to remember, is thoroughly evident in the historical narrative conventions of the nineteenth century; what has changed is the objectifying or rationalizing potential of the pair. The "Nobody" consciousness that narrates nineteenth-century novels reconciles all private and apparently separate times of individual awareness into one and the "same" time. The narrative consciousness of postmodern novels belongs to a changeable reader-writer who is engaged in conspicuous construction. The only "reality" in a postmodern novel is a multiform and metamorphosing reality of language; nothing exceeds its practices or its play, nothing escapes its limitations, nothing acts as a cosmic or natural "ground" and justification.

This reformation that makes time and consciousness into dimensions of language brings into high relief the fact that the powers of language are constitutive of whatever we can make or do. This recognition is quite far removed from any relativist catastrophe. Recalling Cortázar's expression that residence in a language means "residence in reality," one is not overstating the case by saying that postmodern writing seeks to expand our possible reality by rescuing us and our language from the narrow conceptions to which historical habits of thinking increasingly have confined it. This confinement of language to history has been literal in Western languages. By contrast, certain non-Western languages do not make sharp discriminations of tense; and it can be shown that tense itself, as a marked feature of language, is an historically limited phenomenon not only in "nonstandard" languages but also in the early stages of Romance languages, which, though definitely grammatical linguistic systems, had very little to do with tense and where instead the temporal stems in verbs stress *aspect*, a way of viewing language for which process or duration is just one protocol among others. As tense is more marked, aspect recedes. It is demonstrable that, if certain things cannot be expressed *except* in tensed language, certain others are inexpressible in it.[1]

---

[1] See, for example, J. T. Fraser: "Although in Sanskrit, as in Greek, there are five kinds of tenses, they are not sharply discriminated in meaning. To indicate past time, the imperfect, perfect, past participle active, aorist and historical present are used almost indiscriminately. . . . In modern Hindustani as well, we find similar linguistic phenomena" (*The Voices of Time: A Cooperative Survey of Man's Views of Time as Expressed by the Sciences and the Humanities*, [New York: George Braziller, 1966], p. 81); and Stanley McCray on the rarity of well-developed temporal systems (pluperfects and future perfects) in early forms of language that stress aspect—a priority of aspect over tense that may have something to do with a priority of

Borges subtly thematizes these issues in "The Aleph," a story that suggests some ways in which language, and not transcendental consciousness, constitutes social memory. This narrative, which wanders with an erring, metonymic quality from one plot conjunction to another, resembles the long digressive poem being written by Carlos, who has discovered under the nineteenth stair in his basement an Aleph: a white spot of light of less than three centimeters in diameter that contains a complete universe. In a familiar postmodern arrangement, the story provides readers with two alternative modes of consciousness corresponding to two different formulations of temporality. One is associated with Carlos, whose writing becomes labyrinthine in his effort to do justice to the vision available in the Aleph, and the other is associated with the narrator, the fictional Borges, a pompous, regulated, obsessive center-of-the-universe, ruminating on his professional disadvantages. Whereas the Aleph is the secret source of Carlos's writing, Carlos's sister, Beatrice, his blinding heavenly light, is the secret source of the fictional Borges's obsessive story. This narrator grips his marmoreal image of Beatrice, both before and after her death, as a shield against the fact that the universe is moving on—past her, past her death, and past him. An opposite effect is produced by Carlos's vision in the Aleph. There its very simultaneity produces an ever more meandering narrative poem because, while there is simultaneity in the Aleph, in language as in temporal existence there is only succession. The Aleph is all past, present, and future possibility, containing everything and losing nothing. Language, in other words, *is* the successive form of the Aleph, dispersing all "reality" along an infinite web of pathways.[2]

For my purposes the story has important implications about the primacy

---

speech over writing. McCray calls it "a raw speaker strategy" ("Process and Motivation in Early Romance," in *Romanitas: Studies in Romance Linguistics*, Ernst Pulgram, ed. [Ann Arbor: University of Michigan, 1984], pp. 170–79).

McTaggart's famous paradox proving the nonexistence of time is relevant here. This paradox, paraphrased by Richard Gale, rests on the "seeming incompatibility between the dynamic and static conceptions of time." To unravel it we need to "inspect carefully the logic of our tensed and tenseless ways of talking, and, in particular, see how these two different ways of speaking are related." Gale, taking up McTaggart's paradox, aims "to show that the logic of ordinary discourse is such that tenseless expressions are logically dependent upon tensed ones, and also that the fundamental concepts which we employ in talking about the world involve tensed concepts; they could not be expressed except in a tensed language. More specifically, an attempt will be made to show the way in which the tensed distinctions of past, present and future are logically contained in our concepts of precedence and simultaneity, things and events, change, causality, action, intention, knowledge, possibility, truth, propositions and identification. . . . It will show that our dynamic or tensed way of conceiving or talking about time is more basic than our static or tenseless view of time. It will turn out that the concepts of past, present and future are the tree-roots which hold together this multitude of concepts" (*The Language of Time* [New York: Humanities Press, 1968], pp. 7–8).

[2] Borges, *Personal Anthology*, p. 149.

of language over so-called history. Language, to the extent that one knows and uses it, keeps ready at hand the past, the world, all times and spaces. There is no need to cling to what is "past" because it cannot be lost and is not elsewhere. It is in language that the other world surrounds us always, and the problem is not how to recapture the past or to mitigate the disaster of "passing" time but, as for Carlos, only how to manage the formidable power of language. The excitement produced by the Aleph in Carlos and in readers, however, is lost on the Borges narrator, who never gives up his effort to transcend sequence by hanging onto Beatrice just as Cortázar's honest property owner clings to equestrian effigies. Such clinging, the story makes evident, is a crime against language, against the always potentially present past. The Borges narrator regrets something that has not been lost, except through his inexorable regret. He succumbs to what Nabokov calls the most trivial of human emotions, nostalgia for lost opportunity.

"The Aleph" is another instance where, by focusing on the link between language and temporality, a postmodern writer collapses the dualism between words and things. "History" is consigned for better or worse to the sequences of language. Here, and not in some "objective" universe, is moral responsibility really revived and reconceived. One then becomes responsible—because it is now profoundly important—for one's language: for what one reads and writes and imagines and dreams. "The Aleph" presents a major difference and a major choice between two incompatible kinds of attention and activity. As the marvelous vision of a world becomes more wondrous, more awe-inspiring for the respectful amateur, Carlos, it becomes more marginal and irritating for the playless professional narrator, Borges.

Section I: Play and the Crisis of the Sign

Play, however inescapable its value may be in postmodern narrative, has a low status in the world of affairs (the world of the fictional Borges). Play may be something universal—something we already do in ways more or less competent—but it is also something that is, in Western culture and certainly in the United States, widely if not universally discredited. Babies play, women and children play, athletes play, but then one grows up and becomes reasonable, tells "the truth" or appears to, and avoids playing at something that's "only" invented; one learns to remain "in the true," as Foucault says, which is to say, in the received structures that preserve themselves by excluding play. One may play on weekends, but even that recreation is often viewed as essentially a part of (to quote the Michelob beer advertisement) "where you're going." The infinite digressiveness that would be characteristic of a committed full-time player has become associated with those who are marginal to the "serious" world of "work," which is to say, the world of project and conclusion, history and objectivity. Although from a postmodern perspective play belongs to a realm of value, a realm of qualitative values like proportion, complexity, flexibility, pleasure, and eroticism taken in its most expanded sense, viewed from within rationalist discourse (the realm of quantitative values like production, causality, and control), the very word "play," seems almost to gesture toward a realm outside value altogether.

The link of play with pleasure, another depreciated term, belongs to a rooted cultural hostility to whatever threatens to digress. We are not talking about a mere "attitude" here but a much deeper habit of formulating expectations about psychic life. For example, it is notorious in some circles how the Freud industry has codified and purveyed Freud's arbitrary and unbalanced view of digressiveness, playfulness, habitual indirection. According to Freud, such habits have a physiological basis and are a mark of "femininity" and hence of inferiority. With such "reasons," writes Cixous, have they "constructed the infamous logic of antilove."[3] So-called "femininity"—ever the land of exile for depreciated cultural values—has a power of digressiveness that is something people of both sexes might justly resent being exiled from were the value of digressiveness to be unhinged from these dubious anatomical speculations and become a widely available, widely pleasurable, widely valuable practice. Duras has even suggested that the development of such powers is essential to growing up.[4] It is a major effect of postmodern narrative language to privilege precisely such digressiveness.

The radical pluralization to which postmodern writing subjects language puts a strain on meaning in the ordinary sense of "message" and opens up new multilevel employments for language. Characteristic of this new language practice are various forms of doubling in everything from word to sentence to text (no longer "plot") formation; various modes of punning, alliteration, anagrammatical constructions, and parody continually present readers with divergent and digressive claims on their attention, and to such an extent that the term "sign" does not properly describe anything more specific than the site of a certain differential function. Familiar instances of this are the paratactic arrangements already discussed in *Jealousy* and *Hopscotch*, novels whose main demand on reader attention has to do with play in the deployment of language elements or their surrogates. The thematic elements of *Jealousy*, for example, the ice bucket, centipede,

---

[3] Hélène Cixous, "The Laugh of the Medusa," trans. Keith Cohen and Paula Cohen, *Signs* 1, no. 4 (1976), p. 878.

[4] Duras's narrator in *The Lover* says that her mother, for all her valiance and grace, remained a child because she never knew pleasure.

balustrade, and blue letter paper, are "signs" in the sense that they are al-
phabetical elements whose "meaning" arises in their combination and re-
combination. The thematic crossings of *Hopscotch* are another version, as
are the syntactical transgressions and alliterations of *Ada*.

In order to give at the outset some body to this word "play," I want to
consider some actual language: a passage from Nabokov's *Ada*, a novel that
is one long sustained example of the kind of conspicuous construction or
polymorphous play that one finds in postmodern writing. Here Van Veen
is being interrupted (during an assignation with amorous Lucette) by a
telephone call from his secretary, Polly, who is typing his treatise on time.

At this point, as in a well-constructed play larded with comic relief, the brass
campophone buzzed and not only did the radiators start to cluck but the un-
capped soda water fizzed in sympathy.

Van (crossly): "I don't understand the first word. . . . What's that? *L'adorée?*
Wait a second" (to Lucette). "Please, stay where you are." (Lucette whispers a
French child-word with two "p"s.) "Okay" (pointing toward the corridor).
"Sorry, Polly. Well, is it *l'adorée?* No? Give me the context. Ah—*la durée. La
durée* is not . . . sin on what? Synonymous with duration. Aha. Sorry again, I
must stopper that orgiastic soda. Hold the line." (Yells down the 'cory door,' as
they called the long second-floor passage at Ardis.) "Lucette, *let* it run over who
cares!"

He poured himself another glass of brandy and for a ridiculous moment could
not remember what the hell he had been —yes, the polliphone.

It had died, but buzzed as soon as he recradled the receiver, and Lucette
knocked discreetly at the same time.

"*La durée*. . . . For goodness sake, come in without knocking. . . . No, Polly,
knocking does not concern you—it's my little cousin. All right. *La durée* is not
synonymous with duration, being saturated—yes, as in Saturday—with that particular philosopher's thought. What's wrong now? You don't know if it's *dorée*
or *durée?* D. U. R. I thought you knew French. Oh, I see. So long.

"My typist, a trivial but always available blonde, could not make out *durée* in
my quite legible hand because, she says, she knows French, but not scientific
French." (II:v, p. 399)

A whole lot of construction is going on here. With the simultaneous com-
mencement of phone buzz, radiator cluck, soda fizz, and door knock, we
have the emphasis on coincidence, parodying well-constructed plots: a sort
of temporal collage. The soda is "orgiastic" but alas, and despite long anticipation, Van and Lucette are not. The rhymes between "cory door" and
"second floor" link this occasion to an amorous moment with Ada in Ardis. Another conjunction with sense as well as play is the one between
"synonymous" and "sin on," which, though Polly doesn't know it, may be
a good comment on the whole notion of synonymous meaning. "Satura-

tion" and "Saturday" musically join a condition and a moment. The variations on English and French words for temporal persistence (*la durée*, "duration," the "long" of "so long") make a regular little rondo in themselves and allude to variations on the theme of time both in Van's treatise and also in Nabokov's *Ada*. The echo between *la durée* and *l'adorée* is a typist's mistake in the symbolic order but is a luminous conjunction in the Nabokovian play on the theme of time where time and love are the same. Thematically speaking, I am especially grateful for Polly's closing distinction between French and "scientific" French. The whole situation here is not so much a domestic comedy as it is a linguistic self-commentary. There could scarcely be a more literal competition between the rational and playful impulses than the interruption of Lucette's whimper of bliss by the secretary typing a treatise. Of course Lucette's problem always has been that, unlike her sister Ada, she makes eros "mean" something (she turns sex into a symbolic project) and consequently she fails with Van just as she eventually fails with life. Read aloud, the rhythmic and rhyming qualities of this passage are even more insistent than they are for the silent reader.

This process, this play in language that makes way for imagination, is constitutive in *Ada*, a novel that demonstrates the claim Nabokov makes elsewhere that the plot of great literature lies in the style. Nabokov's readers have to be construction workers, not merely consumers. The style of *Ada* is a tissue of little moments that act more like intersections than like stages along the way of plot: moments where several digressions cross, where several thematic voices may sound at once, and where each of them invokes a different coloration, a different frequency. The language moves from one exquisite detail to the next, leaving none of the mnemonic residues of realism. In the polliphone passage the stock plot is no more than a vaudevillian echo; meanwhile alliteration radiates from one center after another. Adoration invokes duration, saturation calls up Saturday, absent Ada is more present than visible Lucette. The clatter of coincidence mimicks the amorous conjunction sought so desperately and fruitlessly by Lucette and makes more poignant still the truly erotic exquisiteness that we experience everywhere in Nabokov's style. One's consciousness cannot properly respond as if it were simply located and single when the narrative reality is multilevel. One's "personal identity, miserable treasure," the conception of identity stated by Lévi-Strauss and alluded to by Kristeva, is not the best equipment for this postmodern expedition.[5]

All this distraction, *this formality of sustained interruption*, dissolves in laughter both transcendental longings and their founding subject. The ef-

[5] This is a reference to Lévi-Strauss's phrase by Julia Kristeva, "From One Identity to An Other," in *Desire in Language: A Semiotic Approach to Literature and Art*, trans. Thomas Gora, Alice Jardine, and Leon S. Roudiez (New York: Columbia University Press, 1986), p. 127.

fort at forward motion is so continually thwarted, the plot-peripheral play so continually sustained that it is impossible to establish any "perspective" with which a more traditional text invites the subject to discover "meaning" and, in the process, literally to found itself. This narrative without meaning confers no identity on a speaking subject because it is not necessary to position that subject as the transcendent motivating and originating agent of meaning, the surrogate provider of thesis and conclusion. The signifying economy that favors play over meaning subverts the speaking subject along with the historical convention of time. The playful disposition of language unsettles this speaking subject (along with meaning and signification) and replaces it with a "questionable *subject-in-process*" (*Desire in Language*, pp. 124, 135), or, more accurately "subject-in-processes." These effects are crucial in postmodern narrative and account for its capacities both to frustrate conventional readers and to delight those who can get beyond reading for ready-made meanings.

The term "play" I use in the sense of the elasticity in a line that is not pulled taut, of the flexibility in a system that can also include its capacity to permit substitutions even to the point of shifting the balance of its so-called structure. (We recall from Part One that this structural evolution, this morphogenesis based on chance interventions, is precisely what characterizes the self-organizing processes of the physical universe according to Prigogine and Stengers.)[6] The power to sustain linear arguments, transfer information, communicate conclusions is only one of language's powers; as a system of signs, language provides a "residence" that is "a reality." A language that is overwhelmingly influenced by rationalism is a language pulled taut to an extent that it impoverishes "reality." Virginia Woolf, a writer admired among postmoderns, already knew this when she wrote, in *The Waves*, "To speak of knowledge is futile. All is experiment and adventure."[7] To emphasize play in a sequence or a discursive system, then, is to restore "experiment and adventure" to that sequence, that discourse.

This definition of play owes much to the theoretical discussions of the subject by Kristeva and Derrida. Kristeva's distinction between the symbolic and semiotic dispositions of language matches to a degree my distinction between historical and rhythmic time. Like historical time, the "symbolic" disposition of language constitutes itself by predication; its emphasis is syntactical, thetic (as, for example, in the dialectical motive of anti- and syn-thetic); it "communicates meaning." By contrast and like rhythmic time, the "semiotic" disposition belongs to the musical, rhythmic, nonsense effects of language, such as those evident in poetry or in the echolalias of children or in "carnivalesque discourse, Artaud, a number of texts by

---

[6] See above Part One, p. 62 and Prigogine and Stengers, *Order out of Chaos*, p. 166.
[7] *The Waves* (New York and London: Harcourt Brace, 1931), p. 118.

Mallarmé, certain Dadaist and Surrealist experiments." This semiotic disposition remains heterogeneous to meaning, which is to say, syntactical production. For the sake of stabilizing terms, it is worth noting that in Kristeva's (as in my) usage poetic language is the *opposite* of symbolic language, not its synonym.[8]

Kristeva distinguishes these two dispositions in order to insist that neither alone exhausts linguistic function, that both are necessary. Her discussion still unfortunately retains dualistic and thus implicitly hierarchical tendencies, a manner of speaking that reinforces the problem she is addressing, but even so her discussion illuminates what is going on in postmodern narrative language: a massive effort to reunite two dispositions that have been severed and, in so doing, to restore health to psychic and social life and to heal the damage done by long-term and ever-increasing discursive emphasis on the symbolic, syntactical, thetic disposition of language at the expense of the semiotic, paratactic, rhythmic disposition.

No postmodern writer, so far as I know, seeks to establish an exclusively semiotic practice either linguistically or in any other terms. Still, to reemphasize the semiotic raises difficulties that demonstrate how far gone we are on the road to the other extreme, that is, toward an exclusively symbolic literary theory and practice, one that masks the semiotic function in order to encode a supposed transcendence that is really a function of linguistic habits. In emphasizing the depreciated half of the double identity of language, postmodern writers move to contain the disrupted representational and symbolic practices (together with the social and political theories such practices confirm) and to restore the semiotic disposition to its function.

The restoration of play to Western discourse is the implicit agenda of Derrida's important and influential analysis of "Structure, Sign, and Play in the Discourse of the Human Sciences." For Derrida, as for Kristeva, the stakes in this discursive reformation are high because, following Lévi-Strauss, Derrida affirms play as the function that distinguishes living systems from dead ones. This play, which provides possibilities of continuing substitution and improvisation, exists in constant tension with structure that limits play. A living system is always in process, incomplete, in play, whereas a system without play is functionally dead: doomed to perfectly rational but lifeless exactitude because it has followed to its conclusion the

---

[8] *Desire in Language*, 132–35. The need for both of these dispositions is often a thematic implication in postmodern narratives, for example, in Borges's "The Aleph," where the Borges narrator shows by his sheer disagreeableness that the symbolic function, or disposition to produce meaning, does not work particularly well alone; and where unchecked responsiveness to the play of language evident in the meandering style of Carlos is a liability that he manages to overcome only after the Aleph is destroyed; it is only then that his literary success begins.

structural impulse to foreclose play and even to foreclose it totally. Derrida's structurality—the very idea of structure—is essentially a rational instrument that has the goal of all putatively rational systems to *exclude* play as much as possible, to the extent of achieving total rigidity. Like Kristeva, Derrida opposes these two motives in an all too familiar dualism, the kind that is the perennial invitation to hierarchy; as Foucault says, it is very, very difficult to say something new. Still Derrida's formulation accomplishes the difficult feat of using essentially rationalizing and representational language to deconstruct such language.

Derrida's argument has the implication that *structure itself is referential* in the sense that it always depends for its stability on reference elsewhere to some justifying absolute that exists "beyond" the structure and exceeds it.[9] It is *this referentiality* to an Elsewhere—to a "full presence," a Beyond in time and space—that validates the structure and justifies its effort to achieve maximum rigidity or perfection or completeness. By referring to something outside it—something like "truth" or "natural law" or "reality" or "Being" or "objectivity" or "history"—structure depends on something that is prior to it, that survives it, and that limits absolutely its play of differentiation. However, to the extent that a structure limits play in the interest of closure, precision, or "perfection," it becomes "ruined" because its very completeness—its "totalization"—uses up its options to the point that no new formulations, no new experiments or adventures are possible. By contrast, the incompleteness of living systems guarantees a continuation because the possibility of play remains open. In other words, and not to put too fine a point on it, systems that seek to exclude play are also seeking death.

The crux of Derrida's (and it is also Saussure's)[10] contribution to the theorizing of postmodern writing is the conception of *supplementarity*, or the process whereby a fixed system or syntax is perpetually renewed by the necessity of substitution: substitution of one term, one experiment, one improvisation after another as dictated by some irreducible ambiguity in the system of signs. This supplementarity, which prevents the system from

[9] This referentiality of all structure means, to put it in Derrida's paradoxical language, that the "center" or "origin" is both unique to a structure and, at the same time, that thing within the structure that "escapes structurality. This is why classical thought concerning structure could say that the center is, paradoxically, *within* the structure and *outside it*. The center is at the center of the totality (is not part of the totality), the totality *has its center elsewhere*. The center is not the center" ("Structure, Sign, and Play in the Discourse of the Human Sciences," in *Writing and Difference*, trans. Alan Bass [Chicago: University of Chicago Press, 1978], pp. 278–79). In spatial and synchronic terms, structure is based on ideas of centrality, whereas in temporal and diachronic terms structures are based on ideas of origin and end.

[10] Derrida's supplementarity, as well as his suppression of speech, derives from Saussure's *Course in General Linguistics* (c. 1906–11), trans. Wade Baskin (New York: McGraw-Hill, 1959), see esp. I.iii and III.

being totalized and "ruined," occurs in "classical" systems because of in-completeness (one grounds the process by positing a completeness that can never be reached); it occurs in postmodern systems as play (infinite, un-grounded substitution that can have the effect of changing the system ["Structure, Sign, and Play," esp. pp. 284–90]). Historical thinking is an example of the "classical" way to avoid totalization by deferral: "truth," whatever it is, will always exceed knowledge at any given moment. This position, which is quantitative, empiricist, and, as Derrida says, "classical," retains the idea of truth by simply deferring its realization and thus, with no final fulfillment, keeps the system in play. The postmodern narrative series is an example of unanchored play. The blue letter paper in *Jealousy* might be a "clue" to adultery-in-progress, except that it appears too often, is too common a detail of life, exactly to fit into such a "plot"; by virtue of its repetition it becomes instead a feature of paratactic not syntactic ar-rangement, an instrument of play not purpose, thereby dissolving any pos-sibility of rationalizing its contradictions in time or consciousness. Another example, mentioned in chapter 73 of *Hopscotch*, is Picasso's bronze statue that makes a toy car into the chin of a baboon. Magritte's famous pipe (his *The Treachery of Images* (c. 1928–29) is subtitled *ceci n'est pas une pipe*) is both a pipe and not a pipe. *The multiplication of semantic contexts multiplies the "identity" of the object*. This multiplication—the "multilevel thinking" discussed in Part Two—is the special province of the characteristic parallel logics of postmodern narrative, for example, parody, where the language is heterogeneous to meaning but always in sight of it, just as Picasso's car is both a car and not a car.

By this logic of multiple semantic "identity," a corporate profit is both a profit and not a profit; a strategic weapon really does point in more than one direction. We see the subversive potential of this postmodern attitude and why it is relatively unpopular at those centers of hegemony where the enterprise of "learning" or "producing" is conceived not in terms of play-ing with given power structures but in terms of reinforcing them and mak-ing them more coherent. It is this play, this overabundance of signifiers, this constant potential for substitution that *uncloses* a system and thus pre-vents it from being "complete and ruined." It is this baggage in excess of what is needed for the definition of structure that makes the system capable of play. It is this supplementary play that accounts for the importance of language as a model in postmodern philosophy and social science, because language is a system that is both finite (quite different from totalized) and capable of an infinite play of substitutions (new sentences, inventions, for-mations). There is "no millenary kingdom," Cortázar writes in *Hopscotch*, there is only "this dirty game of substitutions" (chaps. 71 and 56). We are not going anywhere, we are sitting at home, and home is language. Post-modern writing hovers between the substitution that elaborates familiar historical conventions to the point of parody, on the one hand, and, on the other, the play that generates indeterminacy and its seminal adventure.[11]

These theoretical discussions of language help to locate postmodern narrative habits relative to much larger discursive events. Kristeva's symbolic disposition of language, with its subject and structure, its thetic impulse for results, provides a sort of linguistic Beyond: a guarantee, as she says, of "a transcendence, if not a theology." The semiotic disposition of language, on the other hand, encourages precisely the kind of play that Derrida and Lévi-Strauss theorize: an activity that searches, in Kristeva's words, "within the signifying phenomenon for the *crisis* or the *unsettling process* of meaning and subject rather than for the coherence or identity of either *one* or a *multiplicity* of structures" (*Desire in Language*, pp. 132, 133–35, 125). In other words, what we need is a theory of process rather than of production, *but process forever separated from the product that formerly subverted it*: process conceived as a means whereby meaning and subject cease to be structures of static forms and become permanently questionable, always unfolding activities. Where the symbolic, thetic, dialectical process encourages univocality and rational awareness, the semiotic, anthematic, playful process encourages multivocality and multilevel awareness.[12]

These postmodern efforts to subvert transcendence with language collapse distinctions between language and subjectivity, and between language and time. Those crises of historical time and of individual subjectivity discussed in Parts One and Two—those linked disappearances of historical thinking and its founding subject—materialize in the postmodern reformation of language. The ease with which powerful and longstanding conventions can be erased by changes of linguistic usage dramatizes the powerful if ineffable importance of language to the establishment and renewal of these discursive conventions. It appears that representational language is not something based upon a certain given order of things but that, on the contrary, a certain order of things is based on representational linguistic usages and is changed when that language changes. The Cartesian subject, it seems, can be replaced by a questionable-subject-in-process to the extent that such subjectivity is differently inscribed by language. And the convention of historical time, what Kristeva in "Women's Time" calls "the time of project and history" (p. 18), is a "thetic" or "sym-

---

[11] This power to vary without finality (and defeat) and without mere randomness, this ability to hover between systems, has importance, I think, to feminism and is one more instance of the affinities between feminism and postmodernism. See Ermarth, "On Having a Personal Voice," in Gayle Greene and Coppelia Kahn, eds., *Histories/A History*.

[12] The terms "multilevel" and "multivocal" seem adequate to the descriptive effort here, but terms like "plural" or "pluralized" do not for the reason that, in a nutshell, "pluralism" is merely one of the more seductive forms of historicist and transcendentalist thinking.

bolic" view of temporal process that grounds certain social versions of natural law and disappears when thetic and symbolic language disappears. Whereas representational forms of language and temporality are governed by the necessity to mediate the distance between any moment of awareness and an ever-transcendent "reality," which by definition always exceeds that moment of awareness, postmodern language turns from dialectics and history and the unquestioned subject and finds another way.

The reader of postmodern writing who operates on "the other side" of classical discourse operates very much like Lévi-Strauss's *bricoleur*: like a handyman, without a grand design but instead with whatever tools suffice for the particular task at hand. A *bricoleur*, like a maker of collage or a musician improvising, uses what has situational value and recognizes the limits of every coherence. Such *bricolage* is exactly the kind of arbitrary construction with materials at hand that readers must undertake with the shuffled decks of Nabokov and Cortázar, the mobiles of Butor, the protean intensities of Duras and Hawkes. The *bricoleur*'s opposite, what Lévi-Strauss calls the *engineer*, is the totalizing interpreter whose aspiration is to reduce play and to arrive at conclusions. Scientific language aspires to be totalized and to reduce play absolutely, for example, in botanical notation or mathematics; the myth of "comprehensive evidence" belongs to this faith; for the late-modernist historian-as-(social)-scientist the methodology of history entails the relativization of every system *except history* which itself remains beyond the system. The Renaissance historian's recognition that the past was past—one of the truly original moments in the history of consciousness—included a philological understanding of historical methodology far different from that of later positivist historians backed by two centuries of science.

These theoretical analyses attend to an important synapse between social order and interpretive practice. Disrupted representationalist practices, that is, those that suppress the semiotic in favor of the symbolic function of language, do not in Kristeva's view merely obscure the full range of value in literature, they disturb the renewal of social codes. They block a moral process, and often in the name of morality. The rational discourse that has been privileged in the West by several centuries of positive science has thereby crippled our capability to perceive and sustain what is multivocal, inconclusive, or undecidable; in other words, it has crippled important powers of survival. The semiotic or playful or "poetic language," Kristeva writes, "awakens our attention to this undecidable character of any so-called natural language, a feature that univocal, rational, scientific discourse tends to hide" (*Desire in Language*, pp. 124, 135).

This analysis has certain implications for anyone engaged in interpreting or, even more, in teaching interpretive practice.

> While poetic language can indeed be studied through its meaning, such study reduces it and obscures the very thing that in the poetic function . . . makes of what is known as "literature" something other than knowledge: the very place where the social code is destroyed and renewed. (*Desire in Language*, p. 132)

To "translate" a text into some other language throws emphasis off language and onto information. One translates not only from French to English, one also translates into "meaning" a film or a novel, the value of which lies precisely in its play upon a reader. This value, one that belongs to a process that always exceeds "meaning" in any ordinary sense, is utterly destroyed by the "translation," which often concerns itself primarily with meaning (symbolic value) and relatively little with matters of proportion, complexity, arrangement, relationship, in short, with the *way* of writing. Kristeva's discussion thus dovetails with the epigraph to this section in which Robbe-Grillet describes the common mistake of thinking that there is any difference between the *way* of writing and what it supposedly is "*about*" (*For a New Novel*, pp. 141–42).

Although the theoretical statements of postmodernism often sound apocalyptic, there is no evidence that such activity amounts to a cultural bonfire. On the contrary, current efforts at linguistic restoration could even be one step further in a methodological revolution that began five hundred years ago, that corresponds to the rise of print culture, and that has often been betrayed by a thetic impulse for resolution aimed primarily at saving essences. The continuity of that tradition, its central dispute between dogma, on the one hand, and, on the other, history broadly conceived as open-ended and unrationalizable process, accommodates postmodern theorists and novelists who are sometimes carelessly excised from it. Primary conventions, after all, have massive staying power, and the news of their demise is usually premature.

It *is* true, however, that beyond the Beyond there is no *certainty* of the kind that humanistic traditions have fostered, but only a kind of unanchored play without guarantee. The "post classical" episteme, instead of turning toward origin or end, "affirms play and tries to pass beyond man and humanism, the name of man being the name of that being who, throughout the history of metaphysics or of ontotheology—in other words, throughout his entire history—has dreamed of full presence, the reassuring foundation, the origin and the end of play" ("Structure, Sign, and Play," pp. 278–79). Derrida recapitulates the critique of humanism and of "man" (the very idea of "man") that we found from Nietzsche to Robbe-Grillet. This challenge to humanism is direct and widely misunderstood, but it does sound a knell to certain habits and beliefs, and the challenge is broadly sustained. The problem is not so much whether the challenge can be ignored, because obviously it cannot, but what response to choose. Derrida presents two alternatives that seem to sum up the main options in postmodern narrative. One can cry about it, recapitulating the humanist nostalgia Robbe-Grillet describes—what Derrida calls "the saddened, *negative*, nostalgic, guilty, Rousseauistic side of the thinking of play"—or one can laugh about it—what Derrida calls

> the Nietzschean *affirmation*, that is the joyous affirmation of the play of the world and of the innocence of becoming, the affirmation of a world of signs without fault, without truth, and without origin which is offered to an active interpretation. *This affirmation then determines the noncenter otherwise than as loss of the center.* And it plays without security. For there is a *sure* play: that which is limited to the *substitution* of *given* and *existing*, *present*, pieces. In absolute chance [on the other hand], affirmation also surrenders itself to *genetic* indetermination, to the *seminal* adventure of the trace. ("Structure, Sign, and Play," pp. 292–93)

"The seminal adventure of the trace" is a phrase that evokes the pleasures of postmodern language, an exercise that subverts the sober language of rationalism and seeks to "blow up the law, to break up the 'truth' with laughter" (Cixous, "Laugh," p. 888). Beyond the closed system of controlled play is the realm of "absolute chance," a surrealist's *hasard objectif*, where what has not yet been thought or spoken may materialize, where the reviving, life-giving unknown may come into play.

The cultural implications of postmodern writing—just how relevant poetry may be to the preservation, alteration, and renewal of social economies—generally need to be explored much more than they have been. One suggestive attempt is Lyotard's construction of *The Differend*: an ambitious effort to extend into practical and especially political terms the revolution implied by postmodernism. The postmodern condition, he argues, is a state of *différence* and hence a political condition he calls "the differend," which poses primarily problems of linkage between what he speaks of as "phrases" (rather than "systems"). His ingenious argument makes politics—itself a language or protocol or phrase—the *site* of these intractable, given differences in need of linkage. Politics is "the *threat of the differend*. . . . Politics is not everything, though, if by that one believes it to be the genre that contains all the genres."[13] The problem, as Lyotard acknowledges, is finding language that is not radioactive for writing the new politics. The words "time," "human," and "history," for example, come trailing clouds of discourse from which they can scarcely be detached, and Lyotard's discussion seems to be no exception;[14] even so, the differend seems

[13] Jean-François Lyotard, *The Differend: Phrases in Dispute* (*Le Différend*, 1983), trans. Georges Van Den Abbeele (Minneapolis: University of Minnesota Press, 1988), pp. 137–43, sects. 188–205.

[14] Heidegger's inauthentic time appears in Lyotard's *The Differend* (e.g., "It takes too long to read, when success comes from gaining time" [p. xv]). This would seem to suggest that, as

a postmodern place. Just as the gestalt *figure* operates as a *con-figuration*, as a difference not an identity, so every contemporary situation is a differend, a differential site for systems, usually multiple systems on even the simplest level. For example, an interesting case (Lyotard offers other cases) would be the time differend belonging to gendered temporal constructions ("men's" and "women's" time). Like the other phrase conflicts described by Lyotard where the one threatens the other, this differend is political and involves a threat, one that occurs not so much person to person as system to system (or Lyotard's "phrase" to "phrase"), when a system ("phrase") accepts, even assumes acknowledgment but does not acknowledge in return the presence or even the possibility of an other system, which is to say, doesn't acknowledge difference.[15]

---

with everything else, one deals not with temporal constants but with different kinds of time corresponding perhaps to his "phrase families"; but this suggestion does not seem to be borne out by the rest of the discussion, sect. 235 and "The Sign of History" notwithstanding. Lyotard speaks of "human history" in ways that take "time" for granted, even where all else is consigned to "phrase families." The sign of history is not chronology, Lyotard's "diachronic series" (*Differend*, sect. 235, pp. 161–63) but neutrality and homogeneity. Summarizing Kant, Lyotard seems to speak without qualification of "heterogeneous but compatible phrase families," mediated by "the critical watchman," and thus to slip back into long-familiar habits that raise the familiar questions. From what perspective does one see all this: from that of a "floating intelligentsia"? (as Karl Manheim has called it in *Ideology and Utopia*). Lyotard's "time," like the "critical watchman," seems to transcend the phrases in dispute. This is not surprising considering the difficulty (but not the impossibility) of changing habit. He seems entirely to ignore the narrative reformations of postmodernism ("In the matter of language, the revolution of relativity and quantum theory remains to be made" [p. 137, sect. 188]). One wants to ask Lyotard (as Nabokov asked an interviewer who kept speaking of "reality"), "What time?" "Whose time?" "What time 'phrase'?" (see, for example, *Differend*, sects. 244, 247, p. 175).

[15] "What is subject to threats is not an identifiable individual, but the ability to speak or keep quiet" (Lyotard, *Differend*, p. 11). How easy it is to say, "but *I* didn't threaten you," and yet to threaten by sheer systemic pressure. For example, the cultural construction and gendering of time: "her" time differs in kind from "his" time. "Her" time is the houseperson's time, the time of Adam Smith's "unproductive" labor; "her" time is conformable, flexible, always being adjusted and defined by others, by their needs, by their way of doing things, by their hours. "His" time is the professional's time, common time, universal time, the time of history and project. "Her" system is a system, but it doesn't look that way to the working person whose main business is the bottom line, which is to say, the business of eradicating difference and establishing rational order (making things "work" in politics, finance, construction, etc.). "His" whole effort bends toward conclusion. "Her" whole effort involves keeping multiple systems managed without fatal conflict. Engagement between them is not so much an engagement of persons as it is an engagement of systems. What's at stake is time. "Her" life, its lack of definition—"and, my dear, what do *you* do?"—because it conventionally involves juggling several systems at once (family, household, business support systems, social details, perhaps a job paying or nonpaying). In our bottom-line world, that is perceived as having no bottom line. How easy to assume that (and to slip into habits that say) "you are secondary, your power of attention, your hopes, your fears, and above all your time, is secondary, epiphenomenal, attached parasitically to other more 'real' things. We love you, of

Another formulation of postmodernism's cultural implications comes from "noise" theory and conceives the "noise" of culture in much the same terms as I have described the play of language. William Paulson ably shows that "literariness" is distinctively "noisy" because it does *not* involve exact transmission of messages but instead involves the "play between redundant order and informative surprise."[16] Producing such awareness in readers is the postmodern novelist's project. Paulson generalizes it this way:

> For the reader, one might say that where the seemingly individual fact was, there the intersection of systems shall be. What appears to be a perturbation in a given system turns out to be the intersection of a new system with the first. *The principle of constructing a pattern out of what interrupts patterns is inherent in artistic communication, because this kind of communication arises by deviating from the regularities of non-artistic communication, and this deviation must be the source of whatever advantage or specificity artistic communication possesses.* (p. 87)

Such "literariness" is to culture what the playful and semiotic element of postmodern language is to narrative: the element that forces us not only to "semanticize elements normally unsemanticized" (p. 86) but also to be aware of that tension and that process.

This discussion very much resembles Nabokov's definition of poetry in his book on Gogol, an artist he praises for his high achievement of "complex and unnecessary deception."[17] He calls Gogol's play *The Inspector General* "poetry in action, and by poetry I mean the mysteries of the irrational as perceived through rational words" (p. 55); he is master of "the sudden focal shift" by which the syntax blurs and discloses other meanings (p. 140), literally making "noise" for rational structures in much the same way Nabokov's style does. "Gogol's genius is exactly that ripple—two and two make five, if not the square root of five, and it all happens quite naturally in Gogol's world, where neither rational mathematics nor indeed any of our pseudophysical agreements with ourselves can be seriously said to exist" (p. 145). Nabokov's poet is a postmodern writer and his opposite, for whom two plus two always equal four without any noise whatever or pos-

course, but your time . . . your time, is, well, flexible, infinitely changeable, conformable to *my* time, which is to say *the* time." The ability to stay in the interstices—as Cortázar says—to inhabit the contested space and time and keep well, and even keep alive—this is poetry. In a system dedicated to conclusion it may look like nothing, but it is not nothing as anyone doing unproductive labor can testify; it is the semiotic function; it is an essential half of social health (in personal bodies and in the body politic). "His" time and "her" time usually are divided between men and women, especially husbands and wives, without their ever knowing that they as individuals have nothing to do with it except perhaps, as Borges might say, insofar as they suffer so that a certain formality may repeat itself.

[16] William Paulson, *The Noise of Culture: Literary Texts in a World of Information* (Ithaca: Cornell University Press, 1988), p. 85.

[17] Nabokov, *Nikolai Gogol* (1944) (New York: New Directions, 1961), p. 13.

sibility of sudden focal shift, Lévi-Strauss calls the "engineer." In other words, the paratactical, semiotic, poetic emphasis in postmodern narrative perturbs the conventional narrative system of history with its pseudophysical agreements, causality, and individual subject. One could say that in a given language system play is the "noise" of *logos*; it makes available the power to know the limits of systems, the power to subvert or disrupt their claims to meaning and authority.

It probably goes without saying that if such play (or "noise") actually is essential to the renewal of social codes, then it belongs to an exercise too important to be done badly and on weekends. Anthony Wilden thinks instructively of our cultural situation as an "historical ecosystem" and of its "noise" as the material base from which we derive new, in-process, always unstable, aesthetically, which is to say, qualitatively elected clarity.[18] By thinking of political and other material issues in terms of the model of language, the postmodern writer provides sites for performing new acts of attention that are literally acts of cultural construction and even of political reformation. The play that opens systems, that keeps them alive, is "a phenomenon of language and not one of ideas" (Nabokov, *Gogol*, p. 150). This linguistic basis, whether it is conceived as metaphor and model, in the manner of discourse analysis, or whether it is conceived literally as the practice of writing and speaking, presses toward some powerful revisions of ordinary usages across a whole range of practice.

The stakes in this revision of linguistic practice are nothing less than the revision of social code. The emphasis on reflexive play in postmodern narrative seems to me historically intelligible as a response to the almost insane lengths to which we have transformed language into a symbolic instrument. The postmodern writer's emphasis on artificiality in language, far from being mere dandyism or antibourgeois assault, is an effort at restoration of a language that has been bound by a thousand threads in Lilliput. If postmodern writers are right, that is, if there is more to language than meaning and signification (more than the symbolic disposition), then the unsettling process that Kristeva recommends and that postmodern writers produce is much more than an arbitrary production of an idle French intelligentsia or of novelists who just like to show off; it is fundamental to the functioning of language and its constructions. For postmodern writers these linguistic matters belong at the heart of philosophical, aesthetic, and theological matters, or rather those matters *are* at heart linguistic ones. If all thought is discourse and all discourse is language, then the postmodern exercise of language in its full power as both semiotic and symbolic and

---

[18] "The noise of the historical ecosystem is necessarily engendered by its character of being *out of step* with itself" (*System and Structure*, 2nd ed. [London: Tavistock, 1980], p. 403), cited by Paulson in *Noise of Culture*, p. 181.

understood as a process of construction fundamental to all other conscious construction does not merely point to philosophical, aesthetic, or ethical discourse; it *is* philosophical, aesthetic, and ethical discourse.

Postmodern narrative's linguistic project suggests we exorcise the scientism that has crept into our methodologies and into our practical transactions with the word because that scientism has paralyzed language's potent energies and constrained it to a narrowly conceived representational function: one in which a sign simply refers, without any unsettling influence, to a world where language functions chiefly as an instrument of information. This disrupted representational view of language has done much to compromise the value of literature and even of humanism as it has been taught in certain institutional and disciplinary languages. "If," as Paulson argues, "language is a noisy channel . . . then humanism in its more or less authoritarian avatars and formalism in its more or less scientific avatars are irrevocably compromised—not broken beyond use, but cracked beyond repair" (p. 94). By reinstating semiotic values postmodern writers implicitly displace the disrupted representational view of language, that is, the view that thinks reference or symbolic value is *all* there is to language. With its semiotic disposition restored, language always also refers to itself as an entire formulating system wherein the sign has its place and its function as an instrument of human agency and an entirely human invention, a system where proportion, emphasis and value are as important as information, communication, and meaning.

The effort to reinstate semiosis into the symbolic order is an agenda that postmodern novelists share with certain feminist theorists. Both insist that the discursive problem posed by postmodernism is a problem of language, and both insist on the preeminent importance of writing a new language, one uncontaminated by the old radioactive terms (Irigaray, Cixous, Robbe-Grillet, Derrida explicitly mention this difficulty). New language is precisely what feminist theorists and postmodern novelists invent. By making digressiveness a virtue, by substituting paratactic for syntactic arrangement, and by other means they make it possible for readers actually to perform new acts of attention: to engage attention not in plot and character or other forms of meaning production but instead in the patterning process of repetition and variation as it extends along a linguistic sequence shadowed by other states and modes. Such linguistic sequences bring linear attention to a standstill, like Van Veen "stuck again" on the road, and they invoke from peripheral awareness the materials for constructing the unique and unrepeatable rhythms of a life: insect rhythm of a humid night, heartbeat, breathing, *pneuma* not *logos*. Even though this language reformation is not "political" in the traditional modern sense of the term, its political importance seems clear. If language is where social code is destroyed and renewed, such a reformation of language is a political act.

For feminist theorists, and I think especially of Cixous and Irigaray, changing discursive habits requires more than simply putting new vocabulary into an old system; it absolutely necessitates experimenting with new ways of writing. Cixous and Irigaray not only encourage their readers to "write with the body," they themselves write in a language that has been repressed: a language that stays close to the digressive and dynamic powers of speech, a language with emphatic rhythms and syntactical catastrophes that open the thetic disposition of language, as postmodern narrative language does, to new power, affirmation, and delight in risk-taking. This language can be described as woman's language, in the sense that women who have been "the repressed of culture" may initially use and understand it better; but, like Kristeva, both Irigaray and Cixous explicitly insist that the definition of such language is finally cultural, not biological. Such language is a power available to anyone capable of exercising it and not a biologically determined property of one sex or the other.[19]

This statement by Irigaray on language, for example, would be at home in writing by Cortázar or other postmodern novelists:

> If we continue to speak the same language to each other, we will reproduce the same story. Begin the same stories all over again. Don't you feel it? Listen: men and women around us all sound the same. Same arguments, same quarrels, same scenes. Same attractions and separations. Same difficulties, the impossibility of reaching each other. Same . . . same . . . always the same. . . . This currency of alternatives and oppositions, choices and negotiations, has no value for us."[20]

This language takes risks with the syntax of things; it defies the language that, in everything from academic essays to political speeches to corporate reports, is still the "same . . . same . . . always the same" and that therefore holds in place a structure of discourse, a cultural formation that marginalizes, represses, and otherwise does violence to the powers valorized by postmodern writers. The "same stories" and the "same language" to tell them in may be habits found in recognizably gendered and domestic situ-

[19] At the beginning of her most famous essay, "The Laugh of the Medusa," Cixous says that the important thing for women is not biological destiny but *writing*, and she manages her discussion on language and writing in such a way as to avoid the biological bases that plague so many discussions of gender and language. Cixous's own writing collapses the dualisms that rivet our language in its old postures, including the dualism implied by terms like "women's" and "men's" writing, although this has sometimes been missed by those who do not see beyond Cixous's own use of these hard-to-avoid terms. In short, Cixous's own style actually confirms as it carries out the linguistic reformulation that is her subject. Kristeva treats the gendering of linguistic disposition as a cultural construction. This is not just a French insight. Mary Ellman noted some time ago, speaking of Ivy Compton-Burnett and others, that subtle undermining stylistic preciosity can be found in unorthodox writers of either sex (*Thinking About Women*, 1968).

[20] Irigaray, "When Our Lips Speak Together," p. 205.

ations, as Irigaray's description suggests, but these habits belong to a language of appropriation and grasp that we hear everywhere and from both sexes.

Both Irigaray and Cixous attempt to rewrite a psychiatric practice that tries to rationalize what cannot be rationalized. Both these women write a language worlds away from the conventional language of psychiatry: it is unofficial language, language that is part of a dialogue where there is room for the reader. Even Freud, perhaps the least objectionable of Freudians, by contrast takes a wholly different approach to the problem of writing. Even as he disclaims total knowledge, Freud accounts for everything in generalizations. His discourse is "objective," even including its humilities. It is *not* the language of experience, consciousness, therapy, play; it is the language of lawyers, documents, directions, signatures; it is scientific, reproducible, expert; it is generalizable, if not universal, and in the end this is what is so offensive about it, especially given the fact that his subject matter is psychic life. His language leaves no room for anyone else to speak. Authority speaks; no other voice is invited. To compare small things with great, this is the same language and the same voice we find, in matters of literature and interpretation, in the work of the New Critics. They talk about poetry the way Freud talks about neuroses. In both cases, poetry is repressed.

This reformulation does not simply reinstate digression at the expense of dialectics, any more than it reinstates "women's" writing at the expense of "men's": or at least it avoids these things to the extent that it seeks truly original solutions. And Cixous seems to favor truly original solutions. As Barbara Freeman has persuasively argued, Cixous's purpose is "to assert the inseparability of language and the body"—to define the body linguistically and language viscerally—and thus to collapse the mind-body dualism.[21] If what Cixous says really *isn't* essentialism, then it is shareable; it is not something that belongs to one gender, biologically conceived, but instead it is part of a culturally constructed language—my language, your language, his language, her language—that has been disrupted, ignored, and repressed. It may be that women know it best, for various reasons having to do with hegemonies of long duration, but this *disposition* of language, as Kristeva calls it, is just that—a culturally constructed disposition of language and hardly something "naturally" restricted to women.

The difference in writing that Cixous recommends—the inscription of *jouissance*, diffusion, doubleness—is precisely the difference that is made by postmodern narrative style (even as the gendering of the disposition obscures rather than illuminates these affinities). In the following passage

[21] Barbara Freeman, "Plus corps donc plus écriture: Hélène Cixous and the mind-body problem," in *Paragraph* 11, no. 1 (March 1988), pp. 65, 63.

from *The Newly Born Woman* (Hélène Cixous and Betsy Wing) I have changed the usual English translation of "she" to "it" for purposes of argument:

> [It] has never stayed "in place"; explosion, diffusion, effervescence, abundance, [it] takes pleasure (jouit) in being limitless, outside of [it]self, outside of the same, far from any "center."[22]

As altered, the passage describes a disposition of language. To what extent has it been culturally gendered, severed from its symbolic sibling, stamped with the "female" identity, made into a form of private enterprise? What is it exactly that enables us to work/labor (in) the in-between, to interrogate "the process of the same and of the other without which nothing can live"? Is it women only who want to escape being "fixed in sequences of struggle and expulsion or some other form of death," and who want instead to be "infinitely dynamized by an incessant exchange from one subject to another"? (Cixous, "Laugh," p. 883). What do these important formulations mean, not only for an advance-guard cadre of theorists but for persons at large, pedestrians in Western cities whose daily usages are not, presumably, merely backdrop to a finite drama of opposition but the ground of reiteration or change? When Cixous speaks of the "desire to write . . . to live inside . . . a desire for the belly, for language, for blood" (p. 891), she use metaphors that *can* be assimilated broadly; however, taken exclusively as descriptions of the biological female function, they simply lapse back into the uncontested transcendence that goes with any naturalization of critical terms and thus recapitulate one of the oldest reflexes of the discourse of structure and centrality, *arche* and *eschaton*, appropriation and grasp, history and project.

Where and when does the identification of body and language drop the gendered dualism that reinstates an old essentialism in a new disguise? To say that body and language become one, if this is really to be taken seriously, is to say that language is constitutive; it is to say that language *is* the enterprise, not a secondary reflection of it. It is to commit oneself once and for all to language and to disrupt all distinctions based on biological and metaphysical determinations, abandoning them completely in favor of a new set of multilevel possibilities where the old dualisms and their contests simply do not apply. It may be that the courage to do so has become a matter of survival, one that goes far beyond either women's practice or academic discourse. To insist on terms like "masculine" and "feminine," "women's" and "men's," "maternal" and "paternal" is to insist on gendering dispositions that have been established by the repressions and acceptances of both sexes. Such binaristic and dialectical terms do not rescue

---

[22] Cited in Freeman, "Plus corps donc," p. 63. I am indebted to Barbara Freeman, both in this article and in conversation, for suggesting this illustration.

discourse from transcendence. If we are really looking for a new language, we need to reformulate (using Freeman's words) "the very ways in which categories such as 'corporeal' and 'metaphorical' are thought" (p. 66). Such an effort may even contribute to an end to gendering of the discourse altogether and perhaps begin a new attempt to find a process that can sustain without anarchy the power to proliferate possibilities, the power to diversify and rename old habits, the power to play.

If, as I argue, Cixous's description of "feminine" language describes the usage of postmodern novelists, a usage found quite far from explicitly feminist writing, then one of two things follows. Either these values or formations belonging exclusively to women are gaining ground as women gain ground (*if* they are gaining ground) or else a permanent disposition of language is changing its gender definition or even ceasing to be gendered. Postmodern writing operates in the context of the latter alternative, as it operates beyond various other sorts of dualism (see Part Three, II). To speak of the language of the body, in other words, far from being a way to maintain gender distinctions, instead undoes them with a new emphasis on embodied language. Such language has a rhythm or impulse, an immediacy, an "impetus," to use Breton's word; it functions without the authoritative, objective voice and quite differently from the supposedly neutral instrument with which people of affairs exchange information. It is a disposition that is available to anyone willing and able to assume it. In the terms of former phallogocentric discourse, postmodern writing is "feminine" just as the demand for rational control is "masculine." But what is really at stake here? Not biology, surely, but the demands of discourse on questionable-subjects-in-process. The inexorable demand for public speech—for the language of "rationality"—enforces on all speakers what amounts to a taboo on personal or individual speech, a taboo on the admission of feeling, of fear, of hostility, of love, of need. Where one's "I" must be defined only in rational terms, one's "I" becomes deranged, and this process of derangement begins with the earliest processes of learning language. Women's theoretical writing thus extends the critique of Western metaphysics right into linguistic practice and raises the question, how does one incorporate the powers that we have depreciated? Pursuing a new writing means providing ways to respect and to value the power of passibility and the power to digress or to differ—even to the point of eradicating the "same" as a value; it means to live a new practice by taking up a new residence in a language. This is what takes true courage in our culture; this is the truly radical subversion: to unrepress these powers where they have been repressed, not just in individuals but in the social body itself and in its speech.

Whether postmodern writers are men or women, theorists or novelists, their language changes the world by changing the very tools of thought. This effort avoids the profound mistake that so often undermines efforts at social, cultural, or personal change: the mistake of supposing that cultural formations—sexism, feminism, postmodernism, or for that matter socialism or capitalism—are primarily matters of intellectual formulation. It is only in concrete, material, immediate forms that the embedded practices of a cultural formation may be found. It would be the most serious mistake for feminist or any theory to engage patriarchal and logocentric cultural formations abstractly, in the same way theory has always engaged it, just as it would be the most serious mistake for novelists to go on writing the same forms and the same language, "the same . . . same . . . always the same," as if writing is, to use Cortázar's words, "a pretext for the transmission of a 'message' (there is no message, only messengers, and that is the message, just as love is the one who loves)" (*Hopscotch*, chap. 79). Before the exercise of postmodern language, in novels or elsewhere, there is, as Robbe-Grillet says, "nothing—no certainty, no thesis, no message. To believe that the novelist 'has something to say' and that he then looks for a way to say it represents the gravest of misconceptions. For it is precisely this 'way,' this manner of speaking, which constitutes his enterprise as a writer, an enterprise more obscure than any other, and which will later be the uncertain content of his book. Ultimately it is perhaps this uncertain content of an obscure enterprise of form which will best serve the cause of freedom" (*For a New Novel*, pp. 141–42).

In the discourse of dialectics, metaphysics, and phallogocentrism language functions mainly as a rational instrument, conceived by transcendent subjectivity to serve a discourse that hypostatizes the body of the world itself, converting its impenetrable mysteries into a realm of projected consciousness and intention. Material existence in such a context becomes porous, distinct from mere bodies and, perhaps, even a little immortal. Such language and abstractions distract attention from the mortality of bodies and the materiality of language. In resisting such dangerous deflections Derrida, Kristeva, Cixous, Irigaray, Cortázar, Duras, Robbe-Grillet, Nabokov, Hawkes, and a large illustrious company of other writers defy these conventions of what Kristeva calls "symbolic" language that estrange us from the embodied world, most especially from our embodiment in language, and thus distract attention from that all-important finitude. Irigaray's comment, "Truth is necessary for those who are so distanced from their body that they have forgotten it" ("When Our Lips Speak Together," in *This Sex*, p. 214), applies as well to language, which has material existence and is not a forgettable neutrality.

Section II: *Della Figura* (Time and the Figure)

By collapsing the distance between language and putative referent, by insisting on the play of language as itself constitutive and substantial, postmodern writers do away with the transcendental subject position, and with historical time, the medium of that human transcendence. The problems this creates for readers' habits extend well into the arena of belief and commitment, as those hostile to postmodernism are instinctively aware even when they understand little about the agendas that inform such writing. This section attempts two things: first, to sketch the broad implications of this collapse of transcendence in language, and second, to introduce in place of the representational norm of "image" a new postmodern norm of "figure" to describe the postmodern narrative sequence in which time and consciousness are one with language.

First, the implications of collapsed transcendence. What interests me here is a certain *effect* of semiotic writing that explains its popularity with postmodern novelists, in particular, its tendency to collapse the dualisms between life and art, form and content, primary and secondary text, and the one between subject and object that support representational narrative and language.[23] This collapse serves the not very new idea that "reality" is a construct, that material and mental worlds are less distinguishable than they may appear. A building, to take an obvious example, is both steel and idea, both a given material object and an invention. By pursuing this insight further than ever, postmodern writing denaturalizes constructs like "object" or "self" or "history" that depend on conventional referential usages where it is assumed that language points toward an other, transcendental "reality" that is not language and not constructed. Postmodern writing exchanges "depth," a preeminent value of history, for "surface," and most of all the surfaces of language as they inscribe and reinscribe (or not) discourse in practice. This change introduces a new problematic in place of an old one: in Craig Owens's words, "how to conceive difference without opposition."[24] Owens is formulating the feminist problematic, and the fact

[23] This habit of dualistic distinctions belongs to much older traditions than that of historical conventions as they were conceived after the fifteenth century. Margaret Homans, for example, traces to the root of Western discourse this penchant for dualism and its inevitable production of hierarchy. She concentrates on romanticism and its relation to "the Judaeo-Christian tradition of language" with its discourse of appropriation and mastery. "It is typical of the Judaeo-Christian tradition of language," she writes, speaking of Ralph Waldo Emerson, "that his thoughts should run from poetry to centrality and rule." In that tradition the concept of "center" and "centrality," formations important to Derrida's analyses, stimulates a desire to be at the center, generates hierarchical thinking. But even, and perhaps most insidiously of all, the potentially neutral concept of dualistic opposition also turns into hierarchy because it is impossible ever to be entirely disinterested; one element must be primary and the other secondary ("The Masculine Tradition," in *Women Writers and Poetic Identity: Dorothy Wordsworth, Emily Brontë, and Emily Dickinson* [Princeton: Princeton University Press, 1980], pp. 31–32, 36–39). The unstable dualisms that produce dialectics and all its historical and hierarchical baggage belong to a long tradition of objectification traceable to Plato. Postmodern writing accomplishes its subversion of representational agendas by undermining that tradition.

[24] The critique of binarism, in Owens's words, is "an intellectual imperative, since the hi-

that it could stand as well for postmodern writing indicates the close alliance between the two.

The dualism between life and art is a powerful representational instrument. If we posit a difference between what is invented and what is "real," then we can automatically assume the existence of this thing we call "real" life. This distinction also makes it possible to assume that "real life" has nothing to do with what is invented: nothing to do, that is, with imagination or invention, suffering and endurance, even enjoyment or pleasure. A similar move, positing a distinction between fiction and reality, confines fiction to a secondary role and privileges a vision of "reality" purified as much as possible of such things as "fiction." If art and life differ, it follows that art is not life (that is, something negatively defined—the discredited half of this dualism). This view of the relation between art and life is the one that prevails in our social and political system, where, at least until recently, art has been keep under strict surveillance and policed off the preserve of serious business, which is to say, the empirical world of the schedule and the bottom line. This is not without reason. Hostility to art belongs to this habit of attention by which "life" is purged of imagination; and hostility to art can be expressed in subtle ways, even including the treatment of art as a commodity.[25]

When we posit, as postmodern narrative does, that reality is a construct, we have at one stroke collapsed the dualism between "reality" and "fiction" and introduced ourselves to an entirely new universe of problem solving. There is no longer a stable, immutable, "natural" external referent or objectifier beyond our formulations to take responsibility for what is, after all, only our construction. We can no longer leave the difficult discursive accommodations and resolutions to naturalized entities like Society or The Market or The System, as if those fictional entities were "objectifiers" or cosmic guarantors. It now appears that we have constructed Society, The Market, and The System and are solely responsible for them. The postmodern fact is that our discourse, our terms, our norms for knowing and judging are inventions, constructions, orchestrations in a void. Our norms for knowing and our terms for judgment, in other words, are entirely, and for want of a better word, aesthetic.

Postmodern writing subverts the distinction between fiction and reality by *internalizing* it, thereby casting "reality" as a fictional mode and dem-

---

erarchical opposition of marked and unmarked terms . . . is the dominant form both of representing difference and justifying its subordination in our society" ("Feminists and Postmodernism," in Hal Foster, ed., *The Anti-Aesthetic*, 1983, p. 62).

[25] On the art "market" see Martha Rosler, "Lookers, Buyers, Dealers, and Makers: Thoughts on Audience," in Brian Wallis, ed., *Art After Modernism: Rethinking Representation* (New York: The New Museum of Contemporary Art, with David Godine, Boston: 1984), pp. 311–39.

onstrating that the very distinction between fictional and real is an artifice: one way of arranging relationships, like any other. Postmodern narrative at all levels of magnitude is an art of parallel structure that calls attention to its own subtexts and hence to its arbitrary and constructed nature, thus collapsing any "distance" that it might establish between itself and some "reality" beyond it. The semiotic play in the sequence of the text is a primary, not a secondary, activity. In this play of language each element has a parastructural relation to the others; each element comments on the others, revealing by comparison the self-contained and arbitrary nature of every formulation. Parody, for example, is a way of seeing double: seeing both the formulation, the single structure, and at the same time seeing beyond it. We see the figural entity and we see it *as* figural. From the sentence to the overall arrangement the postmodern novel forks and reforks, like fate in *Lolita*: at every level of magnitude an art of parallel structure.

To take for the present one small example, *Ada* begins with this sentence, supposedly a quotation:

> "All happy families are more or less dissimilar; all unhappy ones are more or less alike," says a great Russian writer in the beginning of a famous novel (*Anna Arkadievitch Karenina*, transfigured into English by R. G. Stonelower, Mount Tabor Ltd., 1880).

The allusion to *Anna Karenina* entirely reverses Tolstoy's language in that novel's first sentence, which reads: "All happy families resemble one another, but each unhappy family is unhappy in its own way." By inverting Tolstoy's first line Nabokov parodically engages Tolstoy's novel as a context for his own, but with a *difference*. Next we are left wondering what "Tolstoy" we actually are talking about when the translator who has "transfigured" it into English bears a name suggestive of the crudest sort of work. Then any question of similarity and difference disappears abruptly as the passage continues, claiming that, in any case, this opening pronouncement "has little if anything to do with the story to be unfolded now, a family chronicle." All this "play" is relevant in the sense that *Ada* takes place in sight of the great realist predecessor precisely so as to depart from it. Another, more "lit-crit" way of saying this is to say that *parody is the ironic mode of intertextuality*, the shadowed form being constantly undermined by the activity of the other one. A problem with describing the action of parody is that it is hard to avoid giving the appearance that one is explaining a good joke, as this paragraph demonstrates.

The kind of perpetual digression that occurs in this passage keeps attention focused in more than one place at a time. On the one hand, there is the putative plot line; on the other, there is the digressive play where the real action is, which remains (using Kristeva's definition of the semiotic disposition of language) "definitely heterogeneous to meaning but always in sight of it" (*Desire in Language*, p. 133). Paratactic, parodic, paralogical writing operates simultaneously in more than one mode, and once such multiplication has taken place, we depart from the Euclidean universe of unity, identity, center, and enter the non-Euclidean universe of pattern, superimposition, and differential function. Instead of continuity we have leaps in space, instead of linear time we have time warps that "superimpose one part of the pattern upon another" (Nabokov, *Speak Memory*, p. 139).[26]

[26] Both Lyotard (*The Postmodern Condition*) and Hutcheon (*Poetics of Postmodernism*) have identified "paralogic" and "parody" as postmodern forms, although for very different reasons. Parody is hard to discuss because its subtle works require more extensive literary explication than is undertaken by either of these theoretical treatments or, for that matter, by the present argument. There are, for example, many ways in which the text undermines itself with laughter; the parodic or paralogical effect in Robbe-Grillet's *Jealousy*, for example, differs considerably from those in, say, Hawkes's *Blood Oranges* or García Márquez's *Chronicle of a Death Foretold*.

My argument diverges from Hutcheon's on the general estimate of parody, which she claims operates in the realm of representation and thus means that parody operates so as to question and even salvage representation. Her intention, however, is to oppose Baudrillard's claim that parody operates in the realm of simulation (it lacks historical specificity and increasingly loses difference, generalization, and equivalence), and other claims that depreciate postmodernism and its parody, and in this more restricted sense our arguments converge. Parody makes subjectivity, narrativity, knowledge sites for questioning.

Hutcheon's argument, like others relying on architectural postmodernism for their definitions, underestimates the historical scope of the difference postmodernism makes. It is debatable whether postmodern parody in architecture is a way of acknowledging the cultural amnesia produced by the razing effects of modernism (was the razing of buildings to create modern ones a demolition of past tradition or merely a consolidation of that tradition's implicit values such that its particulars were no longer needed because its essence could now be fully expressed?). Modernist literature certainly retains the main category of historical time, and in that sense it produced the reverse of cultural amnesia. In razing detail, it can be argued, modernism mythologized and naturalized the structures that bore those details and in which those details had their representational value. Modern discourse in its broad scope was, after all, the discourse that produced belief in general laws and in the power of generalization and rationalization that made all details porous.

Charles Jencks's "double-coding" is a good definition of postmodernism, but again his practical concerns with architecture limit the scope of definition to recent decades (*What Is Postmodernism?*, p. 15). But this commitment to a definition raises long-term historical questions reaching well beyond the period Jencks has in mind. It was precisely such a doubling of the system that was accomplished by the Reformation, and especially for my purposes the historically minded Reformation of transalpine humanism that began construction on historicism in the first place. Henry VIII's declaration of religious sovereignty definitely doubled the system; and one way of thinking about the era since is to regard it as a protracted experiment with the implications of that moment. Paul Ricoer mentions the threat this doubling presents in cultural terms, although the question remains as to how new this is; one must "acknowledge the end of a sort of cultural monopoly. . . . Suddenly it becomes possible that there are just *others*, that we ourselves are an 'other' among others. All meaning and every goal having disappeared, it becomes possible to wander through civilizations as if through vestiges and ruins" in an "interminable, aimless voyage." Quoted from "Civilization and National Cultures," p. 278, in Craig Owens, "Feminism and Postmodernism," pp. 57–58.

Jencks, like Deleuze and Guattari, Baudrillard, Jameson and others, also invokes schizo-

In terms that would be at home in Breton or Cortázar, Nabokov praises Gogol's style for its production of unrationalizable experience and its departure from the norms of objectivity, history, and representation.

> Gogol's world is somewhat related to such conceptions of modern physics as the "Concertina Universe" or the "Explosion Universe"; it is far removed from the comfortably revolving clockwork worlds of the last century. . . . We will find in *The Overcoat* shadows linking our state of existence to those other states and modes which we dimly apprehend in our rare moments of irrational perception. The prose of Pushkin is three-dimensional; that of Gogol is four-dimensional, at least. He may be compared to his contemporary, the mathematician Lobachevsky, who blasted Euclid and discovered a century ago many of the theories which Einstein later developed. If parallel lines do not meet it is not because meet they cannot, but because they have other things to do. (*Gogol*, pp. 144–45)

Although Gogol, Nabokov, Breton, and Magritte did not declare themselves a "school," their writings have strong family resemblances. To give the gist of such non-Euclidean texts as the one Nabokov describes would be pointless because the plot "lies in the style"; what "happens" takes place at the level of language, in other words, at the level where discourse and social codes take shape, not in more transcendent places having to do with "fact," "event," or "information." These agendas in Nabokov's Gogol essay (published in 1944) have much in common with those of surrealism, a movement that had reached verbal expression in Breton's manifestoes only fifteen years before the period of 1938–40 when Nabokov lived in Paris on the rue Boileau.

In addition to the dualism between life and art, postmodern narrative language also collapses another familiar bulwark of representational language and discourse: the dualism between form and content. Like the distinction between life and art, this one establishes transcendence by displacing from the arena of specificity and concreteness some putative substance or essence. Form is the mere means for grasping the "content" that is "in" it, in the same way that "truth" always transcends any particular, always remaining elsewhere as the source and end of effort.[27] The practices of

---

phrenia as a metaphor for postmodernism: a troubling move for various reasons, not least because as a definition of sickness it invokes the discourse that created it. See Gilles Deleuze and Felix Guattari, *Anti-Oedipus: Capitalism and Schizophrenia*, trans. Robert Hurley, Mark Seem, and Peter R. Lane (New York: Viking, 1977); Baudrillard's uses of the term for the "new state of things," in "The Ecstasy of Communication," in Hal Foster, ed., *The Anti-Aesthetic*, p. 132; and Jameson, "Postmodernism, or the Cultural Logic of Late Capitalism," pp. 53–92.

[27] Derrida discriminates play from the "classical" way of coping with this constructed problem, which is to invoke quantitative temporal considerations (i.e., essentially history as I describe it in *Realism and Consensus*). See Kristeva's argument concerning "becoming" in "From One Identity to An Other."

putatively neutral literary study have contributed much to sustaining this dualism of form and content, a local subcontract of the broader dualism between so-called reality (content, substance, Being, truth, "natural," and supposedly unconstructed things-as-in-themselves-they-really-are) on the one hand and, on the other, literature (imaginative writing, form, art, style). Again, despite disclaimers, such literary study reduces language to meaning, thereby reinforcing the separation of form and content and, in the process, destroying the very thing that, in Kristeva's terms, "makes of what is known as 'literature' something other than knowledge: the very place where social code is destroyed and renewed."[28] The postmodern resistance to distinctions between form and content thus belongs to the general attempt to reduce transcendence and to take up the practical consequences and opportunities of that effort.

Postmodern writing, as Robbe-Grillet says of art, "endures no servitude of this kind." The new novel "contains nothing, in the strict sense of the term"; it is not a box, not a "brilliantly colored envelope" containing an author's "message," not "a sauce that makes the fish go down easier. Art endures no servitude of this kind, nor any other pre-established function." Nothing is more absurd than the critical praise, " 'X has something to say and says it well.' "[29] This inseparability in art between the "what" and the "how" is what gives art its freedom and its power, as Robbe-Grillet says in the passage (part of it appears as the epigraph to Part Three of this book):

> Political life ceaselessly obliges us to assume certain known significations: social, historical, moral. Art is more modest—or more ambitious: in art, nothing is ever known in advance.
>
> Before the work of art there is nothing—no certainty, no thesis, no message. To believe that the novelist "has something to say" and that he then looks for a way to say it represents the gravest of misconceptions. For it is precisely this "way," this manner of speaking, which constitutes his enterprise as a writer, an enterprise more obscure than any other, and which will later be the uncertain content of his book. Ultimately it is perhaps this uncertain content of an obscure enterprise of form which will best serve the cause of freedom. But who knows how long that will take? (*For a New Novel*, pp. 141–42)

[28] "While poetic language can indeed be studied through its meaning . . . such a study would, in the final analysis, amount to reducing it to the phenomenological perspective and, hence, failing to see what in the poetic function departs from the signified and the transcendental ego and makes of what is known as 'literature' something other than knowledge: the very place where social code is destroyed and renewed" (*Desire in Language*, p. 132).

[29] Postmodern form is "invention and not formula," as Robbe-Grillet says. "There are not, for a writer, two possible ways to write the same book. When he thinks of a future novel, it is always a *way of writing* which first of all occupies his mind, and demands his hand" (*For a New Novel*, pp. 44–47).

The writer does not first have a message and then find a vehicle. This "gravest of misconceptions" accounts for the popularity of certain writers whose predictability, in Robbe-Grillet's or Nabokov's or Breton's terms, is fundamentally immoral. What any artist has is a language, and an "uncertain enterprise of form," that precedes all other forms and is their basis. And a novel is a specific practice of a more general power of writing in the sense, as Cortázar puts it, that "everything is writing": agriculture, sculpture, literature, pisciculture, "all the tures of this world" (*Hopscotch*, chap. 73). For a reader to "straighten out" the abrupt shifts and irreducible contradictions of a postmodern narrative, or to destroy a digression with a clarification of its (ready-made) "meaning," would be to override the chief purpose of the writing.

A third and final dualism collapsed in postmodern narrative is one with vast political and social reverberations, especially in the United States: the dualism between primary and secondary texts. The question of "Why text?" has already been addressed in the preface. Yet there are profound extensions of the faith in textuality that need to be recognized, especially when the possibility of "a text" is so much in question. The whole practice and profession of literary commentary—what most English professors do when they "write" and at least in part what I am doing now—is based on a division of primary and secondary texts wherein the primary text acts as a sort of stand-in transcendence, an unquestioned given—like "Shakespeare" or "Goethe" or the New Testament—the value of which is taken for granted as an almost natural norm, a given, an essential "truth" that may be interpreted by an infinite play of substitutions but is itself beyond the need for justification.

The practice of literary interpretation, however, is only one version of this dualism between primary and secondary texts. In a constitutionally based political order, public order itself theoretically depends on the "right" or "proper" or "sound" construction of a set of fundamental texts which, like "Shakespeare," are given a special status as unquestioned texts. There is, says Foucault, "scarcely a society without its major narratives . . . formulae, texts," in other words, without some form of those "basic" readings that E. D. Hirsch wants to be sure we all "know." However, the purpose of such founding texts, and thus the purpose of the commentary that confirms them, is to perpetuate a structure, not to confirm its more specific values (for example, maintaining "community" or the like). Foucault's point is important because it focuses on the way in which commentary forecloses on the very surprise or chance element, the very risk-taking power so valued by surrealists and their postmodern successors:

> Commentary averts the chance element of discourse by giving it its due; it gives us the opportunity to say something other than the text itself, *but on condition*

that it is this text itself which is uttered and, in some ways finalized [or "ruined" in Derrida's terms]. The open multiplicity, the fortuitousness, is transferred, by the principle of commentary, from what is liable to be said to . . . the circumstances of repetition.[30]

Legal commentary, a sort of ultimate textual criticism, has a special status and importance in the United States for institutions and citizens alike, especially at the level of the Supreme Court, the last resort of law. Postmodern narrative, by making readers co-authors of the text in the sense that their acts of attention belong to the "text," undermines the distinction between primary (author's) text and secondary (reader's) text. The transcendent "primary" (which is to say, nearly "natural") text, be it *Ecclesiastes*, *Othello*, or Article 1 of the U.S. Constitution, maintains the distinction between primary and secondary that consigns most writing to the latter, less important, less responsible status. Without the transcendent Text, all writing must justify itself and cannot hide from that necessity in the free zones that sacred texts create.

This revision of basic reading habits obviously has certain other implications as well for those who teach language and interpretation. In a language practice where the semiotic function is fully restored, the conventional practices of literary interpretation become impossible, their questions moot. Postmodern language would make such a difference to interpretive (as of many other) practices that I will not attempt a summary here but only a brief speculation. We could imagine, for instance, that instead of talking about things like form and content, or discursive "meaning," or the fourfold distinction between author, audience, work, and world (an appallingly bald application of undiluted Aristotle to unsuspecting young minds), postmodern interpreters would, at the least, be talking about language and its surprises (or lack of them), the presence of messengers instead of messages, the play of the sequence, the nature of the series, the status of reading consciousness or acts of attention, and what it means for an interpreter "to write."

The collapse of these and other dualisms in postmodern writing makes room for a doubling process that operates not as exclusive and totalizing dualisms but as play. Postmodern "doubling" thus pluralizes every arrangement and every system, which are thus constantly shadowed by not one but two, and if two, possibly three or four, and on through the potential mathematical series to infinity. But this pluralization is nothing at all like the "pluralism" or relativism of nineteenth-century discourse, a difference often misunderstood. While physics is beyond the scope of my present argument, the quantum universe does offer especially interesting anal-

---

[30] Foucault, *The Discourse on Language*, published together with *The Archaeology of Knowledge*, trans. A. M. Sheridan Smith (London: Tavistock, 1972), p. 221; italics mine.

ogies with my argument about language and time. The doubled identity of wave and particle, for instance, where "it" moves from one identity to an other (Kristeva's title keeps asserting itself), depending on its phase, has been described by a British physicist in temporal terms: waves (the future) change to particles (the past) right "now" (present), making the "present" always a moment of this particular mutation or doubling of identity.[31] There is an important corollary here, too, in that the doubling activity that does not involve classical "identity" does *not* involve Either/Or choices but instead maintains an improvisatory equilibrium between determinate and indeterminate and, in discursive terms, between meaning and nonsense, symbolic and semiotic, plot and play.[32]

Improvisatory equilibrium between one state and another incorporates what has been sundered; it joins, for example, what Kristeva calls the symbolic and semiotic dispositions of language. Andrea Nye calls this double activity "perilous," and it is; probably that accounts for its vitality.[33] Like Kristeva, Irigaray considers the semiotic or playful half of this doubled process—that is, this doubleness without dualism, this alterability without

[31] Clark, *Einstein*, p. 345. "Everything that has already happened is particles, everything in the future is waves," states Sir Lawrence Bragg, director of the Royal Institution. "The advancing sieve of time coagulates waves into particles at the moment 'now.' "

[32] See Werner Heisenberg, *Physics and Philosophy: The Revolution in Modern Science* (New York: Harper & Row, 1962); and Deborah Morsink, "Indeterminacy: 'La Folie du Jour,' " chap. 4 in her "Science and the Literary Text: Readings of Blanchot's Fiction" (work in progress).

[33] Andrea Nye speaks of "her perilous, simultaneous, participation in and subversion of symbolic structures"; she describes Kristeva's *jouissance* in terms that sound very much like what I am calling parody: "not the joy of a communion in which there are no boundaries but the perverse laugh of someone who knows the clay feet of any male idol" (*Feminist Theory and the Philosophies of Man* [New York: Routledge, 1988], p. 207); also see Nye on Irigaray, pp. 200–201.

Improvisation can modify "normal" language in ineffable ways. An accessible example is Garrison Keillor's rendition of "Tell Me Why the Ivy Twines," on the televised edition of "Prairie Home Companion" of 1 August 1987. This is a widely familiar song: "popular" in the deprecatory sense of that word. Keillor's version, however, was a work of genius and an instance of the healing powers of collective improvisation, construction, multilevel thinking. Standing alone on the stage, he got the audience to sing the well-known first verse (with women doing the "beautiful descant"). Then and without a word he began a second verse that everybody soon joined, singing in the same music the pledge of allegiance (the audience putting together things that didn't normally go together, without being either satirical or "serious" in the sense of having "meaning"). Next he began a verse (it turned out to be a solo) that was to the same music but using the language of airline emergency instructions: "In case of a decrease in cabin pressure" clear through to "breathe normally." Having been thus put on notice, the audience rallied with the next verse; they all knew what to do without a single word of direction, having already grasped the code and needing only the specific cue, which in this case was the prayer, "now I lay me down to sleep." Finally Keillor began the last verse of "Ivy Twines" ("Because God made. . . .")—something that by this time sounded positively, even thunderously new. One might say, if the hermeneutical vocabulary were not so clumsy an instrument for such an event, that it was an act of estrangement that produced renewal.

disperson, this flexibility of category and boundary—as a gender-constructed disposition of language. The repressed of culture are thus profoundly linked with what Stephen Tyler in an elegant phrase calls the "absent potentialities" of discourse, which we can trace back to Saussure's "paradigmatic" or associative ordering which he opposes to the syntagmatic (*Course in General Linguistics*, pp. 123–24). The paradigmatic element, the capacity for alterability, the "absent potentialities" of discourse are the other worlds that, in Nabokov's words, "surround us always."[34]

The emphasis on *practices*, which is one of the most radical powers of both postmodernism and feminism, throws renewed emphasis on speech acts and on the enacted, performative aspect of languages. The emergence of alternative forms—of religion, of culture, of linguistic and habitual usages that remain theoretically unconjugated—are inaccessible by theory alone.[35] To take a salient instance, feminism has provided much more than theoretical alternatives, and its practical experiments bear on new definitions of subjectivity as well as of child care. In Huyssen's words:

> It was especially the art, writing, film making and criticism of women and minority artists with their recuperation of buried and mutilated traditions, their emphasis on exploring forms of gender-and race-based subjectivity in aesthetic productions and experiences, and their refusal to be limited to standard canonizations, which added a whole new dimension to the critique of high modernism and to the emergence of alternative forms of culture.[36]

The importance of practice in postmodernism casts a new light on the depreciation of speech in both Saussure and, following him, Derrida—a depreciation not without its patriarchal point, as Nye cogently observes:

> Feminist critique of a masculine symbolic showed that attention must always be paid to the terms in which we think about what we are doing. It also revealed something about theory itself. Liberalism, Marxism, existentialism and psychoanalysis, tried to make sense of the concrete historical situation of men by searching for origins—of society, consciousness, personality. Some universal constant would rule the variety of cultural and political practice. Lacan's Law of the Father was instantiated in natural law, economic law, Oedipal structures. The phallus,

[34] Tyler, *The Unspeakable*, p. 22. Tyler summarizes usefully as follows the differentiation between syntagmatic and paradigmatic: "Syntagmatic orderings consist in the linear sequence of signs where each sign acquires its value in opposition to preceding and following signs in discourse. Paradigmatic orderings are nonlinear and are formed outside of discourse. They are associated with relations which are not present in the discourse itself. They are absent potentialities, mnemonic wholes in the inner storehouse of ideas that make up language."

[35] See Ermarth, "Feminist Theory as a Practice," in Elizabeth Meese and Alice Parker, eds., *Theorizing Feminist Writing Practices* (London: John Benjamins, 1991).

[36] Huyssen, "Mapping the Postmodern," in Nicholson, ed., *Feminism/Postmodernism*, p. 250.

centre of meaning, became man's identity with himself. 'Man is competitive', 'man is productive', 'man is subject', 'man is Oedipus'—each in turn became the self-evident starting point from which social, economic and psychological theory was derived.

Feminism, in short, reveals "the symbolic form of the philosophy of man" and, Nye continues, it "suggests a new direction for feminist thought. Not only may yet another theory devised by men to rationalise men's activities be rejected as inadequate, but theory itself, as a search for self-present origins" (and deductive laws), is called into question. Feminist theorists have also searched for origins, but these explanations, while they have offered partial illumination of women's problem, "also obscured the various practices, contemporary and historical, Western and non-Western, that might yield new feminist concepts, values and knowledge. Although a deconstruction of the text of patriarchy may be needed to clear the way for these new ideas, a feminine counter-text can only offer a mirror image of masculinist thought" (*Feminist Theory*, pp. 217–18). My point, in collaboration with these theories, is that the emergence of alternate forms (a better word is "series") itself becomes a form (series) in postmodern writing (this is not at all the same thing as the nineteenth-century presentation of shifting form within the constant form of historical time), and this accounts for postmodernism's emphasis on multiple *voices*.

The distinction between speech and writing may itself be a fundamental dualism that postmodern writing works to collapse. Certainly the play in speech between separate but parallel communicating "levels" of language has obvious importance for the new writing. The indeterminacy in language that Paul Friedrich calls "poetry" is not confined to writing but is the condition of language fully sounded and active in speech where its indeterminacy is irreducible. For Friedrich (a linguist, anthropologist, and poet), "poetry" is a term that describes a zone of language, emotion, and cognitive awareness that is "variable, unpredictable, and dynamic" and "significantly beyond the scope of exhaustive description and accurate prediction." Language can be seen as "*rough drafts* for poetry" and "an infinitude of used poems waiting to be molded into new realities as one determines, and fails to determine, the degree and direction to which one will be influenced by them." Friedrich finds in New England dialect, for example, the rhythms of Robert Frost's beloved Horace. The relation between poetic and so-called natural language, in other words, "is not cyclical but rather that of two imperfectly parallel streams, which sometimes are almost out of earshot of each other and sometimes converge."[37] The mul-

[37] *The Language Parallax: Linguistic Relativism and Poetic Indeterminacy* (Austin: University of Texas Press, 1986), pp. 23, 2, 33, 27. Friedrich's argument "presupposes this variable, unpredictable, and dynamic zone, and assumes, in part, that the emotions and motives and

tivocality of postmodernism presses readers for their collaborative addition, something very close to their voice, or at least to a voicedness, and
the emphasis on sound is appropriate when one considers that, in Tyler's
words, "hearing and speaking, in fact, require the simultaneous integration
of paradigmatic and syntagmatic" (p. 23), although it is worth repeating
from an earlier argument that Tyler's "dialogic" is not an adequate word
for what's new. He invokes rhetoric and its artful style because it torpedoes
the "plain style" that "above all else, seeks to erode the presence of the
speaker by eliminating all marks of individuality that speak of the speaker's
difference from the text" (p. 7). This point works illuminatingly with Cixous's emphasis on the lost voice of women, on the difference it makes, and
on the difficulty of speaking in a context where that difference is unvalued
and unacknowledged.[38]

The collapse of these dualisms and other variants on which we rely (for
example, public and private, or between Us [present company] and Them
[politicians, blacks, women, communists, republicans, the neighbors])
transforms the interpretive situation in many ways, not least of which is
the new role of readers as newly self-conscious construction workers, co-
creators of the text. Readers of postmodern writing have no alternative but
to accept the postmodern fact of language as a determining and determinate experience in which the arbitrary, rhythmic, always-subjective process
of thematic substitution constitutes the temporal series. We can no longer
think in the old terms of time and subjectivity and language as separate
entities; we must accept them as dimensions of a single process. The nature
of the sequence in postmodern narrative thus becomes a point of utmost
interest because it is in the management of that sequence that time and
subjectivity take their definition.[39]

This brings me to the second point of this section: the justification for

---

even the cognitive world of a human being are significantly beyond the scope of exhaustive
description and accurate prediction. I have called this indeterminacy "poetic". . . . The present
formulation seeks a balance between the (relativist) determinacy of structure and the (poetic)
indeterminacy of the individual who participates in that structure actively and passively" (p.
2). The arguments of French feminism make a full, if unacknowledged, precedent for this,
although agreement between their usages is problematic because of Friedrich's unquestioning
use of "structure" and "individual," which, I take it, indeterminacy effectively denies from
sheer inability to make the kind of definition such terms require.

[38] On women speaking see Cixous, "Laugh of the Medusa." On Derrida's depreciation of
speech, see Tyler, *The Unspeakable*, pp. 19–20: "What Derrida does not make clear in his
deconstruction of the signified is that speech is the other [that] writing invents in order to
give itself an origin and thus to legitimize itself as the mark of civilization"; and Spanos,
Repetitions, p. 246: Derrideans valorize "writing (*écriture*) as the agency of the free play that
is the imperative of decentered authorship. But the speech they criticize on the authority of
Derrida is a philosophical idea, an abstraction of discourse."

[39] Foucault makes his primary objective the description and differentiation of series in
"L'Ordre du discours," translated by A. M. Sheridan Smith as "The Discourse on Language."

using the term *figure* for the norms of postmodern, as distinct from representational, narrative. The term *figure* (in classical and medieval usage, *figura*) has considerable value in reconceiving the narrative sequence in postmodern terms because it somehow suggests the twist, the network, the crossing line, the two-dimensional flatness, the arbitrary and yet perfectly balanced arrangement possible outside classical models. Matisse's paintings (for example, *Goldfish and Sculpture*, 1911) or his line drawings come to mind as a visual model; so do paintings by Gaugin, Klee, and Miró or prints by Escher; so, for that matter, do *La Madonna dell'Umiltà* by the Sienese painter Giovanni di Paolo (c. 1399–1482) and many a medieval icon. Such constructions call attention not to representational values but to the values their elements have by virtue of their place in an arrangement, in other words, by virtue of a function determined negatively within the construct and only as imagined by viewers. Klee's pictures, for instance, are not pictures *of* something but rather they are figural constructions where linearity has nothing to do with outline or "objects" because the painting erases the difference between form and content. An Escher print collapses the dualism between inside and outside, thus erasing the neutrality and homogeneity of space. The logic of these constructs, like that of a Moebius strip, involves a fundamental contradiction bordering on crisis, a crossing over from one side of a formation or discursive boundary to another that offers considerable potential for wit.

In sequences, where temporality is more at issue, film may provide the most immediate experience of postmodern *figure*. Alain Resnais, the director who has collaborated with postmodern writers like Robbe-Grillet and Duras, speaks of his work in terms that might describe the sequences of postmodern narrative. For example, Resnais describes his super-stylized, melodramatic film, *Melo*, in terms of a figural rather than a representational ambition: "I wanted it to be like a drawing you make without lifting the pen off the paper—I wanted the audience to be moved by the line, the simplicity of the line."[40] Such cinematic sequences have little to do with reassuring viewers about the emergent powers of time and consciousness that belong to the temporal form of realism, that is, to history. Instead viewers are required to find that governing arrangement or figure in which each sign in the series has its differential function, which is to say, has value by virtue of *not being* something else in the sequence. When the sequence (tempo, temporality) includes a viewer's (or reader's) own consciousness, the simplicity of the line becomes more impressive the more it engenders active substitutions on the part of a potential infinity of readers. Chance

[40] Resnais, quoted by reviewer Robert Goldberg in the *Wall Street Journal*, 24 March 1987, p. 34. Goldberg goes on to say: "On the technical level, Mr. Resnais experimented with changing lighting in mid-shot, creating a light as stylized as the action."

thus becomes an element of the text; an art of improvisation is an art of planning creative accidents. Where time, consciousness, and language are one, the reader or viewer operates not in a neutral historical time but in a profoundly differentiated medium.

In heading this section "*Della Figura* (Time and the Figure)," I intentionally invoke the title of a major theoretical statement about modern pictorial art, *Della Pittura* (1435–36) by the Renaissance painter, architect, and theorist Leone Battista Alberti (1404–1472). With the waning of the modern aesthetic, a new statement comparable to Alberti's would introduce in place of *picture* a different term for a different agenda: instead of *pittura*, we can substitute *figura*; instead of the norm of realistic representation, we can substitute figural arrangement. Given the breadth of influence that representation has had across Western cultures, across endeavors, and across centuries, this shift of agenda has monumental implications. I invoke Alberti mainly to suggest the potential scope of the cultural reformation evident in postmodern narrative. Although the term *figure*, like *picture*, conventionally has belonged to a pictorial and spatial idiom, I enlist it here to describe art in a temporal idiom.

Postmodern writers invoke *figura* as an alternative to the conventions of representation, a way of expressing the alternative norms of postmodernism. One such invocation is Cortázar's reference to *figura* in one of the "expendable chapters" in *Hopscotch* where we find this "odd note" from Morelli on how the painter Manet liberates the pictorial image from its representational syntaxes and restores it to the condition of *figure*. In a thrice-bracketed instance of multivocality Cortázar (characteristically ignoring the boundary between "fictional" and "real") quotes the fictional Morelli, who in turn quotes Lionello Venturi on Manet:

> "Lionello Venturi, speaking of Manet and his *Olympia*, points out that Manet did not need nature, beauty, action, and moral intent in order to concentrate on the plastic image. Thus, without his knowing it, he is working as if modern art were going back to the Middle Ages. The latter understood art as a series of images, replaced during the Renaissance and the modern period by the representation of reality. The same Venturi (or is it Giulio Carlo Argan?) adds: 'The irony of history has decreed that in the very moment in which the representation of reality was becoming objective, and ultimately photographic and mechanical, a brilliant Parisian who wanted to be realistic should be moved by his formidable genius to return art to its function as the creator of images. . . .' "

> Morelli adds: "To accustom one's self to use the expression *figure* instead of *image*, to avoid confusions. Yes, everything coincides. It is not a question of a return to the Middle Ages or anything like it. The mistake of postulating an absolute historical time: There are different times *even though* they may be parallel. . . . Painters and writers who refuse to seek support in what surrounds

them, to be 'modern' in the sense that their contemporaries understand them . . . are simply on the margin of the superficial time of their period, and [working in] that other time where everything conforms to the condition of *figure*, where everything has value as a sign and not as a theme of description." (chap. 116, pp. 479–80)

To emphasize "*figure* instead of *image*" means, first of all, that all writing— and, since everything is writing, all discourse ("all the tures of this world")—is reflexive rather than representational, but what exactly does this mean? It means that one exercises language not primarily as a referential pointer, a neutral instrument of information, but primarily as a system of signs, which is to say, as a system of differential values, a design, a discursive arrangement, a constructed system of whatever kind and whatever magnitude (nation state, room arrangement, novel, handshake). A sign (as opposed to an "image"), whether it is an Italian word, a detour arrow, or a skyscraper, is not primarily a sign *of* something, any more than a part of an engine "means" engine. The sign, like the engine part, has a differential function. Its *value* is one of place rather than of representation. The figure describes nothing, it points to nothing. Representational "figures," like metaphor or metonymy or a host of others with lingering Latin names and uncertain identities, all approximate the condition of "image," the representational word Cortázar seeks to avoid.

   Given the relative strangeness of the term *figura*, I begin with a brief discussion of its traditional usage, which is to say, its medieval roots. *Figura*, sometimes used interchangeably with the term "typology," belongs to a medieval aesthetic that, from the point of view of representational conventions, is a strange world indeed. It has quite different implications and serves quite different values from those associated with more familiar representational usages, as D. W. Robertson explains in his essay on "The Aesthetics of Figurative Expression." Robertson uses the example of St. Augustine, who describes holy men as the teeth of the church and praises the church as a beautiful woman whose "teeth are as flocks of sheep, that are shorn, which come up from the washing, all with twins, and there is none barren among them." To a sensibility trained to certain associations, these figures are rather alarming, but Augustine, as Robertson says, is primarily interested in a typological value and an intellectual pleasure and not at all interested in the kind of representational associations that makes such a figure mainly unpleasant to us.

> It is obvious that St. Augustine was not concerned with any spontaneous associations his experience may have led him to have with teeth and sheep. Teeth do not in themselves suggest holy men. In the same way, shorn and washed ewes with twin lambs are neither empirically nor emotionally connected with human perfection. There is, moreover, no surface consistency between teeth and sheep.

But the peculiar configuration of these materials as they are governed by the context does give rise to an abstract pattern which is coherent. The incoherence of the surface materials is almost essential to the formation of the abstract pattern, for if the surface materials—the concrete elements in the figures—were consistent or spontaneously satisfying in an emotional way, there would be no stimulus to seek something beyond them.

With medieval as with postmodern art, then, it is the difficulty and search required that give value to the figure, a purpose that would be unattainable if the figure were merely decorative or emotionally satisfying. The church is a collection of attributes, more or less independent, that can be developed in parallel but quite separate figures of teeth and sheep. "That is, there is no point in dwelling on the various characteristics of teeth and sheep which have no relevance to the abstraction."[41] Surface consistency and "realism" would be not only unnecessary to the figure's effectiveness, they would spoil it.

Of course, in one sense all poetic language (including all the tropes of daily speech) is figural, and in classical rhetoric from Quintilian and the *Ad Herennium* onward *figure* was a large category that included tropes like metaphor or metonymy. But in its more restricted and specific sense, *figura* was a medieval strategy that uniquely operated between Neoplatonic transcendence, on the one hand, and literal events on the other, inseparably bonding them together in ways also found in postmodern narrative. It is this collapse of distinction between the transcendent and the literal, this literalizing of metaphor, that perhaps uniquely maintains what Erich Auerbach calls "the mixture of spirituality and sense of reality which characterizes the Middle Ages and which seems so baffling to us today."[42] In fact it is baffling partly because *figura* collapses the mind-body dualism, the separation of spiritual and material existence maintained by both empiricism and Neoplatonic exegesis.[43]

To this classical configuration the church fathers added history with the idea of *pre*figuration: prefigures not in some transcendental realm but in-

---

[41] D. W. Robertson, *A Preface to Chaucer: Studies in Medieval Perspectives* (Princeton: Princeton University Press, 1962), Part II, "Some Principles of Medieval Aesthetics" pp. 56–57.

[42] Auerbach "Figura," pp. 60–63.

[43] From its classical usages on, as Auerbach explains it, *figura* had the connotation of "something living and dynamic, incomplete and playful . . . the new manifestation [or] changing aspect of the permanent" (Auerbach, "Figura," p. 12), including the ideas of configuration and transformation. Augustine especially develops three stages of historical fulfillment of the Word in which the second, the incarnation, was both fulfillment of the Jewish Law and prefiguration of the Last Judgement (p. 41), thus making a three-fold distinction between literal history, figure which is both literal and fulfilled truth, and finally uncloaked fulfillment or truth. "In this connection," Auerbach writes in a way suggestive for postmodern narrative, "*figura* is roughly equivalent to *spiritus* or *intellectus spiritalis*" (p. 47).

carnate, in this world, something that is, in Auerbach's words, "real and historical" and that announces something else equally real and historical ("Figura," p. 29). Treating Jewish law and history as figurae for Christ and his laws gave Europeans "a basic conception of history" ("Figura," p. 53), an important link between history and religion too often forgotten and one tellingly analyzed in Karl Löwith's *Meaning in History*. Figural interpretation, Auerbach argues, is neither allegorical nor symbolic; its aesthetic is neither the *allegoria* of exegetical tradition nor the *istoria* that Alberti glorifies in *Della Pittura*. Moreover, *figura* is an interpretive practice that has only recently been supplanted and that in most European countries "was active up to the eighteenth century" ("Figura," pp. 26–27).

In Christian doctrine and in Christian humanism alike, the two mutually informative historical instances point to something miraculous that is based entirely outside history, however much specific incarnations may be relevant to its human program. Such figural interpretation moves toward transcendence away from the more classical sense of *figura* as living, dynamic, playful form that can be found in postmodern writing. Auerbach describes this Christian historical figuration as follows:

> Figural interpretation establishes a connection between two events or persons, the first of which signifies not only itself but also the second, while the second encompasses or fulfills the first. The two poles of the figure are separate in time, but both, being real events or figures, are within time, within the stream of historical life. . . . Figural prophecy implies the interpretation of one worldly event through another; the first signifies the second, the second fulfills the first. Both remain historical events; yet both, looked at in this way, have something provisional and incomplete about them. . . . Thus history, with all its concrete force, remains forever a figure, cloaked and needful of interpretation.

The discursive situation changes with the historicist humanism that accompanies empiricism from the seventeenth century onward and finds the transcendent position in the individual consciousness, Foucault's "founding subject," and in its most formidable construct, historical temporality.

Figural interpretation, in other words, belonged to a medieval construction of history quite different from the modern, empiricist construction. This comparison is worth quoting at length:

> In this light the history of no epoch ever has the practical self-sufficiency which, from the standpoint both of primitive man and of modern science, resides in the accomplished fact; all history, rather, remains open and questionable, points to something still concealed, and the tentativeness of events in the figural interpretation is fundamentally different from the tentativeness of events in the modern view of historical development. . . . Whereas in the modern view the event is always self-sufficient and secure, while the interpretation is fundamentally in-

complete, in the figural interpretation the fact is subordinated to an interpretation which is fully secured to begin with: the event is enacted according to an ideal model which is a prototype situation in the future and thus far only promised. . . . Thus the figures are not only tentative; they are also the tentative form of something eternal and timeless; they point not only to the concrete future, but also to something that always has been and always will be . . . This eternal thing is already figured in them.[44]

In short, figural writing was "in constant conflict with the purely spiritualist and Neoplatonic tendencies" because of its preservation of the spiritual *as* something inseparable from the historical and material. In the figuration, the future fulfillment is already present.[45]

[44] "Figura," pp. 53–55, 58–60. Auerbach's distinctions between allegory, symbol, and figure are interesting not only in themselves but for what they may suggest to us about the kind of cultural condition in which *figura* flourishes. "Since in figural interpretation one thing stands for another, since one thing represents and signifies the other, figural interpretation is 'allegorical' in the widest sense. But it differs from most of the allegorical forms known to us by the historicity both of the sign and what it signifies. Most of the allegories we find in literature or art represent a virtue (e.g., wisdom), or a passion (jealousy), an institution (justice), or at most a very general synthesis of historical phenomena (peace, the fatherland)—never a definite event in its full historicity. . . . In biblical exegesis this allegorical method long competed with the figural interpretation" in a tradition including Philo, Homer and Hesiod, and Origen. "But despite the existence of numerous hybrid forms, it [allegory] is very different from figural interpretation. It too transforms the Old Testament; in it too the law and history of Israel lose their national and popular character; but these are replaced by a mystical or ethical system, and the text loses far more of its concrete history than in the figural system" (pp. 53–55). Symbol is the other alternative to figure besides allegory: "the so-called symbolic or mythical forms, which are often regarded as characteristic of primitive cultures, and which in any case are often found in them. . . . The symbol must possess magic power, not the *figura*; the *figura*, on the other hand, must always be historical, but not the symbol. Of course Christianity has no lack of magic symbols; but the *figura* as such is not one of them. What actually makes the two forms completely different is that figural prophecy relates to an interpretation of history—indeed it is by nature a textual interpretation—while the symbol is a direct interpretation of life and originally no doubt for the most part, of nature. Thus figural interpretation is a product of late cultures, far more indirect, complex, and charged with history than the symbol or myth. Indeed, seen from this point of view, it has something vastly old about it: a great culture had to reach its culmination and indeed to show signs of old age, before an interpretive tradition could produce something on the order of figural prophecy" (pp. 56–57).

[45] Auerbach argues that *figura* predominates in and determines the whole structure of Dante's *Divine Comedy*: here Cato, "who in a significant moment in his own destiny and in the providential destiny of the world sets freedom above life, is preserved in its full historical and personal force; it does not become an allegory for freedom"; nor is Virgil "an allegory of an attribute, virtue, capacity, power, or historical institution. He is neither reason nor poetry nor the Empire. He is Virgil himself. Yet he is not himself in the same way as the historical characters whom later poets have set out to portray in all their historical involvement, as for example, Shakespeare's Caesar or Schiller's Wallenstein. These poets disclose their historical characters in the thick of their earthly existence; they bring an important epoch to life before our eyes, and look for the meaning of the epoch itself. For Dante the meaning of every life

This peculiar mixture of transcendental and historical truths in figural language constitutes its value for postmodern writers. Whereas in *allegoria* the linguistic figure is a husk of meaning that becomes discardable when the meaning is retrieved (Robertson, p. 59), and whereas in *istoria* (*littera*) metaphor dematerializes language by naturalizing it, in *figura* such dualisms between language and (transcendent) meaning blur because the incarnation is the spirit, and the spirit is incarnate. The church fathers would have been horrified, no doubt, at the postmodern insistence that there is no exit from language; nevertheless, both medieval and postmodern writing gives a status to language, to the Word, unavailable in the historicist, representational, and empiricist mode. In a Borgesian or Nabokovian figure the husk *is* the meaning, and to discard it would be to produce a blank, not a positivity. Time and subject *are* the figure, and there is no "other side" to it, except in some other figure.

The postmodern usage of the term *figure* is neither scientific nor religious; its meaning can better be sensed than defined and its relation to medieval usage is necessarily problematic.[46] It may seem that there could hardly be a practice farther from postmodernism than one that loves "the truth in words and not the words themselves" (Robertson, *Preface*, p. 63). The differences between medieval and postmodern usages are considerable and include different conceptions of transcendence, "identity," and temporality. Still, the similarities are more than matters of mere technique. Postmodern writers find in medieval techniques ways to cut across time (and space) and to avoid the requirements of narrator (spectator) awareness (we may think of Miró, Kandinsky, or Klee). But in both the postmodern and the medieval senses figural art knows nothing of that rationalization of faculties required by representational conventions, and consequently knows nothing of the particular notion of "identity" that accompanies them. Where we can have an "image" of a character or an event, we can have a "figure" that collects independent attributes in a differential arrangement that gives priority to pattern over discrete objects and subjects and the "neutral" media on which they depend.[47] Postmodern *figura* can

---

has its place in the providential history of the world, the general lines of which are laid down in the Revelation which has been given to every Christian, and which is interpreted for him in the vision of the *Comedy*" (p. 70).

[46] As Maureen Quilligan's *The Language of Allegory* (Ithaca: Cornell University Press, 1979) often reveals, Christian allegory explicitly depends on religious "truth" or Logos in its "eternal dimensions"(p. 153) and is not content with mere mystery. While postmodern writing, like phenomenology before it, could be characterized as a "religious" response to extremes of rationalization in the sense that it insists on the importance of mysteries that baffle reasons and their humanist projections, postmodern writing has no use for Logos.

[47] Each attribute of a given person could belong to a different figure or typological reiteration without necessarily invoking any of the others. On the medieval version of this see *Realism and Consensus*, pp. 8ff.

be understood not as a gesture toward doctrinal truth but as a way of gesturing past the dead ends of representational writing. The objectification of the world and the rationalizations of sight and consciousness that inaugurated centuries of exploration, empiricism, and historicism have no privileged place in an art of *figura*.

The turns of postmodern narrative language do have a sort of strange quality of being like allegory, only without allegory's transcendent world. It is this quality, what I am calling *figural* quality, that makes them so often funny. Cortázar's narrator with his bunnies in the closet, or Van Veen stopped on the road that is *both* a Swiss road and a more spiritual "way," or the narrator-cum-reader in *Jealousy*: these arrangements that double, that multiply their semantic contexts, that refuse to maintain a single identity produce a kind of chronic risibility in readers who are always aware of an alternative plot shadowing the "real" one. This figural turn continuously suggests that the real plot lies not in the ostensible one but elsewhere, and yet the elsewhere is not a Beyond of meaning or other transcendence but simply in the power of language itself to digress infinitely while at the same time remaining syntactical and organized.

These feats of language cannot be demonstrated with the usual short quotations because they mutilate the characteristic syntactical derangements, so in order to give a specific instance of postmodern language producing figural shoots I must quote at some length. This passage from Cortázar's *Hopscotch* not only meanders illustratively, exemplifying the digressive narrative line that keeps turning an apparent logic into something else, it also conveniently uses the term "figure." Here the characteristic digression curls inexorably away from its implied conclusions, passing threshold after threshold and coming to an end, as it were, at the end of a branch:

> Maybe there is another world. . . . That world exists in this one, but the way water exists in oxygen and hydrogen, or how pages 78, 457, 3, 271, 688, 75, and 456 of the dictionary of the Spanish Academy have all that is needed for the writing of a hendecasyllable by Garcilaso. Let us say that the world is a figure, it has to be read. By read let us understand generated. Who cares about a dictionary as dictionary? If from delicate alchemies, osmoses, and mixtures of simples there finally does arise a Beatrice on the riverbank, why not have a marvelous hint of what could be born of her in turn? What a useless task is man's, his own barber, repeating *ad nauseam* the biweekly trim, opening the same desk, doing the same thing over again, buying the same newspaper, applying the same principles to the same happenings. Maybe there is a millenary kingdom, but if we ever reach it, if we are it, it probably will not be called that any more. Until we take away from time its whip of history, until we prick the blister made of so many *untils*, we shall go on seeing beauty as an end, peace as a desideratum, always from this

side of the door where it really is not always so bad, where many people find satisfactory lives, pleasant perfumes, good salaries, fine literature, stereophonic sound, and why then worry one's self about whether the world most likely is finite, whether history is coming to its optimum, whether the human race is emerging from the Middle Ages and entering the era of cybernetics. *Tout va très bien, madame la Marquise, tout va très bien, tout va très bien.* (*Hopscotch*, chap. 71, p. 380)

This passage is not only about figure as an alternative to history, it *is* a figure in the postmodern sense: its linear track branches and branches again, producing several "tries" without conclusion; one can hardly speak of "the" syntax; and rather than being summarizable as "plot" in any conceivable sense of the word, it has to be read and reread, which is to say "generated." The "point"—or rather the fun—of this is in its accumulation of instances, which in the end presents a meaning that digresses from any summarizable point; and that is the point. "It is important to understand," as Robertson says of medieval aesthetics, "that the affective value of this figurative language lies in what is found beneath the language and not in the concrete materials of the figures" (*Preface*, p. 56). The supplemental overload here, the refusal to stick to its ostensible message, *is* the message. In this sense the figure *constructs* (with the reader's indispensable collaboration) consciousness and temporality.

What is "found" beneath this postmodern syntax transgressing across a formerly inaccessible threshold to another side is laughter, eros in the largest sense; not, presumably, at all what was "found" in medieval figures. Robbe-Grillet's, Cortázar's, and Nabokov's syntactical structures undermine themselves in ever more inventive ways. The quiet—even "useless"— space created by these subversions is filled not with dogma but with laughter (although the two may have more in common than may initially appear to rationalist discourse with its more productive similitudes). Into this space, Nabokov says, "rushes all that I love":

I confess I do not believe in time. I like to fold my magic carpet, after use, in such a way as to superimpose one part of the pattern upon another. Let visitors trip. And the highest enjoyment of timelessness—in a landscape selected at random—is when I stand among rare butterflies and their food plants. This is ecstasy, and behind the ecstasy is something else, which is hard to explain. It is like a momentary vacuum into which rushes all that I love. A sense of oneness with sun and stone. A thrill of gratitude to whom it may concern—to the contrapuntal genius of human fate or to tender ghosts humoring a lucky mortal. (*Speak Memory*, p. 139)

The postmodern writer creates such vacuums for willing readers. In these texts and this language, the historical disaster of receding time does not exist but only a sequence definable as a rhythmic repetition or "rush" of "love" that fills the ineffable hollow between two moments.

This language literalizes the metaphors yet keeps in sight their former mimetic function enough for readers to experience a perpetual surprise, a kind of risibility that accompanies the collapse of this fundamental representational achievement. Cortázar's bunnies in "Letter to a Young Lady in Paris" are part of an elaborate analogy between, on the one hand, the fate of personal, private, inspired, creative life in the modern city and, on the other hand, the physical qualities of rabbits and their growth. The bunnies that the hapless narrator vomits up in the elevator aren't simply metaphors for hidden inspiration (for example, my poetic instinct is like an effervescent fluff in the throat); they belong to an extensive development the meaning of which is never translated out of the figural state into portable property: one's creativity (the rabbits) appears between the interstices of rational modern structure (in the elevator between floors); he hides them in the closet; they develop a life of their own, they even pee on the rug; he tries to repair the damage they do with good reliable empiricism (English cement); the more he tries to hide them, the more they take over his life; and so it goes. The fun—must we say "the point"?—is in the infinitely branching, surprising turns this analogy can be made to take, and in the very experience of surprise in the place where convention ought to be.

This disorientation for its own sake is very unlike the effect of medieval *figura*, which makes truth only temporarily inaccessible so that it can be properly valued and not taken for granted as "obvious." Postmodern *figura* makes univocal truth permanently inaccessible. On the "other side" of a medieval figure is a clarifiable structure and a stable, cosmic meaning. On the "other side" of postmodern figures is the marvelous mystery consisting of the fact that these figures *are* the tangible world, and that the tangible world is discourse, is language, is figure. In postmodern writing there is nothing but figure; the figure is the discourse. There are no messages, as Cortázar has it, only messengers. A reader can't throw away the husk after getting its kernel because the dualism between husk and kernel has collapsed.

The short stories of Cortázar and Borges, because they are so short, are especially obvious figurations of this collapse. They are Moebius strips in language that carry the reader right over the boundary of empiricist epistemology to an "other side" where difference cannot be mediated. For example, Borges's story "The South" is about crossing over: crossing geographical barriers, cultural barriers, discursive barriers. Such crossings entirely rearrange the elements of identity, which, far from surviving the transition from one discourse to another, literally finds that crossing a change (as Nabokov says at the end of *Transparent Things*) "from one state of being to another." Borges's story concerns Dahlman, who, after an illness, takes the train south to recover his health, and by chance he gets into an argument that culminates in his picking up a knife, perhaps to kill, perhaps to be killed by an unknown opponent. But putative plot is not where the action lies; the interest for readers lies in the sequence that limns for reading consciousness that threshold, boundary, or shadow line between one reality and another, and also lies in how the "one" turns into the "other," as in the Moebius inside/outside paradox, without fanfare, without as it were lifting the pencil from the paper.

Cortázar's stories, where rational "order" gets twisted into unexpected positions, are virtuoso exercises of this kind. In "Continuity of Parks," a reader moves in two pages from being the detached, spectator-reader of a melodrama to being the victim of the story. The photographer in "Blow-Up," another spectator fixing the world with his lens, loses his subject position—to put it mildly—when the world he has first framed with his lens and then fixed in a photo blow-up turns out to have a life of its own and shatters the only real fixity, which turns out to be his confidence in his "identity" (name, address, nationality, occupation) and in his capability to fix "reality." In "Night Face Up" the narrating consciousness alternates between two states of being, one "modern" and the other "primitive," in a sequence that turns the reader's "reality" into a dream and a putative nightmare into reality. These stories put readers *into* the Moebius strip, the Escher space, forcing them to experience a medium warped by invisible boundaries, a medium of figural not representational value.

One of the more spectacular of the many language experiments in postmodern novels, the interlineated chapter 34 of *Hopscotch*, calls attention to the figural as distinct from the representational power of language in a most remarkable way. In this seven-page chapter two entirely different texts are interlineated, one from a famous nineteenth-century realistic novel and the other part of *Hopscotch*. Printed on alternating lines, the two texts are literally superimposed, to the extent this is possible in inexorably sequential language. If the "meaning" of each text were important each could be presented separately, and if comparisons were valid they could be made in the usual way (comparing and contrasting style, thematic concerns, formal arrangement), but this use of language calls into focus neither the meaning of the individual texts nor the similarities and differences between them but instead their figural relation as "interminable pattern without any meaning." In trying to cope with this sequence it is not enough simply to "follow" it; readers have to perform strenuous acrobatics in order to keep both texts intact and separate, a task that ultimately fails from sheer lack of interest. In the process, however, a reader discovers several things about language: that every unity is exclusive because we have to exclude something every time we construct a "meaning"—and often a meaning less interesting than the textual transaction itself; that residence in a language means "residence in a reality," and realities differ, for example, between the language world of property, ownership, times, places, clothing, degrees, and "nostalgia for vocation and action" (chap. 90, p. 419) and the language world of junk novels and their superannuated ideas about "family warmth," and so forth. The most startling, even eerie, effect, however, is that themes from one text echo in the other to such an extent that these two systems are not entirely separable. A final affront to linear habits appears when the shift from one line and one text to another involves us in this mystery: the experience of a seamless sequence of meaning in what is ostensibly a *chance* conjunction between two "different" texts.[48]

[48] A few excerpts, beginning at the first line, will show how "meaning" takes a back seat to play, and how the sequence thus encourages the perception that language is figure not picture:

> IN September of 1880, a few months after the demise of my
> AND the things she reads, a clumsy novel, in a cheap edition
> father,I decided to give up my business activities,transferring
> besides, but you wonder how she can get interested in things
> them to another house in Jerez whose standing was as solvent
> like this. To think that she's spent hours on end reading
> . . . .
> . . . .

Even though these two texts differ in style and emphasis, still the reader, trying to learn the arbitrary but unavoidable habit of skipping some text in order to "follow" a narrative line, learns the hard way—by practice—that verbal patterns, at least in chapter 34, have paratactic as well as the more familiar syntactic value. We must give up simple reliance on the linear habit of constructing "meaning" because it exists in several different dimensions and is not deployed along a track.

Certain verbal coincidences add complexity to the problem of reading, for example, these three series from the middle of the chapter:

> the properties, transferred my holdings and inventories, and
> *France Soir*, those sad magazines Babs lends her. *And moved to*
> moved to Madrid to take up residence there. My uncle (in truth
> *Madrid to take up residence there*, I can see how after you swal-
> . . . .
> . . . .

> [or]

> warmth when that became essential. The good gentleman lived,
> *family warmth*, that's good, shit if that isn't good. Oh, Maga, I
> should say we lived, in a section that had been built up on a
> how could you swallow this stuff,and what the hell is the charity
> site where the charity warehouse had once been. My uncle's flat
> warehouse, for God's sake. I wonder how much time she spent
> . . . .
> . . . .

> [or]

> irony through the lines you read with great emotion, convinced
> it was no less real because of all this. In a word,my nose had got
> of the fact that you were getting all kinds of culture because

Such figuration all takes place, as Nabokov says of Gogol, at a "super-high level of art" and has nothing to do with the making of "life-like" portraits or of argumentative points. In short, it has nothing to do with the conception of art as container, as envelope, as coating to make the message pill go down.

> So to sum up: the story goes this way: mumble, mumble, lyrical wave, mumble, lyrical wave, mumble, lyrical wave, mumble, fantastic climax, mumble, mumble, and back into the chaos from which they all had derived. At this superhigh level of art, literature is of course not concerned with pitying the underdog or cursing the upperdog. It appeals to that secret depth of the human soul where the shadows of other worlds pass like the shadows of nameless and soundless ships. . . . If you expect to find out something about Russia, if you are eager to know why the blistered Germans bungled their blitz, if you are interested in "ideas" and "facts" and "messages," keep away from Gogol. The awful trouble of learning Russian in order to read him will not be repaid in your kind of hard cash.

A figural language is a language almost entirely resistant to the kind of commentary that banishes the "shadows of other worlds" and sustains the distinction between form and content. Great literature doesn't mirror "the world" because the novel doesn't exist univocally any more than "the" world does; instead, great literature produces an experience in which "normal" functions are displaced by a sudden slant of the "rational plane of life" that reveals the "other side" of the "normal" system and opens up the possibility of perpetual substitution. This tilt of the rational plane, this syntac-

---

the *scent of some European culture*, of well-being, and even
you were reading a Spanish novelist whose picture is on the
riches and hard work.
fly-leaf, but right now the guy is talking about a *scent of Euro-*
    My uncle is a well-known businessman in Madrid. In years
pean culture, you'd convinced yourself that all this reading
past he had held important positions in the government: he had
[italics mine]

. . . .
. . . .

One text ends before the other, reemphasizing the visual dimension of language patterns: not only because (as the nineteenth-century text might say) seeing is believing but also because emphasis on the visual properties of written language mystifies its capability to maintain merely informational value and emphasizes instead its capability of being "interminable pattern without any meaning."

ance, because his three daughters, alas!, were already married.
another direction,and all of this is drawing a picture, a pattern,
something nonexistent like you and me, like two points lost in
Paris that go from here to there, from there to here, drawing
their picture, putting on a dance for nobody, not even for themselves, an interminable pattern without any meaning.

tical detour that has such profound implications, takes place humbly enough in the sentences and paragraphs where a reader's collaboration is called upon. That is where the "action" is.

Rhythmic time and its multilevel consciousness ARE this process of anthematic substitution in which readers maintain simultaneously various different figures.[49] Each time a detail recurs, the reader slips from putative plot (some person's pilgrimage) into wordplay or thematic echo or repetitive figure. The attentive reader—and this act of attention takes practice—experiences a syncopated moment of recognition that breaks with the depths provided by historical time with its always elsewhere past and future, forcing attention back to the surface activity of consciousness where the deliberate focus on the moment includes the flash of memory. This discipline is especially hard to sustain for those in a hurry. But of course if "the other world surrounds us always and is not at all at the end of some pilgrimage," then such rushing is rather like the ear-splitting sound of crickets in *Jealousy*, an erosion of difference that destroys all pattern. Hurtling "toward" a nonexistent future only flattens the poetry of an individual life. A postmodern narrative slows down that forward hurtle by enlarging a reader's stock of elements for thematic construction: of what Nabokov calls "those thematic 'voices' with which, according to all the rules of harmony, destiny enriches the life of observant men" (*Gift*, p. 211). The reader's construction of these "thematic voices" depends, as the sections on surrealism and on *Jealousy* have suggested, on the paratactic treatment of detail, and it is this particular stylistic element that gives postmodern style its strangeness and intensity.

The plots of the elusive masters of postmodern narrative, from the short fictions of Borges to the big books of Nabokov, have the erring, metonymic quality of narrative to the tenth power because they routinely divert the course of conventional sequence by means of these irreducible details; they are the fatal pebbles under the wheel, the spider in the shoe. These details, and the minute, unmediatable differences they make, are all-important because those differences are what *constitute* the discursive system. The ever-digressing narrative line makes *difference* the sublime fact of life in postmodern novels.[50] Postmodern readers are required to participate

[49] "Anthematic" is a term suggested by Nabokov's "thematic anthemion," discussed below in the Rhythm Section on *Ada*.

[50] This emphasis on difference is tantamount, in William Paulson's terms, to emphasizing literariness per se because literature is neither a message nor an object but a source of differences (*Noise of Culture*).

The negative definition of differential "identities" is something that can be found not only in its more familiar poststructuralist sources but also in Heidegger, where the existential basis of *Dasein* "implies that in having a potentiality-for-Being it always stands in one possibility or another: it constantly is *not* other possibilities, and it has waived these in its existentiell

in making the figure, in other words, required *knowingly* to fabricate not just their meanings (nineteenth-century readers sometimes did that) but the systems that produce whatever there is of meaning. This creation and maintenance of difference, through increasing the semiotic "noise" of a narrative, pressures the logic-bound awareness to the point of collapse. Meanwhile, mysterious, meaningless repetitions thread the text with elements of paratactic play that, like alphabets of some mysterious alternate languages, are capable of an infinite number of different arrangements.

The power and excitement of this language comes precisely from its resistance to historico-transcendental longings; it is erotic language, not in the narrow and shabby sense but in the broad and privileged sense of having the capacity to surprise and sustain play. Postmodern narrative maintains eros by sustaining surprise. The constant sense of the arbitrariness of arrangement, the surprising sense that where one thematic echo appears, another might just as well be, the reliance on chance conjunctions in contrast to rationalizable or meaningful ones all are surprising because they are unpredictable. Such reading and writing vastly expand the experience of language as a residence with an inexhaustible range. In this sense the conflict of life and death, eros and thanatos, while it may seem heavy material for a playful art, is definitely relevant to that play. The unique poetry of an individual life, the one constructed from particular thematic voices, can be constructed not with rational explanations but with reliance on chance (*hasard objectif*) and on what Nabokov and Breton both call "love."

Its erotic value may be the most unsettling effect of postmodern narratives, even more unsettling than the necessity to confront one's own value structures. By yanking readers out of their armchairs and forcing them to play at, to participate in, literally to co-author a narrative, postmodern writers confront readers with another demand because questions of value inevitably lead to questions of *pleasure*. That, I think, is one surprise historical thinking protects us from; it rationalizes activity in terms of open-ended production by deferring questions of value to the future. But postmodern narrative by emphasizing play lets questions of value creep in, and so questions of pleasure creep in, too.

What do I mean by pleasure? What does pleasure have to do with work? The question itself is exceedingly historical because it implies precisely the kind of deferrals that historical thinking has masked in order to maintain. And there is good reason for this complex and paradoxical maneuver. Pleasure and play, as some theorists have noted, are explosive; they are subversive of the law; they create new and provisional dispensations. In a culture that places strong emphasis on linear, productive, progressive models,

---

projection" (*Being and Time*, p. 331; II.2.58). "Conscience" itself may have such "a 'negative' character" (p. 340; II.2.59); and the discussion of "guilt" (pp. 329–31).

pleasure has been culturally depreciated along with play and relegated to the arts and leisure section of the Sunday paper. In fact, the insistent separation between work and play is one telltale sign of this cultural deflection of pleasure, one that has special importance in a discourse that privileges putatively public values. Reading narrative subversive of this distinction between work and pleasure can be very intimidating because it carves up so-called public time and denaturalizes every undertaking, even one's "work." In postmodern play every endeavor shows its surprising side—and some endeavors more than others.

The capability for surprise is *erotic* in the large sense of eros as opposed to thanatos, of life affirmation in the face of death.[51] Attali opposes pleasure to death conceived in his terms as the stockpiling of "time": "*the stockpiling of use-time in the commodity object is fundamentally a herald of death*. In effect, transforming use-time into a stockpilable object makes it possible to sell and stockpile rights to usage without actually using anything, to exchange ad infinitum without extracting pleasure from the object, without experiencing its function."[52] Pleasure, surprise, and play are watchwords of postmodern narrative and they are what its critics most often find objectionable. Reading this writing requires reconsideration of both what it means to enjoy and what it means to write. To enjoy is to grasp the quality created by limitation: "Death is the mother of beauty," says Wallace Stevens in a patriarchal phrase; in Miguel de Unamuno's more elegant words, "Death is the great economist."

The sense of beauty and economy encouraged in postmodern writing laughs in the face of the more sober discourse of production and its denials. While no one claims that laughter can or should destroy production, it has the power to alter the context in which various forms of production are conceived. The reaction against the postmodern effect, both inside and outside the university, might be explainable partly as a deep and insecure

[51] Whatever the historical situation, this old sense of eros conflicts fundamentally with that discourse of "distance" that can be found in the thirteenth century but was not broadly based until the seventeenth or even eighteenth centuries, a period that saw (among other things) T. S. Eliot's famous "dissociation" of sensibility and the separation of "aesthetics" into a separate field by Baumgarten and others. William Barrett, discussing the existentialist move to reassimilate "aesthetics" and "life," finds their separation taking place as late as the eighteenth century (*What Is Existentialism?* [New York: Grove Press, 1964], pp. 118ff.).

[52] "No human act, no social relation, seems to escape this confinement in the commodity, this passage from usage to stockpiling. Not even the act that is the least separable from use-time: death. . . . Repetition today does indeed seem to be succeeding in trapping death in the object and accumulating its recording. This is a two-step operation: first, repetition makes death exchangeable, in other words, it represents it, puts it on stage, and sells it as a spectacle. . . . Then in the second step, not yet realized, death will become repeatable, capable of trapping use-time; in other words, purchasing the right to a certain death will become separable from its execution" (Attali, *Noise*, p. 126).

suspicion that activities like counting currencies (including information) or planning explosions may be among the world's more simpleminded and tedious activities. While postmodernism does not mean the end of counting or planning, it certainly means a major revision of goals: something understandably threatening to those comfortably at rest in various forms of discursive sleep or privileged by the prevailing hegemonic arrangements. It is no accident that universities have maintained historical thinking by disciplinary means in the epoch of capitalist and empiricist hegemony, or that the university is largely seen as a prevocational instrument.

To enjoy, to take pleasure in, to see the changeability or, in other words, the play in any system of appropriating and grasping the world is something we have learned to avoid. And our reluctance has its logic because to turn away from the production model is to accede to a radical revision of a primary cultural formation. To state the crux as baldly as possible, value and pleasure have radical implications precisely because, while habits are passive, enjoyment is not. To savor the arbitrariness of an activity—to receive its surprises with pleasure rather than denial—is not easy work. It involves a capability for equipoise, for flexibility, and for small-scale improvisation that are not currently primary values of the cultural formation in which we presently operate our universities, watch our markets, and pursue our careers.

The details of style in postmodern narrative language, then, are not just fancy dress for deeper thoughts; they accomplish more important work. The digressive, paratactic detail or sequence that resists generalization and rationalization becomes intensely surprising and thus confers an exquisite pleasure by relieving the mind of its already recognizable (ready-made) "meanings" and its dialectically inspired flight from the concrete present moment. To restore to language its electricity, what Breton calls its "power to shock," to derail it from the track of conventional formulas, is the job accomplished by the anachronistic, digressive language so characteristic of postmodern narratives. Details that resist the assimilating power of context or chrontext retain their surprising, erotic power, which is to say, their power of life affirmation in the widest sense. They serve Eros, not Evidence.

Love and chance go together in postmodern writing, just as they do in surrealism. "The ideal equipment for the surrealist personage," writes J. H. Matthews, "is lucidity in the pursuit of knowledge, with reliance on the generous gifts of love and objective hazard 'beyond,' as Gracq puts it, 'the paltry discrimination of good and evil.' "[53] The surrealists obviously knew their Nietzsche, and perhaps their Heidegger for that matter ("fate" is an-

---

[53] J. H. Matthews, *Surrealism and the Novel* (Ann Arbor: University of Michigan Press, 1966), p. 10.

other name for *Dasein*), and they passed along in new terms a similar critique of transcendental metaphysics and its discursive practices.[54] Contingency in chaos theory, as we saw in Part One, is the key to continuing life in an always evolving and often far from equilibrium physical universe. In describing what is needed for this postmodern enterprise of language, postmodern novelists, like the surrealists, use the twin terms of love and fate in similar ways, ways that have little to do with their values in the discourse of history and objectivity. They invoke, in place of the historical emphasis on past and future, the focus on the present moment in its concreteness (Breton's "concrete intensity") and, in place of the heroic effort to master fate, the improviser's reliance on what comes "to hand" (Breton's "objective chance" or Lévi-Strauss's *bricoleur*). Where historical linearities, and their ever-transcendental impulse, move away from present concreteness and complexity, the thematic figure of the postmodern narrative sequence supports a constant, multilevel play of substitution. Where the representational effort requires understanding, projection, identification, the figural effort requires ardency, intensity, resignation. Nabokov describes the necessary act of attention in these words, describing his own early experience:

> To love with all one's soul and leave the rest to fate, was the simple rule she heeded. "*Vot zapomni* [now remember]," she would say in conspiratorial tones as she drew my attention to this or that loved thing in Vyra—a lark ascending the curds-and-whey sky of a dull spring day, heat lightning taking pictures of a distant line of trees in the night, the palette of maple leaves on brown sand, a small bird's cuneate footprints on new snow. As if feeling that in a few years the tangible part of her world would perish, she cultivated an extraordinary consciousness of the various time marks distributed throughout our country place. . . . Thus, in a way, I inherited an exquisite simulacrum—the beauty of intangible property, unreal-estate—and this proved a splendid training for the endurance of later losses. (*Speak Memory*, p. 40)

The details remembered rather than lost in their development become the "time marks" of "an exquisite simulacrum" (not a meaningful history) and constitute a basis of affirmation and endurance. Similarly in *Hopscotch*, where the power to love and the terms of fate or chance are constant themes, emblematic moments are those where Horacio and La Maga set out to meet by chance, and the one where, while the philosophical Club debates ontological questions with a ceaseless circularity, La Maga looks out the (closed, Euclidean) window at the "ardently useless night" (chap. 141).

---

[54] For Heidegger, "Dasein *is* fate" and "fate" is "*authentic historicality*" (*Being and Time*, pp. 436ff.; II.5.74).

The discourse of ardent intensity and objective fate must remain incomprehensible to a mind intent solely upon a representational, which is to say, a "natural" itinerary for language (whether its language system is French or English, businessese or legalese, certain interpretive languages of the academy or political conventions in several senses); such a mind has a vested interest in not comprehending the arbitrariness and the constructedness of sign systems. But happily for postmodern novelists most readers, however unquestioningly empiricist they may be in their conventions, experience subjectivity as precisely the digressive impulse that postmodern style traces. Such readers are forced to give up the representational itinerary and to accept the power and the burden of postmodern consciousness; forced, rather like Borges's Funes the Memorius, to sustain an unaccustomed intensity: to be "the solitary and lucid spectator of a multiform world which was instantaneously and almost intolerably exact" (*Personal Anthology*, p. 114). It is this surreal exactitude, this precise specificity of detail that prevents the formation of any transcendent rationalizing system, that gives postmodern narrative language its particular quality and postmodern readers their particular exercise. It is a narrative world that is too "multiform" for the power of thought to maintain its control, so other powers come into play. Postmodern figural art is an art of language without transcendence; one simply does not, as in representational art, slip into the "depths" of this or that history, this or that message. Unlike the representational field, where putative openness is actually closed by its dependence on a single system of rationalization that brooks no contradiction, the figural arrangement invites the play of substitution in which one thing can turn into another and the outside can become the inside in a boundaryless but finite play.

The question inexorably arises for such readers, how does one get along socially, morally, without rationalizing classifications or without the monuments and markers of historical time? Devising an art of "chance" seems a little like trying to calculate accidents, and in fact the digressive figures of postmodern style with their perpetual surprises do seem a bit like an art of accident in the traditions of surrealism and even Buster Keaton. Whatever the metaphors for it, the multilevel thematic practices of postmodern narrative language enforce a rhythmic attention. Once we have given up antidotes to finitude—Kantian categories and vodka—we face finitude and its opportunities. In postmodern narrative that finitude is never far from awareness, in everything from the theme of death to the uncollated precision of descriptive language that inscribes the particular, and no other, figure. In *Transparent Things*, Nabokov's last, vast little book, the elusive "Mr. R." (the "R" a reversed mirror image of the Russian word for "I") explains his writing as a response to such unthinkable, unmediatable death:

Total rejection of all religions ever dreamt up by man and total composure in the face of total death! If I could explain this triple totality in one big book, that book would become no doubt a new bible and its author the founder of a new creed. Fortunately for my self-esteem that book will never be written—not merely because a dying man cannot write books but because that particular one would never express in one flash what can only be understood *immediately*.

There can be no linear understanding of an "exquisite simulacrum" of the kind that "prodigious individual awareness" constructs; one must be content with that process of construction, that game of substitutions, that postmodern narrative necessitates for readers. Life in postmodern narratives is a continuing experience of this unanchored precision.

The figure that binds both time and consciousness is a turn of language: a turn to be found in local shifts within sentences and in the overall radiating, paratactic patterns of attention. The play of language puts the representational sign in crisis by disturbing its univocality, and this play during the course of even a short narrative collapses the dualisms that support representational "distance" and its mediations, especially including the mediations of historical temporality, its objectivity, and its founding individual consciousness. In postmodern narrative readers must experiment with the formulations of time and subjectivity as dimensions of a process of figuration and not apart from it. Language is the determining experience: its substitutions are the events of rhythmic temporality, and its figures are the unique poetry of an individual life. These postmodern *figurae* are, to use Saussurian dialect, more than *parole* but less than *langue*, which is to say, more than individual speech acts and less than a system of potentiality. These *figurae* in the sequences of language, as a participant co-creates them, constitute for their duration all there is of time and consciousness.

Rhythm Section: Vladimir Nabokov's *Ada: A Family Chronicle*

Postmodern narrative sequences include the active engagement of readers who, as they attend to varying thematic voices, construct from the paratactic elements *sequential figures that differ with each reader and reading*. This constructive activity takes place at a level of complexity impossible to summarize. Reading *Jealousy* or *Hopscotch* or *Ada* engages readers in sustained feats of multilevel thinking, a complex discipline of consciousness resembling the power of good chess players. Not only must the player remember accumulated patterns and frequencies, with each new variation he or she must also keep in view the possible developments of which these themes might still be capable. The more themes or details one becomes aware of, the more multi-thematic power one has.

Nabokov's term for this patterning, "thematic anthemia," fits nicely both the characteristic sequence of postmodern narrative and also the reader's enterprise. The "polliphone" passage, cited in the first section of Part Three, demonstrates the digressive play of Nabokov's language, but that example was relatively, even uncharacteristically, contained, like a set piece of stage parody. In general, Nabokov's development of multilevel thematic patterns resembles those in *Jealousy* and *Hopscotch*; various details and in varying frequencies are repeated through the course of *Ada*, creating vast paratactic, digressive networks sustaining a many-colored, manifold sequence in language. These thematic developments are so embedded in the progression of sentences that a selection of examples undermines the rhythmic sense these apparitions present fully only in the actual moment of reading. I want to select two kinds of example to at least suggest, however unsatisfactorily, the range and complexity of this effect: first, by isolating one or two threads from the grand design, and second, by considering a single passage where typically several thematic voices occur.

Of the many thematic voices that constitute every sentence in *Ada*, the two I want to isolate are the yellow-and-black theme and the mosquito theme, each of which occurs in a different frequency. The yellow-and-black theme, for example, appears more than a dozen times and the mosquito theme at least eight; both always intersect with several other themes. The dozen or so yellow-and-black themes, for instance, occur in the following forms: Aqua going to commit suicide in a pinewood "put on yellow slacks and a black bolero" (p. 31); the scene of important erotic exploits is the daybed in Ardis library "covered in black velvet, with two yellow cushions" (p. 44); Ada's larvarium contains a lovely worm with "black coat" and tufts colored "red, blue, yellow" (p. 60); the firefly's lemon light in the darkness (p. 78); the wasp (p. 81); Professor Brown's "slap-bang Original Description" of the Chateaubriand mosquito "(small black palpi . . . hyaline wings . . . yellowy in certain lights)" (p. 112); Van's remembered candlestick shadow in "black geometry . . . along the yellow wall" (p. 221); Van reclines "clad in a black training suit, with two yellow cushions propped under his head" (p. 243); Ada's outfit for her sixteenth birthday party, "maize-yellow slacks" and "a rumpled ribbon of black silk" in her hair (p. 281); Van sees "a black-haired girl of sixteen or so, in yellow slacks and black bolero" (p. 313) who reverses the colors two pages later and is "the girl in black slacks and yellow jacket" (p. 315); Van and Ada's drawing room has "its black divan, yellow cushions" (p. 450); Lucette's "divan is black with yellow cushions," in ominously exact repetition (p. 493); and Lucette, on the brink of suicide, "changed into black slacks and a yellow shirt" (p. 523). These references come in several batches, three quarters of them in the first half of the novel and widely spaced thereafter. The theme is varied with different colors and repeated twice in connection with suicide, which is only one of the various other themes evident even in this selection, such as the insect theme (wasp, fireflies, larvarium, mosquito), the clothing theme, the fingernails theme, the balcony theme, the becoming-adult (also related to the larval) theme, the time (also related to the larval and becoming-adult) theme. Such details gain tremendous energy from being part of paratactic sequences, even though they occur in the text at very wide intervals.

Another thematic voice (bear with me) is the mosquito theme, which recurs at least eight times: five in the first half, twice associated with the Chateaubriand theme (pp. 78, 92, 112–13, 191, 297); one lost in the late middle (p. 454); and two relatively near the end at moments of utmost importance (pp. 598, 623). One mosquito is memorably slain on Ada's shin; the Chateaubriand, its bite, and Ada's scratching later receive an epic two-page description; on another occasion Van battles another bug and kisses one of Ada's bites in tribute; one occurs in a movie plot summary; and at the end, a mosquito bite is the occasion for the plot resolution that has been suspended in midair for hundreds of digressive pages of "life" (Van and Ada do not grasp at "happiness"). Finally, the narrator-Van, speaking of the idea of a hereafter, employs what is by then the mosquito "signature."

There are literally hundreds of these themes playing in every sentence and paragraph of the novel. There are lavenders and orchids, there are velvets and armloops, there are nineteen butterflies and forty-eight greens, there are hammocks and honey, there are labyrinth mazes, circuses, incest, time, paradise, death, handkerchiefs, picnics, fatal gunshots, walkings on hands, stage sets and immortality, suicides, pencils, water, telephones, windows and rain, sandals and shoes. And as usual in Nabokov there also are anagrams and alliterations blooming along each trail, not to mention dual and triple language arrangements. To the tuned-in reader, these thematic traceries accumulate resonance from the suggested presence of alternate systems spinning along just outside the line of putative plot in a realm where immortal Van and Ada, and comprehending reader, enjoy their unexpected conjugations and remain precariously invulnerable to those linear habits to which everyone else in the novel falls mortal victim. These thematic voices, like colored rhymes of different frequencies, provide a patter and an exercise that are anything but "background." It is enough to make one suspect that Nabokov wrote on 3x5 cards so he could interlace his themes in a surrealist manner by shuffling them.

In the following passage we can watch the comings and goings of thematic voices in just one clip of sentences. The narrative voice(s) ruminate(s) on the pointlessness of histories, especially "natural" ones, and the supremacy of details:

Natural history indeed! Unnatural history . . . because the detail is all: The song of a Tuscan Firecrest or a Sitka Kinglet in a cemetery cypress; a minty whiff of Summer Savory or Yerba Buena on a coastal slope; the dancing flitter of a Holly Blue or an Echo Azure—combined with other birds, flowers and butterflies: *that* has to be heard, smelled and seen through the transparency of death and ardent beauty. And the most difficult: beauty itself as perceived through the there and then. The males of the firefly (now it's really your turn, Van).

The males of the firefly, a small luminous beetle, more like a wandering star than a winged insect, appeared on the first warm black nights of Ardis, one by one, here and there, then in a ghostly multitude, dwindling again to a few individuals as their quest came to its natural end. Van watched them with the same pleasurable awe he had experienced as a child, when, lost in the purple crepuscule of an Italian hotel garden, in an alley of cypresses, he supposed they were golden ghouls or the passing fancies of the garden. Now as they softly flew, apparently straight, crossing and recrossing the darkness around him, each flashed his pale-lemon light every five seconds or so, signaling in his own specific rhythm. (pp. 77–78)

The familiar reader of *Ada* recognizes several thematic voices in this passage, and perhaps some new ones. Making one transition after another, from one frame to another, this passage shifts from the dancing flitter of a Holly Blue, to the dance of death and ardent beauty, to the joint narrators of *Ada*, to firefly biology, to Italian twilight memories, to the specific rhythm of a life: themes that strike readers differently, if at all, depending on what attention or development he or she has already given them. Just getting through a syntactical unit (sentence, paragraph) requires one to keep simultaneously in play several separate thematic voices. And these voices occur in different frequencies: lemon light in the darkness belongs to two themes, the illuminations in the dark theme and the yellow-black theme last stated seventeen pages ago and destined to be restated four pages hence; the butterfly theme fifteen pages ago and thirteen pages before that; this is the first statement of the mosquito theme. The repetitive interval in the theme involving the narrators differs from the repetitive interval involving insects (the whole larvae-adulthood theme is only faintly echoed here), or the repetitive interval implied between Van's deliberate present in the garden and its mnemonic echo. These complexities are not lost even on the careless first-time reader and are harder and harder to avoid on a second or third reading. Thus the style digresses elaborately, always heterogeneous to but in sight of the vestigial plot line which submits to perpetual interruption. These accumulating thematic voices become paramount, developing a rhythmic, multilevel play that substantially overtakes the shadow plot. Like the firefly, each theme signals in "its own specific rhythm" and also in cumulative relation to all the other rhythms, each with its own frequency. By the end of the novel the complexity of this colored anthemion is immense.

"Anthemion" is Nabokov's term for the figure composed by these relationships. Originally the title of his autobiographical narrative, *Speak Memory*, "anthemion" is the name of a honeysuckle ornament, consisting of elaborate interlacements and expanding clusters. *Ada* is such a figure: a vast *anthematic* system of intersecting parallels, the "thematic anthemia" that define a life or a work of art (p. 77). The paratactic details of postmodern narrative are precisely *anthematic* in their arrangement, consisting of expanding clusters, elaborate interlacements. A reader's attention in this complex figure moves out from local details to other remembered thematic iterations and at several levels simultaneously, exploring the repetitive intervals, not gathering meanings. Nabokov's "anthemion" is like Cortázar's "polychromatic rose" design understood "as a figure" (*Hopscotch*, chap. 109), where every departure implies a return, not in terms of a single pattern of rationalized space or time but in terms of a multiplex figure-in-process. The key activity is the reader's digression and return following the trace of elaborate interlacements in a rhythmic manner, and one made as arbitrary as possible by various forms of figural doubling, parody, or contradiction. Awareness flashes past one intersection after another at hair-raising speed until one is "lost again" by any linear standard of measurement; at the same time and in unexpected places the familiar themes repeat and repeat. Like "Fate," the syntactical line "forks and re-forks" in ways that increase the complexity and valences in a growing structure of differential relationship. Each reader of these sequences constructs from the given alphabet of elements and by her/his own acts of attention a unique discourse of paratactic value: each, like the firefly, in her/"his own specific rhythm."

This "anthematic" language gives readers quite a range of vantage points from which to glimpse alternative semantic systems. The use of Russian and French interpolations, for example, is more than caviar for the general (Nabokov certainly knew that most of his readers would not know three languages), because languages do something other than reinforce "meanings."

> The details that shine through or shade through: the local leaf through the hyaline skin, the green sun in the brown humid eye, *tout ceci*, *vyso eto*, in tit and toto, must be taken into account, now prepare to take over (no, Ada, go on, *ya zaslushalsya*: I'm all enchantment and ears). (p. 77)

The English sentence contains little French and Russian departures that almost, but not quite, replicate the English. Alternate semantic systems come momentarily into view, ones with a different look, a different quality than the system they complicate. Other such intersections appear in the geographical, chronological, and identity scrambles or anagrams: with Van and Ada (Vaniada); with America and Russia (Amerrussia, the ultimate Moebius trip, complete with its Kaloga, Maine); with the early nineteenth-century persona taking a trip by airplane; with Terra and Anti-Terra (invoking the Future, its History and "Heaven" on the one hand, and, on the other, the definitely Deliberate Present that belongs to "Hell"—the Russian "ada" is translated "hell" and here suggests a situation preferable in every way to its opposite, "Heaven"). The reader must constantly cross over and back between these "doubles": others include Aqua and Marina Durmanov, Ada and Lucette Veen, and the pluralizing, alliterative, constantly tropic language, with its "thetic anthemion" and its beautiful doubleness.

On the larger scale, readers of *Ada* will find similar digressiveness, including varieties of the plot contradictions found in *Jealousy*: "specious lines of play," with which *Ada* frustrates any lingering goal orientation in readers.[55] Van does and doesn't shoot himself; Marina seems to discover the illicit affair, then doesn't, but, as we discover hundreds of pages later, actually has. At the fatal moment when he is about to discover the love affair of Ada and Van, Demon Veen pauses for a long digression on Bosch and butterflies while we and the Veen children are wishing he would depart; and after the inevitable discovery we are treated not to the outcome but to a long digression on the Black Miller. This kind of distraction is typical of a language that is always digressing from the straight-and-narrow linear development, sentence after sentence, so that a reader invariably becomes "lost again" like a disappointed beagle on the trail of plot. What seems ancillary momentarily becomes focal and then gives way to something else apparently "ancillary." Events, those things for which historically minded readers hanker—discovery, consummation, death, marriage—elude us; meanwhile, delay turns into digression and digression into an experience in its own right. The mysterious mental maneuver of imagination becomes primary, the history of climaxes irrelevant. At the same time, the anthematic repetitions create multiple patterns outside the line of putative plot, where the paratactic realm of value multiplies and breaks up any lingering linear, historical, or directional interest.[56]

Because of the multilevel figure being constructed in each passage, this always digressing language requires of readers a close-grained effort of imagination and concentration. The reward is laughter. The fun of taking the little excursions and surprise crossings is the only "point" of reading, once plot has been let out the door. Reading is then a question of getting

---

[55] *Speak Memory*, p. 290.

[56] For the argument that Nabokov preserves the representational agenda that I say he leaves behind see Hayles, "Ambivalence: Symmetry, Asymmetry, and the Physics of Time Reversal in Nabokov's *Ada*," in *Cosmic Web*, esp. pp. 120–26.

the rhythm in one after another such description. In this one, for example, the description is shadowed by now well-developed anthematic patterns (balcony, larva, desire, etc.) and other incipient puns:

> On another terrace, overlooking another fabled bay, Eberthella Brown, the local Shah's pet dancer (a naive little thing who thought "baptism of desire" meant something sexual), spilled her morning coffee upon noticing a six-inch-long caterpillar, with fox-furred segments, *qui rampait*, was tramping, along the balustrade and curled up in a swoon when picked up by Van—who for hours, after removing the beautiful animal to a bush, kept gloomily picking itchy bright hairs out of his fingertips with the girl's tweezers. (p. 477)

Among the various erotic amplifications here the primary one is linguistic and discursive: the series of surprising right turns from terrace (a variant of the important balcony theme), to parenthesis for the naive on the subject of desire, to spilled coffee, to description of the gorgeous caterpillar *qui rampait*, to swooning girl imitating a caterpillar, finally to the effect of this particular pubescent insect on Van's fingers. On each detour, moreover, we pick up another thematic voice (balcony, sex, fur, larvae), each of which has various attending themes (perspective, play, touch, time). The amusement here does not come from any trivial snicker. The novel consists of one passage after another like this in a series of waves, and the reader, as one wave goes, catches another, and then another.[57] The activity of reading is an experience of completion and departure, completion and departure, completion and departure taking place over and over again through sequences of (*vot zapomni*, "now remember") intensely specific intersections of this kind. In the specific activity generated in this language Nabokov's multilevel, multicolored, other world takes shape.

The digressiveness of this language calls attention to the *surpluses* of linguistic systems, both of language as such and, by implication, of discursive structures that operate like language. The play in anagrams and alliterations, to take the simplest examples, brings into view the variety of possible arrangements, as do thematic voices on a larger scale. *Ada* encourages us to resign our interest in structure, center, origin, and end and to choose a process of endless differentiation and play that is neither structured nor chaotic in any classical sense. Nabokov's style makes the semiotic play of language unavoidable for readers and it makes available exactly that power of diffusion and escape from "sense" or ready-made "meaning" that surrealism sought.

Because the growing multilevel awareness blocks the rationalization on which history depends, a reader has an entirely new experience of temporality. Time in *Ada* is a dimension of its language, and this bonding of language and time emphasizes both the materiality of language and its vast

---

[57] This analogy I owe to my surfer friends, Katerina Kunska and Kathryn Fisher.

mnemonic capacity. Every language moment is saturated with memory: with personal memory but also with "social memory" which, we recall, is Borges's definition of language. In *Ada* this is no abstraction. Each iteration of a thematic voice, subtly colored by the presence of past iterations, literally reenacts the mnemonic function to produce a temporality inseparable from language and its artifices. The paratactic elements, converted by readers into the rhythms of attention, charge each moment with a multifold complexity that surrounds and multiplies its identity. The momentariness of such experience is only problematic for chronophiles or for those who are habitually guilty of " 'looking forward to a promotion or fearing a social blunder,' as one unfortunate thinker puts it" (p. 585). Each description has a momentary impact: "sudden ice hurtling down the rain pipe; brokenhearted stalactite." It appears and dissolves and becomes part of a thematic fund that echoes in different amplifications through hundreds of pages. The time of one's tense-willed mind, the momentary time of poise and focus succeeded by another and then another in a rhythm like heartbeats, the time of the Tender Interval: *that* time does not transcend the text. Past and future are present in the figure.

It is not desirable, consequently, to "understand" this style because such distance from the style is simply pointless. Nicholas Rowe, although he calls this temporality "timelessness," captures admirably the reader's growing sense of a multiform (and always linguistic) world:

> The sense of timelessness in Nabokov's works also derives from carefully controlled echoes. A tiny detail, a shape, a vivid little phrase will appear and reappear—*almost* unnoticed. The present is thus subtly colored by the past, and the reader himself tends to experience and reexperience the story within its own perceptual framework. And the future is continually prefigured. Time becomes a series of superimposed translucent layers, shifting just enough to reveal unexpected, familiar glimpses. Such echoes, which often range across hundreds of pages, can be almost diabolically teasing. . . . It should be emphasized that in context such little touches are both more subtle and more suggestive. Even less careful readers presumably experience a vague, atmospheric recognition as a piece of familiar scenery flashes past.[58]

Rowe's description of the "intricate network of echoes" (pp. 75–76) suggests how "timelessness," by which I take him to mean the absence of time conceived as history and project, is achieved by means of language. The

---

[58] Nicholas Rowe, *Nabokov's Deceptive World* (New York: New York University Press, 1971), p. 78.

Brian Boyd disagrees with Rowe's general argument. I discovered Boyd's book on *Ada* and his biography of Nabokov (see bibliography) too late for them to influence my argument here, but I find in both a heartening estimate of Nabokov's greatness and of *Ada*'s importance: heartening because I have never understood the grudging reception of books like *Ada* or that flawless gem, *Transparent Things*.

temporal framework depends on the forward and backward action of consciousness constructing its "thematic anthemia," working cumulatively and by superimposition to create not the neutral medium of history but a medium where so-called "rational" perspectives are perpetually tilted and distorted, a medium where little things become great, and great things little, and the shadows of other worlds can be seen.

Time is the subject of the short fourth book of *Ada*, composed of Van Veen's "Treatise on Time." During his long separations from Ada, Van seeks a definition of time adequate to his experience of separation and loss. He ruminates on the dangers of getting lost on the linear track (Swiss road map no help here), all the while pursuing the "track" of time and getting lost, in a figural moment, on the way.

> Lost again. Where was I? Where am I? Mud road. Stopped car. Time is rhythm: the insect rhythm of a warm humid night, brain ripple, breathing, the drum in my temple—these are our faithful timekeepers; and reason corrects the feverish beat. . . . Maybe the only thing that hints at a sense of Time is rhythm; not the recurrent beats of the rhythm but the gap between two such beats, the gray gap between black beats: the Tender Interval. The regular throb itself merely brings back the miserable idea of measurement, but in between, something like true Time lurks. How can I extract it from its soft hollow? The rhythm should be neither too slow nor too fast. One beat per minute is already far beyond my sense of succession and five oscillations per second make a hopeless blur. The ample rhythm causes Time to dissolve, the rapid one crowds it out. Give me, say, three seconds, then I can do both: perceive the rhythm and probe the interval.

This sophistication of the idea of rhythmic time is important in its deflection from the "black beats" and their "miserable" invocation of measurement: like language, this time is a perception of rhythmic intervals.

This "tangible time," time of the Tender Interval, has almost nothing to do with the linear and historical conventions of temporality:

> The irreversibility of Time (which is not heading anywhere in the first place) is a very parochial affair. . . . Pure Time, Perceptual Time, Tangible Time, Time free of content, context, and running commentary—this is *my* time and theme. All the rest is numerical symbol or some aspect of Space. . . . My time is also Motionless Time. . . . The time I am concerned with is only the Time stopped by me and closely attended to by my tense-willed mind. Thus it would be idle and evil to drag in "passing" time. . . . The "passage of time" is merely a figment of the mind with no objective counterpart, but with easy spatial analogies. It is seen only in rear view, shapes and shades, arollas and larches silently tumbling away: the perpetual disaster of receding time. (pp. 572–79)

Like a heartbeat (but not to be confused with it [p. 573]), the paratactic style creates a persistent sequence of Tender Intervals. Van's whole discourse on time takes place in suspension ("a half-day's break in a crucial journey" [p. 575]) as he drives along the road to the plot climax of his life, an opportunity he nearly loses by grasping at it. His situation here thus parodies that of the reader who is also suspended between the black beats of plot, situated perpetually in a complex of Tender Intervals. Our sense of being harried by habitual expectations along the track of plot, our deflection from the "track" or "road", from the idea of "life as a kind of journey," find certain parallels in Van's harried sense of the "impatient sedan" (p. 580) at his bumper—"Cretin behind me"—and his getting "lost again" on the road to this too urgently sought destination.

Rhythmic time is at once artificial and intimately personal, but its uniqueness lies in its being sublimely accidental. The patter of its rhymes, its enticing "poetry" are evoked in this description from Nabokov's *Speak Memory* of the "moment" that his first poem began:

> A moment later my first poem began. What touched it off? I think I know. Without any wind blowing, the sheer weight of a raindrop, shining in parasitic luxury on a cordate leaf, caused its tip to dip, and what looked like a globule of quicksilver performed a sudden glissando down the center vein, and then, having shed its bright load, the relieved leaf unbent. Tip, leaf, dip, relief—the instant it all took to happen seemed to me not so much a fraction of time as a fissure in it, a missed heartbeat, which was refunded at once by a patter of rhymes: I say "patter" intentionally, for when a gust of wind did come, the trees would briskly start to drip all together in as crude an imitation of the recent downpour as the stanza I was already muttering resembled the shock of wonder I had experienced when for a moment heart and leaf had been one. (*Speak Memory*, p. 217)

The act of attention here described is the artistic (rhythmic) moment. Life rhymes: not because it has inherent poetry but because the "prodigious individual awareness" (*Ada*, p. 76) can occasionally focus down from History to the life-sustaining interval where imagination and knowledge meet and where subjectivity gets into process.

This time of a tense-willed mind Van Veen calls the Deliberate Present (compare the inadvertencies of one's historical so-called present):

> To give myself time to time Time I must move my mind in the direction opposite from that in which I am moving, as one does when one is driving past a long row of poplars and wishes to isolate and stop one of them, thus making the green blur reveal and offer, yes, offer, its every leaf. Cretin behind me.
>
> This act of attention is what I called last year the "Deliberate Present." . . . This nowness is the only reality we know; it follows the colored nothingness of the no-longer and precedes the absolute nothingness of the future. Thus, in a quite literal sense, we may say that conscious human life lasts always only one

moment, for at any moment of deliberate attention to our own flow of consciousness we cannot know if that moment will be followed by another. . . .

Our modest Present is, then, the time span that one is directly and actually aware of, with the lingering freshness of the Past still perceived as part of the nowness. (pp. 584–86)

Nabokov's reader, passing these rows of poplars, stops one figure after another with a tense-willed mind, working against forward momentum, elaborating a design or figure outside the track of plot. In the act of focusing on the detail and its every potential alliteration, its "every leaf," we stop to perceive our inertial system, the plot-and-character view of time with all its correlatives of "reality," "transcendence," and "depth." This Deliberate Present, like that "intrinsically artistic moment where imagination and knowledge meet" (*Speak Memory*, p. 167), *is* that syncopated, rhythmic attention enforced by the "anthematic" style.[59]

Such a rhythmic conjugation supports the whole parodic sequence in *Ada*. Both in overall arrangement and immediate language *Ada* forces readers into a situation where any temporal estimate is a function of position. *Ada*'s temporal figuration comes in a sequence of five "books," each half the length of the last and corresponding to twice as much chronological "time." In other words, there is an *inverse relation* between the length of the book and the history supposedly "passing" in it. The "more" chronological time passes, the less rhythmic time it takes. Book One (two years) takes up half the novel; Book Two (four years) takes up a quarter, whereas the final Book Five (an indefinitely long chronological period running from Van and Ada in their nineties into reader's time) takes less than 1/25 of the text. In addition, there are huge gaps in chronological time (nearly three decades unaccounted for during Books One through Four, and three more decades between the last two books). The elements of historical time and conventional narrative (these consist of amorous meetings between Van and Ada) are parodic, that is, they provide a linear track whose arbitrariness is constantly illuminated by the digressive play of the reader's text. There is a representational echo here; the inversions between chronological and perceptual time *do* resemble the experience of moving, as Van and Ada do, from childhood to adulthood. There is a density to the childhood experience, an erotic value, that threatens to evaporate in later years, except for the fortunate Van and Ada, who just manage not to decline into that particular sort of adulthood. The novel in this sense enacts a familiar distortion; one year is a quarter of a life to a four-year-old, whereas to a forty-year-old it is a mere flicker in the span. But the representational elements

[59] This treatment of time differs from that of Proust, for whom the recovery of time past is involuntary, not Deliberate. "Beware the marcel wave" and "the Proustian Bed," Nabokov quips in *Ada*, p. 575.

in this novel, like the erotic climaxes that belong to the putative plot, are only figures for the real action here, which is the tactile, surprising eroticism of language. The incestuous play of the siblings, Van and Ada, is a figure for the play of language with its own self that constitutes the primary reading experience in *Ada* and that amounts, for those embedded in historicist conventions, to a breaking of taboo.

The novel turns on whether its participants, Van and Ada and their reader (and our stand-in, Lucette, who, like us, privileges the pair by constant surveillance), can successfully maintain the Deliberate Present and its rhythmic acts of attention or whether they will succumb to the disaster of receding time, its projects, and its death. The rhythm of life in defiance of death is *Ada*'s project and theme. The telescoping of time suspends Van's "Treatise" (all of Book Four) between beats of his most important rhythm and on the eve of his reunion with Ada after a separation of more than twenty years. This plot element is one of the large and parodic iterations of the theme of erotic play that is demonstrated every step of the way in the sequences of language that maintain for willing readers a Deliberate Present full of epithelial alliteration. This reunion means for a reader the recovery of that aura of eroticism, of surprise, joy, and play that saturate the first half of the novel and that disappear in the shadow of Van's jealousy and the conventional fatherly interference from Demon Veen, the conventional rake.

What jeopardizes reunion—that moment where the life-giving play of a system is maintained—is here not outside interference but a dangerous lapse on Van's part into historical thinking and consequent efforts to "manage" the course of events. Odious control, as Breton says, "does not work all that well." The linear abstractness of Book Four, a theoretical description of what Van has lived, is, at least by comparison with the rest of the novel, an ominous symptom of slippage. Van's whole reflective and philosophical effort in his "Treatise" is generated by (as for readers it generates) absence and separation. When finally they are reunited, Van, who has looked forward intensely to this moment, can find no happiness in it. He has "lost" Ada.

> Nothing remained of her gangling grace, and the new mellowness, and the velvet stuff, had an irritatingly dignified air of obstacle and defense. He loved her much too tenderly, much too irrevocably to be unduly depressed by sexual misgivings; but his senses certainly remained stirless. . . . At their earlier reunions the constraint, subsisting as a dull ache after the keen agonies of Fate's surgery, used to be soon drowned in sexual desire, leaving life to pick up by and by. Now they were on their own.

He only regains his opportunity with help from astute Ada. After she retreats with invented reasons and feigns departure for another hotel, Van spends a bad night reflecting on his losses until, next morning, the moment surprises him out of calculation:

> Should he ring her up at her hotel before starting? Should he rent a plane? Or might it, perhaps, be simpler——,
>
> The door-folds of his drawing room balcony stood wide open. Banks of mist still crossed the blue of the mountains beyond the lake, but here and there a peak was tipped with ocher under the cloudless turquoise of the sky. Four tremendous trucks thundered by one after another. He went up to the rail of the balcony and wondered if he had ever satisfied the familiar whim by going platch—had he? had he? You could never know, really. One floor below, and somewhat adjacently, stood Ada engrossed in the view.
>
> He saw her bronze bob, her white neck and arms, the pale flowers on her flimsy peignoir, her bare legs, her high-heeled silver slippers. Pensively, youngly, voluptuously, she was scratching her thigh at the rise of the right buttock: Ladore's pink signature on vellum at mosquito dusk. Would she look up? All her flowers turned up to him, beaming, and she made the royal-grant gesture of lifting and offering him the mountains, the mist and the lake with three swans.
>
> He left the balcony and ran down a short spiral staircase to the fourth floor. In the pit of his stomach there sat the suspicion that it might not be room 410, as he conjectured, but 412 or even 414. What would happen if she had not understood, was not on the lookout? She had, she was.
>
> When, "a little later," Van, kneeling and clearing his throat, was kissing her dear cold hands, gratefully, gratefully, in full defiance of death, with her dreamy afterglow bending over him, she asked:
>
> "Did you really think I had gone?" (pp. 592–98)

The complex orchestration in this passage sounds many familiar thematic voices, including the balcony and the insect themes (we recall the caterpillar *qui rampait*), the contest between life and death, the role of chance, and the crucial presence of alternate semantic systems extending from four tremendous trucks to three swans. This reunion scene, he at the window above and she on the balcony below, echoes their situation in Manhattan at their parting years earlier, he standing by the third-floor window and she waiting in the room below (p. 466). The same casement and placement may occur in the tense-willed reader's mind, or perhaps another iteration like the photo of Ada on the balcony painting flowers (p. 425), or the balcony that Van and Ada studiously avoid during their penultimate reunion (p. 554), one foiled as former ones were by the forkings of fate. These moments are *privileged purely by attention*. Another dominant theme also echoes here, that of the mosquito and, with it, important moments in Ardis (home of eros, ardor, ardent beauty) when Ada scratches into pink mounds the mosquito bites on her leg. This rhyme with the past enables Van to regain the Deliberate Present and all the thematic threads of his life.

With "Ladore's pink signature on vellum at mosquito dusk," the past once more shines through the transparent moment instead of being blocked by crude historical loss. Like chess masters, Van and Ada manage by another digression to reopen play and resume life "in full defiance of death." This "rhyme" is the key to recovery of the Deliberate Present and its eroticism. With that recovery, the intervening periods of loss disappear into the time warps of the text. There is even here, for the attentive reader, practical reiteration of the Tender Interval and Deliberate Present themes of Van's "Treatise on Time." What precedes the resumption of their rhythm is the precise and unprecedented perception of lake and sky, four tremendous trucks, and three swans held, as it were, in this hollow of time. After this, Van's anxious search for the right opening in the numerical sequence (room 410, or is it 412, or 414?) is merely more vaudevillian parody.

Another thematic dimension of this passage is its echo of an alternative case from a much earlier passage that describes in similar terms Demon and Marina Veen's failure to retain in later decades the rhythm of their initial "three-year affair." Stuck in the disaster of passing time, each strives to mask its inevitable consequences with various cosmetic effects but thus insuring only that they have already lost to nostalgia the very thing they attempt to grasp. Compare Van's final "recognition" of Ada with this baffled response of Demon Veen as he looks at an aging Marina:

> Her singularly coarsened features, her attire, that sequin-spangled dress, the glittering net over her strawberry-blond dyed hair, her red sunburnt chest and melodramatic make-up, with too much ochre and maroon in it, did not even vaguely remind the man, who had loved her more keenly than any other woman in his philanderings, of the dash, the glamour, the lyricism of Marina Durmanov's beauty. It aggrieved him—that complete collapse of the past, the dispersal of its itinerant court and music-makers, the logical impossibility to relate the dubious reality of the present to the unquestionable one of remembrance. (pp. 264–65)

Unable to sustain in a Deliberate Present those all-important thematic threads linking present and past details, Demon experiences the "complete collapse of the past," in other words, the complete collapse of time's rhythm. No detail reminds him of Marina Durmanov. No rhythmic iteration or rhyming echo maintains true time and the pleasure preserved in its hollows. No Tender Interval keeps the past a lingering freshness of the "larval now," or provides the gap into which can rush all that he loves. So literally has their power to love, hence their "time," come to an end that their material survival even seems a bit obscene. In contrast with their parents, Van and Ada survive the threat of that complete collapse of the past, but just barely, and therein lies the interest of their effort at reunion, literally at restatement of their theme: in that effort we see the potential fatality of one slip of a detail, one lapse from the Deliberate Present.

What Van and Ada regain, and with them their lucky attentive readers, is a particular language, and with that language they regain their immortality. Van's comment suggesting that immortality belongs only to this language and this life sounds like an echo of the same theme in passages cited earlier from Duras and Heidegger (Part One, I above).

> You lose your immortality when you lose your memory. . . . The transposition of all our remembered relationships into an Elysian life inevitably turns it into a second-rate continuation of our marvelous mortality. Only a Chinaman or a retarded child can imagine being met, in that Next-Installment World, to the accompaniment of all sorts of tail wagging and groveling of welcome, by the mosquito executed eighty years ago upon one's bare leg, which has been amputated since then and now, in the wake of the gesticulating mosquito, comes back, stomp, stomp, stomp, here I am, stick me on. (pp. 622–23)

Demon and Marina fall victim to that predictable Next-Installment World but Van and Ada, almost miraculously, manage to remain in this always surprising one because they are prepared to be surprised. The sustaining rhythms of a life literally are constructed of those intervals into which rush whatever exists of affirmation or "love."

Perhaps what is most deathlike in *Ada* is the loss of that aura of confident play, the eroticism that Van and Ada reaffirm at their reunion and that surrounds them to the end: an "end" that is a "preface" and thus also a beginning to another story, perhaps one on "the other side" of their material death and continuing in the language of readers of *Ada*. The rhythms of life and love are not for them explanations or instruments of control to be shouldered and wielded; their mysterious magic exceeds any such explanation or control and requires a highly disciplined effort to remain, as the narrator says in *Transparent Things*, "in the now" and "at the exact level of the moment" (chap. 1). Immersion in that Next-Installment World means the loss of the rhythm of life. The complexity of thematic voices spiraling through a life cannot be appropriated or grasped; only a disciplined readiness sustains them, as quick-thinking Ada knows.

The constant in *Ada* is the language where rhythmic time takes shape. The Veen children maintain a constant verbal maturity from prepubescence to old age, and in the face of potential separation and loss the constancy of the language maintains their peculiar power: a power to live without grabbing at things, without insisting on various results and closures, intent instead upon the manifold rhythms of experience in the Deliberate Present. The same tone and style hold on both "sides" of so-called age, as narrators Van and Ada write this novel in their nineties; there is nothing between their "now" and their "then" but the warp of an occasional parenthesis or quotation mark. At the beginning of *Ada* there are many of these time warps where the two aged but still glorious narrators appear in constant company with themselves as glorious children.[60] The temporal gap between youth and age, like the long chronological periods in which they are separated for most of their adult life, evaporates and is of no importance in the text. In all these ways *Ada* cultivates the Deliberate Present to an extent that it has nothing to do with chronological distinctions and instead is synonymous with the power of language.

The eroticism in this novel, then, has little to do with the sexual relish of the two young Veens any more than the eroticism of *Lolita* is confined to, or even mainly apparent in, the immature sexual fantasies of that murderer of imagination, Humbert Humbert. The erotic plot is a figure for the play of the novel—its perpetually surprising language and its capacity, like that of the ever young Van and Ada, to lose every project in some anthematic arrangement or Deliberate Present. This play affirms what is momentary and defies every marmoreal effort to fix or hold it. In *Ada* the detail is not a base for transcendental excursion but rather a moment among paratactic moments; it belongs not to the development-and-climax plot that Nabokov parodies but to the imaginative activity involved in riding through one anticlimactic departure after another. Surprising, digressing, recurring, Nabokov's details and sentences support a thematic anthemion, a floral figure where words do not point to a Beyond of structure and meaning but are, in the essential participation of readers, the construction materials of a Deliberate Present. This novel often makes us aware of the contrast between the linear track, on the one hand, with its defiance of surprise, and, on the other, the semiotic play that generates those moments of highest awareness that, in *Speak Memory*, Nabokov describes as follows:

> It is certainly not then—not in dreams—but when one is wide awake, at moments of robust joy and achievement, on the highest terrace of consciousness, that mortality has a chance to peer beyond its own limits, from the mast, from the past and its castle tower. And although nothing much can be seen through the mist, there is somehow the blissful feeling that one is looking in the right direction. (p. 50)

Such consciousness is possible in the rhythmic tempo of paratactic, anthematic, semiotic play: the "tumescent" time where thematic voices thread the darkness. "Let's not squander," says Van to Cordula, "the tumescence of retrieved time on the gush of small talk. I'm bursting with energy" (p. 486). The figure of fun here has its other implication that small talk trivializes the power of life in its glorious assertion against stirless materiality.

The unique poetry of an individual life, consisting of its various "the-

---

[60] Not counting either the shifts to the fictional "editor" of their memoir or the presence of the conventional narrator implied by the past tense but merging uneasily with the two fictional narrators, there are, roughly, twenty-eight such time warps in Book One, seven in Two, two in Three, and none in the last two books.

matic designs" (*Speak Memory*, p. 27), may include some tender intervals borrowed by readers from a text. The power of play, of constructive imagination and its "unreal-estate," and not anything more rational, constitutes the unique poetry of an individual life as it traces its thematic spirals in the "brief crack between two eternities of darkness" (*Speak Memory*, pp. 126, 19). That brief illumination is one that takes place over and over again in the course of this novel in one rhythmic interval after another, and usually several at once. The compounding anthematic figures that lead nowhere beyond momentary satisfaction nevertheless require a lifetime of temporal discipline to maintain. The detail is all, but only to a certain readiness: as it is "seen through the transparency of death and ardent beauty" (p. 77). If "conscious human life lasts always only one moment," then these crossings between moments bridge a shadowy zone that contains time in its hollow. Perhaps this is what Ada means when she says, "I am because I die" (p. 164).

Nabokov's writing engenders that "mysterious mental maneuver needed to pass from one state of being to another" recommended in the final sentence of *Transparent Things* (chap. 26). This maneuver of imagination at play in language is one that does without history, without a millenary kingdom, without Kantian categories or vodka, without Marx, Freud, or "all the religions dreamt up by man" (*Transparent Things*, chap. 21). In their place this postmodern writing offers its precision, its erotic (chance) conjunctions, its rhythmic series: the colored bits or elements of kaleidoscopic arrangement, and whatever patterns emerge. These are the materials for the anthematic figure, a mandala, a polychromous rose design, a rhythmic, momentary, fleeting, life-affirming arrangement. Trying to give these arrangements fixity, or to control this rhythm in advance, would be like trying to redirect the arrow after it has left the bow.

Coda

On Contingency

IN HIS BOOK on the paleontological wonders of the Burgess Shale, Stephen Jay Gould explores some of its revisionary implications for our assumptions about history. Key to this revision is the role of contingency in the survival of species. With *Homo sapiens*, for example, many chance events during billions of years gave our species its opportunity: events that might have happened otherwise, like a comet shower or a change of climate in Africa. But for such events, life on earth could have developed without ever favoring the development of consciousness and, like most species, *Homo sapiens* would have perished: "one little twig on the mammalian branch, a lineage with interesting possibilities that were never realized, joins the vast majority of species in extinction. So what? Most possibilities are never realized, and who will ever know the difference?"[1] And even though *Homo sapiens* has flourished, there is no particular biological or geological reason to expect the species to survive forever. Even our sun, which has shone on the development of conscious life for only a split second of geological time, has itself run more than half its life's course and, like other, similar stars, probably will explode (in about five billion years), taking with it whatever is left, if anything, of *Homo sapiens*; as Gould observes, "geological time may be long, but it is not infinite" (p. 233). At so many junctures "the unpredictability of evolutionary pathways asserts itself against our hope for the inevitability of consciousness" (p. 316). The denial of this hope, however, far from discouraging aspiration, may be precisely the circumstance to increase it. Gould puts it this way: "*Homo sapiens*, I fear, is a 'thing so small' in a vast universe, a wildly improbable evolutionary event well within the realm of contingency. Make of such a conclusion what you will. Some find the prospect depressing; I have always regarded it as exhilarating, and a source of both freedom and consequent moral responsibility" (*Wonderful Life*, p. 291).

Something like this assertion, and something like its attendant acceptance of contingency, can be felt in the ebullient pathways of postmodern writing. Whereas historical sequences, with their insistent rationalizations, convert chance into causality, the multivalent frequencies of rhythmic improvisations with their obscure enterprise of form find their opportunity

[1] Stephen Jay Gould, *Wonderful Life: The Burgess Shale and the Nature of History* (London, Sydney, Auckland, Johannesburg: Hutchinson Radius, 1989), pp. 318–20.

in what is accidental, surprising, contingent. Where historical conventions formulate most questions in terms of quantity and extension in a neutral horizon overseen by a detached (potentially neutral) consciousness that is "in" history but not of it, rhythmic time, which focuses questions in terms of qualitative difference and precise, systemic differentiation, treats such detachment as an artifact and inscription of particular values. Where historical conventions use (more or less discrete and simply located) events, texts, and persons as bases for key rationalizations, rhythmic conventions of temporality—parataxis on the move—depend on local arrangements whose amplifications are unpredictable. The rhythmic sequence forks and reforks, exfoliating, proliferating details and thematic threads and then coming to an end that is by any rational standard arbitrary. Rhythmic time incorporates the convention of history—internalizes it as one game, one set of rules among many. Confined to a rhythmic sequence, history is a thematic formulation, like any other, and no longer a commanding (determining) premise.

Postmodern writing thus erases the privilege of certain ideas and habits of mind that have long seemed natural: those associated with the great rationalization of faculties accomplished in the Renaissance and Reformation and codified since in a thousand practices across cultures congenial to empiricism and capitalism. Postmodern narrative language raises unsettling and unsettled questions that reach the root of our assumptions about language and time. Narratives that circumvent "meaning" and confine attention to the detail and the moment undermine the traditional humanistic bases of subjectivity, temporality, and familiar forms of social order. This comes to the crux of the postmodern difficulty for readers. We are asked to give up logocentric, dialectical, dualistic, and other transcendental habits; we are asked to give up plot and character, history and individuality, perhaps even "meaning" as we have long conceived it. In their place we are offered "interminable pattern without meaning": an atomized system of details patterned paratactically, which is to say, asyntactically, which is to say, meaninglessly. While such narrative sequences seem to offer few footholds for habitual humanist readers, it is essential equipment for the postmodern person who, coerced perhaps by an emergent *episteme*, begins anew and at the root of the obscure discursive enterprise of form.

In demonstrating the powers of rhythmic temporality, then, I certainly do not mean to say that "history" no longer exists, although a nontrivial case can be made for this view. In attempting to convey a detailed impression of a new experience of temporality, one relatively independent of the usual historical conventions that we so easily assume in so many practical ways, my intention has nothing to do with trashing history and its cultural dispensation or with substituting play as the commanding mode of a new world. The multilevel play described in this book belongs to an effort to renew social codes by restoring powers that have been suppressed; it is not an effort to enforce another repression.

But this effort *does* involve a major revision of hegemonic arrangements. Systems that valorize production, progress, mobility, capitalization, and related ideas of identity have tended to depreciate and marginalize multilevel thinking, conceptions of personhood rooted in local systems and processes, and the capacity for play. The reinstatement of the repressed in this case is momentous because it involves a reformation of assumptions that have the most rooted practical exercise: for example, and to suggest only a few, the assumption that history is a single public medium, to which private histories are tributaries or "in" which they operate; the assumption that public can be more or less easily distinguished from private or the individual from the social; the assumption that losses can be sustained by regarding them as preparation for an as yet unfinished future gain; the assumption that, acknowledged complexities notwithstanding, psychic identity is as simply located and invariant as somatic identity; the assumption that there are regularities in experience, whether individual or collective, that enable us to learn from the past and control the future; the assumption that we can learn from the past in the first place because it is like the present and past persons are like us. In postmodern writing these things can no longer be taken for granted.

The rhythmic conventions of time offer new starting points for discursive reformation. To expand the richness of the moment, as multilevel thinking does, is not stupidly to stop all forward motion or to suppose that there is no "after" and "before"; instead, that expansion makes available more starting points and more alternative routes. Such a reformation is not without precedent. An historical sense quite different from the one implied by the term "history" is evident in the philological comparisons of Renaissance scholarship, which as yet had little or nothing to do with the teleological motives that later inspired the seventeenth-century vision of "time" as a universal constant both in the physical and the social universes. The fate of this time as "history" is linked with the fate of "humanism": and both are terms in need of significant reevaluation and redefinition. Rather than embalming the past in a commanding structure of significance, rhythmic time keeps its precise, concrete details in play and in process of constant renewal. In a complex and specific rhythm each sequence works out its exploratory repetition, its obscure enterprise of form, uniquely specifying the discursive potentials that belong to a collectivity, a text, a life. The result is an ineffably social achievement. It could never be achieved in solitude or by calculation alone or by a mob. It is, like a sentence, a unique specification of discursive possibility.

The challenge to the hegemony of historical thinking may seem to some like a challenge to be resisted. It seems to me like an invitation to take responsibility for conventions that we have naturalized, which is to say, assigned to a realm of undisputed truth where they need not be consciously maintained, modified, or managed. The challenge points up their fragility, their contingency, to be sure, but we do not alter that contingency by ignoring it. In any case, the contingency of all arrangements in rhythmic time seems appropriate to our circumstances.

The postmodern restoration of language attempts to bring back from repression an enduring creative power. If true exploration and experiment—that openness sometimes attributed to "thought"—really are a phenomenon of language in the widest sense of that term, then the creative originals of discourse are those who enable it to renew and not merely perpetuate itself, those who manage some play with the sign systems in which we operate day to day, and who manage some correction of habitual usages. The play of postmodern writing seeks to guarantee vitality, to affirm what remains open to surprise and capable of new formation.

Selected Bibliography

Adams, Parveen, and Beverly Brown. "The Feminine Body and Feminist Politics." *m/f* 3 (1979): 35–50.

Alter, Jean. "The Treatment of Time in Alain Robbe-Grillet's *La Jalousie*." *C.L.A. Journal* 3 (1959): 46–55.

Altieri, Charles. "Wittgenstein on Consciousness and Language: A Challenge to Derridean Literary Theory." *Modern Language Notes* 91 (1976): 1397–1423.

Arac, Jonathan, ed. *Postmodernism and Politics*. Minneapolis: University of Minnesota Press, 1986.

Asher, Lyell. *Ethics/aesthetics: Post-modern Positions*. Washington, D.C.: Maisonneuve Press, 1988.

Attali, Jacques. *Noise: The Political Economy of Music* (*Bruits: essai sur l'économie politique de la musique*, 1977). Trans. Brian Massumi. Minneapolis: University of Minnesota Press, 1985.

Attridge, Derek, Geoff Bennington, and Robert Young, eds. *Post-Structuralism and The Question of History*. Cambridge: Cambridge University Press, 1987.

Auerbach, Erich. "Figura" (*Neue Dantestudien*, 1944). Trans. Ralph Manheim. *Scenes from the Drama of European Literature*, 11–76. New York: Meridian, 1959.

Bakhtin, Mikhail. *The Dialogic Imagination: Four Essays*. Trans. Caryl Emerson and Michael Holquist. Austin: University of Texas Press, 1981.

Balakian, Anna. *Literary Origins of Surrealism*. New York: New York University Press, 1967.

———. *Surrealism: The Road to the Absolute*. New York: Dutton, 1970.

———. *André Breton: Magus of Surrealism*. New York: Oxford University Press, 1971.

Barfield, Owen. *Saving the Appearances*. New York: Harcourt, Brace and World, n.d.

Barth, John. "The Literature of Replenishment, Postmodernist Fiction." *The Atlantic* (January 1980): 65–71.

Barthes, Roland. "The Death of the Author." In *Image, Music, Text*, 142–48. Trans. Stephen Heath. Glasgow: Fontana/Collins, 1977.

Bartowski, Frances. "Feminism and Deconstruction: 'a union forever deferred.' " *Enclitic* 4 (1980): 70–77.

Baudrillard, Jean. "The Implosion of Meaning in the Media." *All Area* 2 (1983): 118–21.

———. "The Ecstasy of Communication." In Hal Foster, ed. *The Anti-Aesthetic: Essays on Postmodern Culture*.

———. "The Precession of Simulacra," *Art & Text* 11 (September 1983): 3–47. Also in his *Simulations*. Trans. Paul Foss and Paul Patton. Repr. in Brian Wallis, ed. *Art after Modernism*, 253–81.

———. *In the Shadow of the Silent Majorities . . . Or, the End of the Social, and Other Essays*. New York: Semiotext(e), 1983.

Baudrillard, Jean. *Selected Writings*. Various translators. Mark Poster, ed. Stanford, Calif.: Stanford University Press, 1988.

Belsey, Catherine. "Constructing the Subject." In Judith Newton and Deborah Rosenfelt, eds. *Feminist Criticism and Social Change*, 45–64. New York and London: Methuen, 1985.

Benhabib, Seyla. "Epistemologies of Postmodernism: A Rejoinder to Jean-François Lyotard." In Linda J. Nicholson, ed. *Feminism/Postmodernism*, 107–32. Repr. from *New German Critique* 33 (1984): 103–26.

Bland, Jay. "Up Against the Wall: The Ethical Limits of Rational Objectivity." *SciFi* 5 (1983): 96–101.

Borges, Jorge Luis. *Ficciones* (1956). New York: Grove Press, 1962.

———. "From Allegories to Novels." In *Other Inquisitions: 1937–1952*. Trans. Ruth L. C. Simms. New York: Simon & Schuster, 1964.

———. *A Personal Anthology* (*Antología Personal*, 1961). New York: Grove Press, 1967.

Borges in/and/on Film. Edgardo Cozarinsky, ed. Trans. Gloria Waldman and Ronald Crist. New York: Lumen Books, 1988.

Boyd, Brian. *Nabokov's "Ada": The Place of Consciousness*. Ann Arbor, Mich.: Ardis, 1985.

———. *Vladimir Nabokov: The Russian Years*. Princeton: Princeton University Press, 1990.

Brée, Germaine. "New Blinds or Old." *Yale French Studies*, no. 24 (Summer 1959): 87–91.

Breton, André. *Nadja* (1928). Trans. Richard Howard. New York: Grove Press, 1960.

———. *Manifestoes of Surrealism* (1924 and 1930). Trans. Richard Seaver and Helen Lane. Ann Arbor: University of Michigan Press, 1972.

———. *Surrealism and Painting* (1965). Trans. Simon Watson Taylor. New York: Harper & Row, 1972.

Bronner, Stephen Eric. "Martin Heidegger: The Consequences of Political Mystification." *Salmagundi*, no. 38–39 (1977): 153–74.

Brumbaugh, Robert S. *Unreality and Time*. Albany: State University of New York Press, 1984.

Buchloh, Benjamin H. D. "Figures of Authority, Ciphers of Regression: Notes on the Return of Representation in European Painting." *October*, no. 16 (Spring 1981): 39–68. Repr. in Brian Wallis, ed. *Art after Modernism*, 107–35.

Bürger, Peter. *Theory of the Avant-Garde*. Minneapolis: University of Minnesota Press, 1983.

Burgin, Victor. *The End of Art Theory: Criticism and Postmodernity*. Atlantic Highlands, N.J.: Humanities Press International, 1986.

Carr, David. *Time, Narrative, and History*. Bloomington: Indiana University Press, 1986.

Casparis, Christian Paul. *Tense without Time: Present Tense in Narration*. Bern: Francke, 1975.

Cixous, Hélène. "The Laugh of the Medusa." Trans. Keith Cohen and Paula Cohen. *Signs* 1, no. 4 (1976): 875–93.

Cixous, Hélène, and Catherine Clement. *Newly Born Woman* (*La jeune née*, 1975). Trans. Betsy Wing. Minneapolis: University of Minnesota Press, 1986.

Clark, Ronald W. *Einstein: The Life and Times*. New York: World Publishing Company, 1971.

Cortázar, Julio. *Hopscotch* (*Rayuela*, 1963). Trans. Gregory Rabassa. New York: Random House, 1966.

————. *Blow-Up and Other Stories*. Trans. Paul Blackburn. New York: Pantheon, 1967.

Cortázar-Hawkes Special Issue. *Review of Contemporary Fiction* 3, no. 3 (Fall 1983).

Coward, Rosalind, and John Ellis. *Language and Materialism: Developments in Semiology and the Theory of the Subject*. London, Henley, and Boston: Routledge and Kegan Paul, 1977.

Crary, Jonathan. "Spectacle, Attention, Counter-Memory." In *October* 50 (Fall 1989): 97–107.

————. "Eclipse of the Spectacle." In Brian Wallis, ed. *Art after Modernism*, 283–94.

Cruchfield, James P., J. Doyne Farmer, Norman H. Packard, and Roger S. Shaw. "Chaos." *Scientific American* 255 (December, 1986): 46–57.

Dallmayr, Fred. *Twilight of Subjectivity: Contributions to a Post-Structuralist Theory of Politics*. Amherst: University of Massachusetts Press, 1981.

Davies, Paul. *Superforce: The Search For a Grand Unified Theory of Nature*. New York: Simon & Schuster, 1984.

Deleuze, Gilles, and Felix Guattari. *Anti-Oedipus: Capitalism and Schizophrenia*. Trans. Robert Hurley, Mark Seem, and Peter R. Lane. New York: Viking, 1977.

Delevoy, Robert L. *Dimensions of the Twentieth Century, 1900–1945*. Trans. Gilbert Stuart. Geneva: SKIRA: Art, Ideas, History Series, 1965.

Delphie, Christine. *Close to Home: A Materialist Analysis of Women's Oppression*. Amherst: University of Massachusetts Press, 1984.

Derrida, Jacques. *Of Grammatology* (*De la Grammatologie*, 1964). Trans. Gayatri Spivak. Baltimore: Johns Hopkins University Press, 1967.

————. *Writing and Difference* (1967). Trans. Alan Bass. Chicago: University of Chicago Press, 1978.

————. *Margins of Philosophy* (1972). Trans. Alan Bass. Chicago: University of Chicago Press, 1982.

Donoso, José. *The Latin American "Boom": A Personal History* (*Historia personal del "boom"*, 1972). Trans. Gregory Kovolakos. New York: Columbia University Press in association with the Center for Inter-American Relations, 1977.

Dort, Bernard. "Are These Novels 'Innocent'?" *Yale French Studies*, no. 24 (Summer 1959): 22–30.

Duras, Marguerite. *The Lover* (*L'Amant*, 1984). Trans. Barbara Bray. New York: Random House, 1985.

Eagleton, Terry. *Criticism and Ideology*. London: New Left Press, 1976.

Ermarth, Elizabeth Deeds. "Fictional Consensus and Female Casualties." In *Representation and Women* (English Institute Essays 1981), 1–18. Carolyn Heilbrun and Margaret Higgonet, eds. Baltimore: Johns Hopkins University Press, 1982.

————. *Realism and Consensus in the English Novel*. Princeton: Princeton University Press, 1983.

————. "The Solitude of Women and Social Time." In *Taking Our Time: Feminist Perspectives on Temporality*, 37–46. Frieda Forman, ed., with Caoran Jowton.

Ermarth, Elizabeth Deeds. "Conspicuous Construction, or Kristeva, Nabokov, and the Anti-realist Critique." *Novel* (Winter–Spring 1988): 330–39. Repr. in *Why the Novel Matters: A Postmodern Perplex*. Bloomington: Indiana University Press, 1990.

———. "Feminist Theory As a Practice." In Elizabeth Meese and Alice Parker, eds. *Theorizing Feminist Writing Practices* (London: John Benjamins, 1991).

———. "On Having a Personal Voice." In Gayle Greene and Coppelia Kahn, eds. *Histories/A History: The Making of Feminist Criticism* (forthcoming).

Fabian, Johannes. *Time and The Other: How Anthropology Makes Its Object*. New York: Columbia University Press, 1983.

Faris, Wendy B. *Labyrinths of Language: Symbolic Landscape and Narrative Design in Modern Fiction*. Baltimore and London: Johns Hopkins University Press, 1988.

Féral, Josette. "The Powers of Difference." In Hester Eisenstein and Alice Jardine, eds. *The Future of Difference*. New Brunswick, N.J.: Rutgers University Press, 1985.

Ferris, Timothy. *The Red Limit: The Search for the Edge of the Universe*. New York: William Morrow, 1977.

Flax, Jane. "Postmodernism and Gender Relations in Feminist Theory." *Signs* 12, no. 4 (Summer 1987): 621–43.

Fletcher, John. *Claude Simon and Fiction Now*. London: Calder and Boyars, 1975.

Forman, Frieda, ed., with Caoran Jowton. *Taking Our Time: Feminist Perspectives on Temporality*. Oxford and New York: Pergamon Press, Athene Series, 1989.

Forster, E. M. *A Passage to India*. New York: Harcourt Brace, 1925.

Foster, Hal. "Re: Post." *Parachute* 26 (Spring 1982): 11–15. Repr. with slight alterations in Brian Wallis, ed. *Art after Modernism*, 189–201.

Foster, Hal, ed. *The Anti-Aesthetic: Essays on Postmodern Culture*. Port Townsend, Wash.: Bay Press, 1983.

Foucault, Michel. *The Order of Things: An Archaeology of the Human Sciences* (*Les Mots et Les Choses*, 1966). New York: Random House, 1970.

———. *The Archaeology of Knowledge and The Discourse on Language* (originally *L'Archaeologie du Savoir*, 1969, and *L'Ordre du discours*, 1971, Paris: Gallimard). Trans. A. M. Sheridan Smith. London: Tavistock, 1972.

———. *Language, Counter-Memory, and Practice: Selected Essays and Interviews*. Trans. Donald F. Bouchard and Sherry Simon. Ithaca, N.Y.: Cornell University Press, 1977.

———. "My Body, This Paper, This Fire." *Oxford Literary Review* 4, no. 1 (1979): 9–28. Trans. Geoff Bennington.

———. "What Is an Author?" In Josué Harari, ed. *Textual Strategies*. Ithaca, N.Y.: Cornell University Press, 1979.

———. *Power and Knowledge: Selected Interviews and Other Writings, 1972–1977*. Colin Gordon, ed. Trans. Colin Gordon, Leo Marshall, John Mepham, and Kate Soper. New York: Pantheon Books, 1980.

———. *This Is Not A Pipe: With Illustrations and Letters by René Magritte* (1973). Trans. James Harkness. Berkeley: University of California Press, 1982.

———. "Final Interview" (with Gilles Barbardette and André Scala). *Raritan Review* 5, no. 1 (1985): 1–13.

Fraser, J. T., ed. *The Voices of Time: A Cooperative Survey of Man's Views of Time as Expressed by the Sciences and by the Humanities*. New York: George Braziller, 1966.

Fraser, Nancy, and Linda. J. Nicholson. "Social Criticism without Philosophy: An Encounter between Feminism and Postmodernism." In Nicholson, ed. *Feminism/Postmodernism*, 19–38.

Freeman, Barbara. "Plus corps donc plus écriture: Hélène Cixous and the mind-body problem." *Paragraph* 11, no. 1 (March 1988): 58–70.

Friedrich, Paul. *The Language Parallax: Linguistic Relativism and Poetic Indeterminacy*. Austin: University of Texas Press, 1986.

Fukayama, Francis. "The End of History?" *The National Interest* (Summer 1989): 3–18.

Gaggi, Silvio. *Modern/postmodern: A Study in Twentieth Century Arts and Ideas*. Philadelphia: University of Pennsylvania Press, 1989.

Gale, Richard M. *The Language of Time*. New York: Humanities Press, 1968.

———, ed. *The Philosophy of Time: A Collection of Essays*. New Jersey: Humanities Press, and Sussex: Harvester, 1968.

Gallop, Jane. "*Quand nos lèvres s'écrivent*: Irigaray's Body Politic." *Romanic Review* 74 (1983): 77–83.

García Márquez, Gabriel. *One Hundred Years of Solitude* (*Cien Años de Soledad*, 1967). Trans. Gregory Rabassa. New York: Harper & Row, 1970.

Gardner, John. *On Moral Fiction*. New York: Basic Books, 1978.

Gershman, Herbert. *The Surrealist Revolution in France*. Ann Arbor: University of Michigan Press, 1969.

Gillespie, Michael Allen. *Hegel, Heidegger, and the Ground of History*. Chicago: University of Chicago Press, 1984.

Gould, Stephen Jay. *Wonderful Life: The Burgess Shale and the Nature of History*. London, Sydney, Auckland, Johannesburg: Hutchinson Radius, 1989.

Graff, Gerald. "The Myth of the Postmodern Breakthrough." *Triquarterly*, no. 26 (Winter 1973): 383–417.

———. *Literature Against Itself*. Chicago: University of Chicago Press, 1979.

Grossman, Manuel L. *Dada: Paradox, Mystification, and Ambiguity in European Literature*. New York: Bobbs Merrill Pegasus, 1971.

Grossvogel, David I. *Limits of the Novel: Evolutions of a Form from Chaucer to Robbe-Grillet*. Ithaca, N.Y.: Cornell University Press, 1968.

Habermas, Jürgen. *The Philosophical Discourse of Modernity: Twelve Lectures* (*Der philosophische Diskurs der Moderne: Zwölf Vorlesungen*, 1985). Trans. Frederick Lawrence. Cambridge, Mass.: M.I.T. Press, 1987.

———. "Modernity versus Postmodernity." *New German Critique* 22 (Winter 1981): 3–14. Repr. as "Modernity—An Incomplete Project." In Hal Foster, ed. *The Anti-Aesthetic*, 3–15.

Hassan, Ihab. "The Question of Postmodernism." In *Romanticism, Modernism, Postmodernism*, 117–26. Harry R. Garvin, ed. Lewisburg, Toronto, London: Bucknell University Press, 1980.

———. *The Postmodern Turn: Essays in Postmodern Theory and Culture*. Columbus: Ohio State University Press, 1987.

Hawkes, John. *The Blood Oranges*. New York: New Directions, 1970.

———. *Travesty*. New York: New Directions, 1976.

Hawking, Stephen. *A Brief History of Time: From the Big Bang to Black Holes*. New York: Bantam, 1988.

Hayles, N. Katherine. *The Cosmic Web: Scientific Field Models and Literary Strategies in the Twentieth Century*. Ithaca, N.Y.: Cornell University Press, 1984.

———. *Chaos Bound: Orderly Disorder in Contemporary Literature and Science*. Ithaca, N.Y.: Cornell University Press, 1990.

Hayman, David. "An Interview with Alain Robbe-Grillet." *Contemporary Literature* 14, no. 3 (Summer 1975): 273–85.

Heath, Stephen. *The Nouveau Roman: A Study in the Practice of Writing*. London: Elek Books, 1972.

Hebdige, Dick. "Postmodernism and 'The Other Side.' " In *Hiding in the Light: On Images and Things New*. New York and London: Routledge, 1988.

Heidegger, Martin. *Being and Time (Sein und Zeit*, 1926). Trans. John Macquarrie and Edward Robinson. New York: Harper & Row, 1962.

———. *Identity and Difference (Identität und Differenz*, 1957). Trans. Joan Stambaugh. New York: Harper & Row, 1969.

———. *On the Way to Language*. Trans. Peter D. Hertz: includes Heidegger essay "Words." Trans. Joan Stambaugh. New York: Harper & Row, 1971.

———. *Poetry, Language, Thought*. Trans. Albert Hofstadter. New York: Harper & Row, 1971.

———. "Letter on Humanism" (1947). Trans. Edgar Lohner. In William Barrett and Henry D. Aiken, eds. *Philosophy in the Twentieth Century, An Anthology*. 3rd ed. New York: Random House, 1962. Also in N. Langiulli, ed. *The Existentialist Tradition* (Garden City, N.Y.: Doubleday, 1971).

———. *The Question Concerning Technology: Heidegger's Critique of the Modern Age*. Trans. William Lovitt. New York: Harper & Row, 1977.

———. *History of the Concept of Time: Prolegomena* (1925 lectures, published as *Prolegomena zur Geschichte des Zeitbegriffs*, 1979). Trans. Theodore Kisiel. Bloomington: Indiana University Press, 1985.

Heisenberg, Werner. *Physics and Philosophy: The Revolution in Modern Science*. New York: Harper & Row, 1962.

Homans, Margaret. *Women Writers and Poetic Identity: Dorothy Wordsworth, Emily Brontë, and Emily Dickinson*. Princeton: Princeton University Press, 1980.

Huizinga, Johan. *The Waning of the Middle Ages*. Trans. F. Hopman. London: Edward Arnold and Co., 1937.

Hutcheon, Linda. *Narcissistic Narrative: The Metafictional Paradox*. New York: Methuen, 1984.

Hutcheon, Linda. *A Poetics of Postmodernism: History, Theory, Fiction*. New York and London: Routledge, 1988.

Hutcheon, Linda. *A Theory of Parody*. New York: Methuen, 1985.

Huyssen, Andreas. "Mapping the Postmodern." In Linda J. Nicholson, ed. *Feminism/Postmodernism*, 234–80. Repr. from *New German Critique*, no. 33 (1984): 5–52; also in his *After the Great Divide*, 179–221.

————. *After the Great Divide: Modernism, Mass Culture, and Postmodernism*. Bloomington: Indiana University Press, 1986.

Irigaray, Luce. *This Sex Which Is Not One* (*Ce Sexe qui n'est pas un*, 1977). Trans. Catherine Porter with Carolyn Burke. Ithaca, N.Y.: Cornell University Press, 1985.

Jacobson, Roman. "Closing Statement: Linguistic and Poetics." In Thomas A. Sebeok. *Style in Language*. Cambridge, Mass.: M.I.T. Press, 1960.

Jacobson, Roman, and Morris Halle. *Fundamentals of Language*. The Hague: Mouton, 1956. 2nd ed. 1971.

Jacobus, Mary. "Is There a Woman in This Text?" *New Literary History* 14 (1982): 117–41. Repr. in *Reading Woman*, 83–109. New York: Columbia University Press, 1986.

Jameson, Fredric. "Imaginary and Symbolic in Lacan: Marxism, Psychoanalytic Criticism, and the Problem of the Subject." *Yale French Studies* 55/56 (1977): 338–95.

————. *The Political Unconscious: Narrative as a Socially Symbolic Act*. Ithaca, N.Y.: Cornell University Press, 1981.

————. "Postmodernism and Consumer Society." In Hal Foster, ed. *The Anti-Aesthetic: Essays on Postmodern Culture*, 111–25.

————. "The Politics of Theory: Ideological Positions in the Postmodernism Debate." *New German Critique*, no. 33 (Fall 1984): 53–66.

————. "Postmodernism, or the Cultural Logic of Late Capitalism." *The New Left Review* 146 (July–August 1984): 53–92.

Jardine, Alice. *Gynesis: Configurations of Woman and Modernity*. Ithaca, N.Y.: Cornell University Press, 1985.

Jay, Martin. "Habermas and Modernism." Repr. from *Praxis International* 4, no. 1 (April 1984): 71–82. In *Habermas and Modernity*. Richard J. Bernstein, ed. Cambridge, Mass.: MIT Press, 1985.

Jencks, Charles, and Nathan Silver. *Adhocism: The Case for Improvisation*. Garden City, N.Y.: Doubleday, 1972.

Jencks, Charles. *The Language of Postmodern Architecture*. London: Academy Editions, 1981.

————. *What Is Postmodernism?* New York: St. Martin's Press and London: Academy Editions, 1986.

————. *Postmodernism: The New Classicism in Art and Architecture*. New York: Rizzoli, 1987.

Kant, Immanuel. *A Critique of Pure Reason* (*Der Kritik der Reinen Vernunft*, 1781). Trans. F. Max Muller (1881). New York: Doubleday, 1966.

Kaplan, Ann, ed. *Postmodernism and Its Discontents: Theories, Practices*. London and New York: Verso, 1988.

Kariel, Henry S. *The Desperate Politics of Postmodernism*. Amherst: University of Massachusetts Press, 1989.

Keller, Alex. "Continuity and Discontinuity in Early Twentieth-Century Physics and Early Twentieth-Century Painting." In Martin Pollock, ed. *Common Denominators in Art and Science*, 97–106. Aberdeen: Aberdeen University Press, 1983.

Klinkowitz, Jerome. *Rosenberg/Barthes/Hassan: The Postmodern Habit of Thought*. Athens and London: University of Georgia Press, 1988.

Koselleck, Reinhart. "Neuzeit." In *Futures Past: On the Semantics of Historical Time*, 231–66, Cambridge, Mass.: MIT Press, 1985.

Kozloff, Max. "The Authoritarian Personality in Modern Art." *Artforum* 12, no. 9 (May 1974): 40–47.

Krauss, Rosalind. "The Originality of the Avant-Garde: A Post-modern Repetition." *October*, no. 18 (Fall 1981): 47–66. Repr. in Brian Wallis, ed. *Art after Postmodernism*, 13–29.

Kristeva, Julia. *Desire in Language: A Semiotic Approach to Literature and Art* (essays published in French in 1969 and 1977). Leon S. Roudiez, ed. Trans. Thomas Gora, Alice Jardine, and Leon S. Roudiez. New York: Columbia University Press, 1980.

————. "Women's Time" ("Les temps des femmes," 1979). Trans. Alice Jardine and Harry Blake. *Signs* 7, no. 1 (Autumn 1981): 5–35.

Kroker, Arthur, and David Cook. *The Postmodern Scene: Excremental Culture and Hyper-Aesthetics*. New York: St. Martin's Press, 1986.

Kuenzli, Rudolf E. "Derridada." *L'Esprit Créateur* 20, no. 2 (Summer 1980): 12–21.

Lacan, Jacques. "Hommage fait à Marguerite Duras, du Ravissement Lol V. Stein." *Cahiers M. Renard et J-L Barrault* 52 (December 1965): 9–13.

————. "Of Structure as an Inmixing of an Otherness Prerequisite to Any Subject Whatever." In Richard Macksey and Eugenio Donato, eds. *The Language of Criticism and the Sciences of Man: The Structuralist Controversy*, 186–95. Baltimore and London: Johns Hopkins University Press, 1970.

Lawson, Hilary. *Reflexivity: The Postmodern Predicament*. La Salle, Ill.: Open Court, 1985.

Lawson, Thomas. "Last Exit: Painting." *Artforum* 20, no. 2 (October 1981): 40–47. Repr. in Brian Wallis, ed. *Art after Modernism*, 153–65.

Lévi-Strauss, Claude. *Myth and Meaning*. New York: Schocken Books, 1979.

Levitt, Morton P. *Modernist Survivors: The Contemporary Novel in England, the United States, France, and Latin America*. Columbus: Ohio State University Press, 1987.

Linker, Kate. "Representation and Sexuality." *Parachute*, no. 32 (Fall 1983): 12–23. Repr. in Brian Wallis, ed. *Art after Modernism*, 391–415.

Lippard, Lucy. "Trojan Horses: Activist Art and Power." In Brian Wallis, ed. *Art after Modernism*, 341–58.

Lippard, Lucy, ed. *Surrealists on Art*. Englewood Cliffs, N.J.: Prentice-Hall, 1970.

Löwith, Karl. *Meaning in History*. Chicago: University of Chicago Press, 1949.

Lukács, Gyorg. "Preface." *Studies in European Realism* (1948). New York: Grosset and Dunlap, 1964.

————. "The Ideology of Modernism." In *Realism in Our Time: Literature and the Class Struggle* (1956). Trans. John Mander and Necke Mander. New York: Harper & Row, 1971.

Lyotard, Jean-François. "One of the Things at Stake in Women's Struggles." *Substance* 20 (1978): 9–17. Repr. in *The Lyotard Reader*, 111–21.

————. *The Postmodern Condition: A Report on Knowledge*. Trans. Geoff Benning-ton and Brian Massumi. Theory and History of Literature, vol. 10. Minneapolis: University of Minnesota Press, 1984.

————. *The Differend: Phrases in Dispute* (*Le Différend*, 1983). Trans. Georges Van Den Abbeele. Minneapolis: University of Minnesota Press, 1988.

————. *The Lyotard Reader*. Andrew Benjamin, ed. Oxford: Basil Blackwell, 1989.

MaCallum, Pamela. "Indeterminacy, Irreducibility and Authority in Modern Lit-erary Theory." *Ariel* 13, no. 1 (January 1982): 73–84.

MacCannell, Dean, and Juliet MacCannell. *The Time of the Sign: A Semiotic Inter-pretation of Modern Culture*. Bloomington: Indiana University Press, 1982.

Marcus, Greil. *Lipstick Traces: A Secret History of the Twentieth Century*. Cambridge, Mass.: Harvard University Press, 1989.

Martin, Stephen-Paul. *Open Form and the Feminine Imagination: The Politics of Reading in Twentieth-Century Innovative Writing*. Washington, D.C.: Maison-neuve Press, 1988.

Matthews, J. H. *Surrealism and the Novel*. Ann Arbor: University of Michigan Press, 1966.

————. *Languages of Surrealism*. Columbia: University of Missouri Press, 1986.

McCray, Stanley. "Process and Motivation in Early Romance." In Ernst Pulgram, ed. *Romanitas: Studies in Romance Linguistics*, 170–79. Ann Arbor: University of Michigan Press, 1984.

McHale, Brian. *Postmodern Fiction*. New York: Methuen, 1987.

Medina, Angel. *Reflection, Time and the Novel: Toward a Communicative Theory of Literature*. London and Boston: Routledge and Kegan Paul, 1979.

Mercier, Vivian. *A Reader's Guide to the New Novel: From Queneau to Pinget*. New York: Farrar, Straus, and Giroux, 1971.

Joan Miró: A Retrospective. New York: Solomon R. Guggenheim Museum and New Haven: Yale University Press, 1987.

Miyoshi, Masao. *Accomplices of Silence: The Modern Japanese Novel*. Berkeley: Uni-versity of California Press, 1974.

Moi, Toril. *Sexual/Textual Politics: Feminist Literary Theory*. London and New York: Methuen, 1985.

Momigliano, Arnaldo. "Time in Ancient and Modern Historiography." In *Essays in Ancient and Modern Historiography*, 179–204. Middletown, Conn.: Wesleyan University Press, 1977.

Montrelay, Michèle. "Recherches sur la femininité." *Critique* 278 (July 1970), Trans. Parveen Adams as "Inquiry into Femininity." *m/f* 1 (1978). Repr. in *Se-miotext(e)* 10 (1981).

Mook, Delo E., and Thomas Vargish. *Inside Relativity*. Princeton: Princeton Uni-versity Press, 1987.

Morris, C. B. *Surrealism and Spain, 1920–1936*. New York: Cambridge University Press, 1972.

Morrissette, Bruce. *Les Romans de Robbe-Grillet*. Paris: Les Editions de Minuit, 1963.

Morsink, Deborah. "Indeterminacy: 'La Folie du Jour.' " In her "Science and the Literary Text: Readings of Blanchot's Fiction" (work in progress).

Mulvey, Laura. "Visual Pleasure and Narrative Cinema." *Screen* 16, no. 3 (Autumn 1975): 6–18.

Nabokov, Vladimir. *Nikolai Gogol* (1944). New York: New Directions, 1961.

———. *The Gift* (1937–39). Trans. Michael Scammell with the collaboration of the author. New York: Capricorn Books, 1963.

———. *Despair* (1936). New York: G. P. Putnam and Sons, 1966.

———. *Ada, or Ardor: A Family Chronicle*. New York: McGraw-Hill, 1969.

———. *Speak Memory: An Autobiography Revisited* (1947). New York: Capricorn Books, 1970.

———. *Strong Opinions*. New York: McGraw-Hill, 1973.

———. *Transparent Things*. New York: McGraw-Hill, 1972.

Näigle, Ranier. "The Scene of the Other: Theodor Adorno's Negative Dialectic in the Context of Poststructuralism." In Jonathan Arac, *Postmodernism and Politics*, 91–111.

New French Feminisms: An Anthology. Elaine Marks and Isabelle de Courtivron, eds. Amherst: University of Massachusetts Press, 1980, and New York: Schocken Books, 1989.

Newman, Charles. *The Postmodern Aura*. Evanston, Ill.: Northwestern University Press, 1985.

Nicholson, Linda J. *Gender and History*. New York: Columbia University Press, 1986.

———, ed. *Feminism/Postmodernism*. New York: Routledge, 1990.

Nietzsche, Friedrich. *"On the Genealogy of Morals" and "Ecce Homo"* (originally published in German in 1887 and 1908 respectively). Trans. Walter Kaufman and R. J. Hollingdale, and Walter Kaufman. New York: Random House, 1967.

———. *Untimely Meditations* (1873–76). Esp. "On the uses and disadvantages of history for life"(1874), 57–124. Trans. R. J. Hollingdale with an introduction by J. P. Stern. Cambridge: Cambridge University Press, 1983.

Nye, Andrea. *Feminist Theory and the Philosophy of Man*. New York and London: Routledge, 1988.

Owens, Craig. "The Discourse of Others: Feminists and Postmodernism." In Hal Foster, eds. *The Anti-Aesthetic: Essays on Postmodern Culture*, 57–82.

Park, David. *The Image of Eternity: Roots of Time in the Physical World*. Amherst: University of Massachussetts Press, 1980.

Parker, Barry. *Einstein's Dream: The Search for a Unified Theory of the Universe*. New York and London: Plenum Press, 1986.

Parrinder, Patrick. *The Failure of Theory: Essays on Criticism and Contemporary Fiction*. Brighton, Sussex: Harvester Press, 1987.

Paulson, William. *The Noise of Culture: Literary Texts in a World of Information*. Ithaca, N.Y.: Cornell University Press 1988.

Pavel, Thomas. "Fiction and the Ontological Landscape." *Studies in Twentieth-Century Literature* 6, no. 1 (Fall–Spring 1982): 149–63.

Paz, Octavio. *The Labyrinth of Solitude: Life and Thought in Mexico* (*El Laberinto de la Soledad*, 1959). Trans. Lysander Kemp. New York: Grove Press, 1961.

Perloff, Marjorie. *The Futurist Moment: Avant-Garde, Avant Guerre, and the Language of Rupture*. Chicago: University of Chicago Press, 1986.

Prigogine, Ilya. *From Being to Becoming: Time and Complexity in the Physical Sciences*. San Francisco: W. H. Freeman, 1980.

Prigogine, Ilya, and Isabelle Stengers. *Order out of Chaos: Man's New Dialogue with Nature* (*La Nouvelle Alliance*, 1979). New York: Bantam, 1984.

Quilligan, Maureen. *The Language of Allegory*. Ithaca, N.Y.: Cornell University Press, 1979.

Quinones, Ricardo J. *Mapping Literary Modernism: Time and Development*. Princeton: Princeton University Press, 1985.

Rapoport, Anatol. *Two-Person Game Theory*. Ann Arbor: University of Michigan Press, 1966.

Ray, Paul C. *The Surrealist Movement in England*. Ithaca, N.Y.: Cornell University Press, 1971.

Read, Herbert. *A Concise History of Modern Painting*. New York: Thames and Hudson, 1968.

Reiss, Timothy J. *The Uncertainty of Analysis: Problems of Truth, Meaning, and Culture*. Ithaca, N.Y.: Cornell University Press, 1988.

Ricoer, Paul. *History and Truth* (*Histoire et Vérité*, 1955). Includes "Civilization and National Cultures." Trans. Charles A. Kelbley. Evanston, Ill.: Northwestern University Press, 1965.

———. "The Model of the Text: Meaningful Action Considered as a Text." *Social Research* 38 (1971): 229–62.

———. "The Configuration of Time in Fictional Narrative," part III of *Time and Narrative*, vol. 2 (*Temps et Récit*, 1984). Trans. Kathleen McLaughlin and David Pellauer. Chicago and London: University of Chicago Press, 1985.

Robbe-Grillet, Alain. "Note sur la notion d'itinéraire dans Lolita." *L'Arc* 24 (1964): 37–38.

———. *Two Novels ("Jealousy" and "In the Labyrinth")* (*La Jalousie*, 1957, and *Dans le labyrinthe*, 1959, Paris: Les Editions de Minuits). Trans. Richard Howard. New York: Grove Press, 1965.

———. *For a New Novel: Essays on Fiction* (essays from 1953–63 published as *Pour un nouveau roman*, Paris: Les Editions de Minuits, 1963). Trans. Richard Howard, 1965. Repr. Evanston, Ill.: Northwestern University Press, 1989.

Robertson, D. W. *A Preface to Chaucer: Studies in Medieval Perspectives*. Princeton: Princeton University Press, 1962.

Robinson, Lillian, and Lise Vogel. "Modernism and History." *New Literary History* 3, no. 1 (Autumn 1971): 177–200.

Rorty, Richard. "Postmodernist Bourgeois Liberalism." *Journal of Philosophy* 80, no. 10 (October 1983): 583–89.

———. "Habermas and Lyotard on Postmodernity." Repr. from *Praxis International* 4, no. 1 (April 1984): 32–44. In *Habermas and Modernity*, 161–76. Richard J. Bernstein, ed. Cambridge, Mass.: M.I.T. Press, 1985.

Rosler, Martha. "Lookers, Buyers, Dealers, and Makers: Thoughts on Audience." *Exposure* 17, no. 1 (Spring 1979) 10–25. Repr. with slight revisions in Brian Wallis, ed. *Art after Modernism*, 311–39.

Ross, Andrew. *The Failure of Modernism*. New York: Columbia University Press, 1986.

Ross, Andrew, ed. *Universal Abandon? The Politics of Postmodernism*. Minneapolis: University of Minnesota Press, 1988.

Ruthof, Horst. *The Reader's Construction of Narrative*. London: Routledge and Kegan Paul, 1981.

Roudiez, Leon S. *French Fiction Today: A New Direction*. New Brunswick, N.J.: Rutgers University Press, 1972.

Rowe, Nicholas. *Nabokov's Deceptive World*. New York: New York University Press, 1971.

Sachs, Curt. *Rhythm and Tempo: A Study in Music History*. New York: Norton, 1953.

Sarraute, Nathalie. *L'ère du soupçon*. Paris: Gallimard, 1956.

de Saussure, Ferdinand. *Course in General Linguistics* (c. 1906–1911). Trans. Wade Baskin. New York: McGraw-Hill, 1959.

Schapiro, Meyer. "Nature of Abstract Art." *Marxist Quarterly* 1 (1937): 77–98.

Schecker, Richard. *The End of Humanism: Writings on Performance*. New York: Performing Arts Journal Publications, 1982.

Schleifer, Ronald. "The Space and Dialogue of Desire: Lacan, Greimas, and Narrative Temporality." *MLN* 98, no. 5 (December 1983): 872–90.

Schoenfeld, Jean Snitzer. "André Breton, Alchemist." *French Review* 57, no. 4 (March 1984): 493–502.

Scholes, Robert. *Fabulation and Metafiction*. Urbana: University of Illinois Press, 1979.

Scott, Geoffrey. *The Architecture of Humanism: A Study in the History of Taste* (1914). 2nd ed. New York: Doubleday Anchor, 1924.

Scott, Joan Wallach. *Gender and the Politics of History*. New York: Columbia University Press, 1988.

Seem, Mark D. "Liberation of Difference: Toward a Theory of Antiliterature." *New Literary History* 5, no. 1 (Autumn 1975): 119–33.

Shapiro, Gary, ed. *After the Future: Postmodern Times and Places*. Albany: State University of New York Press, 1989.

Shattuck, Roger. *The Banquet Years: The Arts in France, 1885–1918 (Alfred Jarry, Henri Rousseau, Erik Satie, Guillaume Apollinaire)*. New York: Doubleday, 1961.

Silverman, Hugh J., and Donn Welton, eds. *Postmodernism and Continental Philosophy*. Albany: State University of New York Press, 1988.

Smith, Barbara Herrnstein. "Value without Truth-Value." In John Fekete, ed. *Life After Postmodernism: Essays on Value and Culture*. New York: St. Martin's Press, 1987.

Sonnenschein, Edward A. *What Is Rhythm?* Oxford: Blackwell, 1925.

Soper, Kate. *Humanism and Anti-Humanism*. La Salle, Ill.: Open Court, 1986.

Spanos, William V. *Repetitions: The Postmodern Occasion In Literature and Culture*. Baton Rouge: Louisiana State University Press, 1987.

Spencer, Sharon. *Time, Space and Structure in the Modern Novel*. New York: New York University Press, 1971.

Stern, Robert. "The Doubles of Post-Modern Architecture." *Harvard Architectural Design* (1981): 63–68.

Tani, Stefano. *The Doomed Detective: The Contribution of the Detective Novel to Post-*

modern American and Italian Fiction. Carbondale and Edwardsville: Southern Illinois University Press, 1988.

Taylor, Mark. C. *E[Я]RING, A Postmodern A/Theology*. Chicago: University of Chicago Press, 1984.

Thiher, Allen. *Words in Reflection: Modern Language Theory and Postmodern Fiction*. Chicago: University of Chicago Press, 1984.

Tyler, Stephen A. *The Unspeakable: Discourse, Dialogue, and Rhetoric in the Postmodern World*. Madison: University of Wisconsin Press, 1987.

Ulmer, Gregory L. "The Object of Post-Criticism." In Hal Foster, ed. *The Anti-Aesthetic: Essays on Postmodern Culture*, 83–110.

Venturi, Robert, Denise Scott-Brown, and Steven Izenour. *Learning from Las Vegas*. Cambridge, Mass.: MIT Press, 1972.

Wallis, Brian, ed. *Art after Modernism: Rethinking Representation*. New York: The New Museum of Contemporary Art with David Godine, Boston, 1984.

Waugh, Patricia. *Feminine Fictions: Revisiting the Postmodern*. London and New York: Routledge, 1989.

Weedon, Chris. *Feminist Practice and Poststructuralist Theory*. Oxford and New York: Basil Blackwell, 1987.

Wilde, Alan. *Horizons of Assent: Modernism, Postmodernism, and the Ironic Imagination*. Baltimore: Johns Hopkins University Press, 1981.

Woolf, Virginia. *The Waves*. New York and London: Harcourt Brace, 1931.

Xenos, Nicholas. *Scarcity and Modernity*. New York: Routledge, 1989.

Yeatman, Anna. "A Feminist Theory of Social Differentiation." In Linda J. Nicholson, ed. *Feminism/Postmodernism*, 281–99.

Young, Iris Marion. "The Ideal of Community and the Politics of Difference." In Linda J. Nicholson, ed. *Feminism/Postmodernism*, 300–23. Repr. from *Social Theory and Practice* 12, no. 1 (Spring 1986): 1–26.

Index